Birth, Death, and Motherhood in Classical Greece

Ancient Society and History

NANCY DEMAND

Birth, Death, and Motherhood in Classical Greece

The Johns Hopkins University Press
Baltimore and London

© 1994 The Johns Hopkins University Press
All rights reserved. Published 1994
Printed in the United States of America on acid-free paper

Johns Hopkins Paperbacks edition, 2004
9 8 7 6 5 4 3 2 1

The Johns Hopkins University Press
2715 North Charles Street
Baltimore, Maryland 21218-4363
www.press.jhu.edu

Library of Congress Cataloging-in-Publication Data will be found at the
end of this book.

A catalog record for this book is available from the British Library.

Contents

Contents

Seven
The Attitudes of the *Polis* to Childbirth: Putting Women
into the Grid

Eight
Women and Children: Issues of Control

Preface

I n the case histories detailed in the Hippocratic *Epidemics*, forty patients suffered complications of pregnancy or childbirth; of these women, twelve died. A number of Greek funerary reliefs appear to commemorate such women; a few even portray women in the throes of labor. Do these sources reflect the actual risk in childbirth in Greece? Do they allow us to determine what caused the death of these patients? Why did families choose to portray scenes of labor on funerary memorials when the Greek commemorative tradition otherwise avoided references to suffering and illness? Could it have been, as Nicole Loraux and Ursula Vedder claimed, that the Greeks equated the death of women in childbirth with the heroic death of young men in battle? These questions arose as I taught courses on women in antiquity and on Greek medicine, and, because I could find no satisfactory answers to them in the existing literature, they provided the impetus for the present study.

My search for answers to these questions has led me in an outwardly spiraling path from the women's quarters in the *oikos*, or family/household, to the institutions and interests of the elite male community—pederasty, philosophy, and the *polis*. Thus the first chapter begins by tracing the life of a Greek woman in the *oikos*.

Spiraling out from this center, later chapters consider helpers who came from outside the *oikos* to assist with childbirth, including female neighbors and kin, the traditional midwife, and, supplementing these in the case of complications by the late fifth century, the male doctor. Following a brief introduction to the basic concepts and methods of Hippocratic medicine and the Hippocratic texts in chapter 2, chapters 3 and 4 analyze the case histories and consider the problems of retrospective diagnosis. Continuing the outward spiral, chapter 5 considers the two principal gods to whom women appealed for help in conceiving or for an easy and successful delivery, Artemis and Asclepius. Chapter 6 focuses on another aspect of divine assistance—the role cult played in the acculturation of women to their allotted role as childbearers, and the contribution of the Hippocratic doctor to this acculturation. Chapter 7 investigates the attitudes of the wider male community to childbearing, using the evidence of the grave monuments that portray labor scenes as well as the concept of male pregnancy as it was employed in male coming-of-age customs and in the philosophy of Socrates/Plato. Chapter 8 reinforces some of the conclusions of the preceding chapters by a brief investigation of Hippocratic pediatrics (or rather, the lack of a Hippocratic pediatrics), and, reaching the outer ring of the spiral, offers a hypothesis in explanation of the coincidence between the acme of the classical male *polis* and increased restrictions on the lives of its women/childbearers. Thus the spiral path goes from the innermost reaches of the *oikos*, where women were confined (at least ideally), to the public (male) world of the *polis*.

In investigating these questions, I have made use of a broad range of ancient evidence, including medical and literary texts, funerary monuments, and inscriptions. I present a general discussion of this evidence in the Historiographical Introduction, where I also discuss relevant research in the history of medicine and gender studies. More detailed discussions of particular aspects of the sources and of modern studies appear in context in the various chapters.

One general issue pertaining to the evidence should be addressed here, however. Much of the nonmedical evidence (especially that in the first chapter) is Athenian, and this raises the question whether the result can justifiably be called "Greek" in the wider sense. The situation is a dilemma. Labeling the entire study "Athenian" would mean overlooking the fact that the bulk of the specific evidence on childbirth experience is non-Athenian: the Hippocratic writings, which were the product of itinerant doctors whose location, when it can be established, was mainly in northern Greece; the cure records from Epidauros; and some of the tombstones portraying scenes of labor (Atticizing, but not all Attic). On the whole, therefore, it seems that the term "Greek" provides a fairer description of the subject matter than would "Athenian," despite the predominance of Athenian evidence on some specific questions.

In referring to the Hippocratic texts, I have cited book and chapter numbers as they appear in the Littré edition; this coincides in most cases (but not in *Epidemics* I and III) with the Loeb numbering. All references to the Hippocratic treatises are followed by Littré pages in parenthesis, with the exception of the childbirth cases, where the Littré references can be found, along with the translations, in Appendix B. In the transliteration of Greek names and words I have adopted the traditional Latinized form when this seemed likely to be most familiar to readers. The abbreviations used in citing ancient authors are those of *The Oxford Classical Dictionary* or H. G. Liddell, R. Scott, and H. S. Jones, eds.; *A Greek-English Lexicon*; abbreviations of modern journals are those used by *L'Année Philologique*.

Acknowledgments

I have crossed a number of disciplinary boundaries in this study and I am heavily indebted to the many scholars who have generously contributed their specialized knowledge, provided encouragement and support, and in some cases read and commented on individual chapters. These include Ernst Badian, T. V. Buttery, Christoph Clairmont (who provided advice on Greek funerary reliefs and read and commented on chapter 7), Sterling Dow, Christos Goulios, Monica Green, Richard Hamilton (who read and commented on chapter 6), Barbara Hanawalt, Anne Hanson, George Hart, Brendan Nagle, John Scarborough, Ronda Sims, Wesley Smith, Heinrich von Staden, Martha Taysom, Ursula Vedder, Martha Vinson, and Eugene Weinberg (who read and commented on chapter 4 and contributed his expertise on the dangers of malaria in pregnancy). I owe a special debt of gratitude to Eugene Borza, to the anonymous readers of Johns Hopkins University Press, who offered many valuable suggestions, and to the editor, Eric Halpern.

Indiana University generously provided Grants-in-aid of Research and a Research Supplement, and a fellowship from the National Endowment for the Humanities enabled me to have an uninterrupted year to work on the project. The Classics Department at

Yale granted me the privileges of a Visiting Fellow, which helped to make that year productive. I also wish to thank the American School of Classical Studies in Athens for assistance in gaining permission to study the funerary monuments in Greece; and Dr. Daoud, director of the Alexandria Archaeological Society, Dr. Rodziewicz of the Egyptian Antiquities Organization, and Mme. Doreya, the director of the Alexandria Archaeological Museum, for their generous help and hospitality in Alexandria. Finally, I am grateful to my husband for his continuing interest, encouragement, and patience.

Thanks are due to the following for permission to reproduce photographs: plate 1: The Metropolitan Museum of Art, New York, Fletcher Fund, 1924 (24.97.92); plate 4: photograph of the Musées Nationaux, Paris; plate 5: The Arthur M. Sackler Museum, Harvard University Art Museums. Gift of Edward W. Forbes in Trust to the University; plate 8: "The Ny Carlsberg Glyptotek," Copenhagen; plates 2, 3, 6, 7, 9, 11, 12: the Greek Archaeological Service, TAP; plate 10: the Alexandria Archaeological Museum, for permission to photograph. The text of the cases in *Epidemics* I and III is reprinted by permission of the publishers and the Loeb Classical Library from W. H. S. Jones: *Hippocrates*, vol. 2, translated by W. H. S. Jones, Cambridge, Mass.: Harvard University Press, 1962.

Historiographical Introduction

ntil recently, childbirth in classical Greece was virtually ignored by classicists, historians, and even medical historians, even though the gynecological treatises make up a large portion of the Hippocratic Corpus.[1] Today this situation has changed dramatically: under the influence of the women's movement and the New History, work on Greek gynecology is flourishing. In fact, the work has become so extensive that I note here only those studies that I have found of particular relevance to my own work.[2]

Hermann Grensemann provided the basis for further work on the major gynecological treatises, *Diseases of Women* I and II and *Nature of Woman*, by his identification of various strata within these works,[3] and I. M. Lonie's edition and translation of the embryological treatises provided the further necessary foundation for work on reproductive issues.[4] Ann Hanson has published numerous articles analyzing this material, and her work in progress includes a new edition and translation of *Diseases of Women* I. G. E. R. Lloyd has put the gynecological material into its broader intellectual context,[5] and Helen King has followed in this direction by her application of structuralist analysis in a series of stimulating articles based on her dissertation.[6]

Aline Rousselle was the first to argue that the gynecological treatises derive from a female oral tradition,[7] while Paola Manuli saw them as an expression of a male voice of social and sexual domination.[8] Attempts to resolve this apparent contradiction by postulating a "common" (and thus essentially male) oral tradition were made by Lloyd, Hanson, and King. John Riddle's work on the contraceptive and abortifacient recipes in the gynecological treatises seems, however, to offer a new and convincing argument for Rousselle's claim that the source of the tradition is female lore. I have argued that this allows us to see Rousselle and Manuli as simply the products of different perspectives on the same situation—the raw material of the gynecological treatises was information discovered and passed on by women, but doctors perceived that raw material through the conceptual lens of the Greek male and of Hippocratic theory. In that sense, the gynecological treatises do speak with a male voice, but we can also reclaim the basic elements in the tradition for women.

This book continues and extends the work done in earlier studies in a number of other ways as well. Perhaps most important to note is a difference of orientation: my focus is on the case histories in the *Epidemics* rather than on the gynecological treatises themselves. Although Hanson's work established that the women's cases reflect the same medical orientation as that found in the gynecological treatises,[9] no one has previously studied the cases involving pregnancy and childbirth as a group.[10] A second general way in which this book differs from previous studies is in its extension of the scope of the investigation to a wider range of nonmedical evidence and, in particular, to iconographical evidence. While both Danielle Gourevitch and Valerie French made use of pictorial evidence in discussing childbirth,[11] their view was both more limited (to the technical aspects of delivery itself) and more extensive (to Soranus and later Roman material) than mine. In its focus on Greece, as well as in the degree to which it makes use of iconographical evidence, this book perhaps comes closest to that of Eva Keuls, although she refers only briefly to the Hippocratic material and does not explicitly employ an iconographical method.[12]

The field of general medical history provided another important framework for this book. The case histories of complications in pregnancy and childbirth offer material for retrospective diagnoses that shed new light on the risks that childbearing women ran from general illnesses in the community as well as from specifically obstetric emergencies. For example, it was possible to answer Calvin Wells's claim that the risk to childbearing women in antiquity was slight because epidemic childbed fever did not exist[13] by pointing out not only the evidence for puerperal fever, but also that for other diseases, and especially malaria. In this I have applied the findings of Eugene Weinberg on the suppression of cell-mediated immunity in pregnancy,[14] linking them with the conclusions of Eugene Borza on the prevalence of malaria in the area where the Hippocratic doctors were practicing.[15]

Models and Methodology

A number of disciplines beyond history are also relevant to the history of childbirth. Feminist scholarship in particular has long struggled with the problems of the muted population that is the subject of this study, and it has been especially helpful in matters of methodology. Anthropology, from studies of modern Greek village life to the investigations of medical anthropology, has also proved useful. Finally, I have borrowed from the methods of literary analysis and iconography in making sense of the rich but varied and often fragmentary evidence about attitudes toward childbirth in Greece and the role it played in the general culture.

The concept of the cultural construction of gender, developed by feminists, has become a fundamental axiom of social analysis in Classics and across the disciplines, especially in the form adopted by postmodernist anthropology.[16] Unfortunately, its feminist origins have often passed unnoted; as Amy Richlin so appropriately put it, "Much like Zeus swallowing Metis and bringing forth Athena, this work reinvents what feminists have done before."[17] Thus I want particularly to stress the feminist origins of the constructionist approach that I have employed in a number of ways in my investigation: in the cultural construction of gender; in application to childbirth itself; and, in a form adopted from medical anthropology, in the concept of the social construction of illness.

The recognition of the crucial role played by patriarchal society in the shaping of female experience is another contribution of feminist theory. In particular, the male concern about control of female reproductivity that marks the ancient evidence has been recognized as a frequent characteristic of patriarchal societies.[18] Male concern took an especially acute form in classical Athens, where it was aggravated by the restrictions on citizenship imposed by the Periclean law, but this situation was by no means uniquely Athenian: Aristotle tells us that such restrictions were a common feature in *polis* development.

The effects of male anxiety over the control of female sexuality appears in the Hippocratic doctors' involvement in women's reproductive care and in their creation of the gynecological treatises. Here Foucault provides a model in his account of the development of the discipline of medicine as a means of exercising social control.[19] Although framed in terms of eighteenth-century French history, Foucault's ambiguous concept of a discipline as both a body of knowledge created through writing and record keeping, and the application of that knowledge as a mode of exercising power over (disciplining) a subclass, is confirmed by, and enlightens, the activities of the Hippocratic doctor. Thus we can see in that doctor one who exercised power both over women as individuals, as he assumed care of their illnesses,[20] and over the field itself, through the transformation of women's lore into the male form of the medical treatise.

In my interpretation of women's lives in Greece, I have followed the lead of many scholars who have used anthropological studies of modern Greek village life as clues in filling the gaps in the ancient evidence.[21] Most of these modern village studies themselves point out the similarities with antiquity, which are numerous and sometimes striking.[22] Whether the likenesses reflect actual continuity from antiquity, result from conscious archaism by modern political leaders, or arise simply from a similarity of response to village life in the same environment[23] are questions that I have not attempted to answer. I have simply offered the parallels for their heuristic value in clarifying and bringing life to the fragmentary ancient evidence.[24]

The field of medical anthropology offers models that are especially useful for the investigation of medical systems, like the Greek, that are structured in ways quite different from our own. Thus the concept of illness as a cultural construct has proved helpful in clarifying the relationship of the womb-centered Hippocratic illnesses to the modern diagnosis of hysteria, and the distinction between illness and disease was useful in assessing Wells's claim that childbed fever did not pose a threat to Greek women. On a more general level, I am indebted to Arthur Kleinman's model of a medical system as one encompassing overlapping sectors—professional, popular, and folk. Kleinman's approach facilitates a more holistic view of the various healing alternatives that were available to the Greek patient.[25]

Kleinman's model is particularly useful in explicating the relationship between the "professional" male Hippocratic doctor and those midwives who moved at this time from the folk sector to the professional as doctors' assistants. In Kleinman's model, "folk" is not a pejorative term. As a member of the folk sector, the traditional midwife controlled a well-developed body of information and had skills that were recognized and valued, especially in the community of women. My claim that some midwives rose in status and became professional through their association with Hippocratic doctors is made in the context of Kleinman's model: I am arguing that these women probably moved up in status in the male patriarchal society by associating themselves with the sector that was recognized as most prestigious by that society, which for that reason we identify as professional in Kleinman's terms. This by no means implies that as traditional midwives operating in the folk sector they had lacked knowledge or skills; on the contrary, it was their knowledge that became gynecology when male doctors took it over and incorporated it into the form of the Hippocratic treatise.

The investigation of the larger cultural context of childbirth required the use of a number of different types of evidence: inscriptions recording cures at the temple of Asclepius at Epidaurus, vase paintings portraying activities in the celebration of the Arkteia at Brauron, literary expressions of male attitudes, and the portrayals of women in labor on funerary monuments. In dealing with this varied material I have borrowed methodology eclectically as it seemed likely to be helpful. For example, in the investigation of acculturation through cult observances and initiation rites, I have made use of the structuralist analyses of Froma Zeitlin and the Foucaudian studies of John Winkler as springboards for my own interpretations.[26] In my analysis of the iconographical evidence of the funerary monuments, I was especially influenced by Christiane Sourvinou-Inwood's structuralist methods of reading the Greek material within the context of Greek culture. I have adopted and adapted her metaphor of a grid for my analysis of the labor scenes, even though I often find myself in disagreement with her conclusions.

It was my attempt to see the scenes on Greek tombstones in terms of Greek iconographical conventions ("through a Greek perceptual screen," as Sourvinou-Inwood expresses it), rather than in terms of modern preconceptions, that led me to challenge the recent widely accepted interpretation of these monuments by Nicole Loraux and Ursula Vedder, which sees them as expressions of a Greek male equation of death in childbirth with the heroic death of young men in battle. Far from agreeing that the *polis* made civic heroes of the victims of childbirth, I follow those feminist scholars who look for the causes of the subordination of women in the development of the state, and, in particular, in the state as patriarchal.[27] In the long course of history, fifth-century Greece, and especially Athens, is only a small note, yet the pattern of its history confirms the larger hypothesis of a connection between state formation and the subordination of women. Moreover, one change that occurred as the *polis* became more restrictive had effects that have extended to this day and to our own lives: the appropriation of female lore about childbearing into the male form of Hippocratic gynecology.

In this discussion of women's reproductive lives, I have sought to go beyond a narrow focus on the childbirth experience itself to consider women's relationship to the broader community in their fulfillment of the role that their society assigned to them. My aim in thus casting the net wider is to suggest the broader social impact of the socially constructed childbearing role on the lives of Greek women.

Birth, Death, and Motherhood in Classical Greece

One

The Lives of Greek Women

irth is a natural physiological process, but for human beings it is also a social event.[1] Culture intervenes in countless ways to shape and structure the experience. We have a good illustration of this in our own society, where we have seen both the "medicalization" of childbirth, with its emphasis on monitored and doctor-controlled delivery, and, in reaction, efforts to make the experience more "natural," ranging from home birth attended by a midwife to hospital care in homelike birthing rooms with father-assisted delivery. Giving birth is not so much a "natural" event as a "cultural construction" (or, in our case, a choice between cultural constructions).[2] As a consequence, the study of the way in which a particular society perceives and manages childbirth reveals fundamental aspects of its cultural and social values. Such a study is especially valuable for classical Greece, where women's central role was as childbearers and little other evidence exists for them. Greek women seldom appear as public figures in the traditional history of the classical period, nor, as has often been noted, do we "hear their voices" in our literary sources. If we are to have a history of Greek women, childbirth must form a central part of it.

The cultural context of childbirth in classical Greece was the

1

polis, or autonomous city-state, made up of individual households, or *oikoi*.[3] Men lived in the dual world of *polis* and *oikos*, but women's status and role was determined entirely in terms of membership— or lack of membership—in an *oikos*. The *oikos* provided the cultural context of reproduction for all women: from citizen wife to slave worker, all had some role within an *oikos* or were defined negatively in terms of their roles outside the *oikos* in the public world of men. Moreover, the interests of the *oikos* as an institution determined such crucial societal factors as optimal age at first childbirth, nutritional status of females, and the forms of assistance available during pregnancy and childbirth. These factors affected all women, from the privileged citizen wife anxious to produce a legitimate heir for the *oikos*, to the slave singer seeking to avoid or terminate a pregnancy that would endanger her owner's profits. Thus we need to begin our investigation with a consideration of the norm, the life of the free woman of citizen birth who lived within the *oikos* as the wife of a citizen, pledged to him by her father for the propagation of legitimate children.[4]

The Oikos and Its Women

The *oikos* consisted of the house itself, its land, and the people, animals, and objects that it housed. It was headed by a male landowner and its continuity depended upon the continuation of this man's line, but it was not simply a family of kinship. Membership involved a combination of blood relationship and physical residence, for nonkin (including slaves) who lived in the house were regarded as part of the *oikos*, while those who lived in other *oikoi* were considered to be outsiders and rivals even if they were kin. Consequently, when a woman went in marriage to the *oikos* of her husband, she became a member of that household and ceased being a member of the household of her birth (although the break was not complete: emotional ties remained, as attested by the dedication of the funerary monuments for married women by parents, and a woman could return to her birth *oikos* when her marriage was terminated by divorce or the death of her husband). Each *oikos* ideally functioned as a self-sufficient unit, and relationships between *oikoi* were more competitive than cooperative: each household vied with every other in a jealous competition for honor, and in the contest each was continually vulnerable to loss.

The weakest point in the strong front that the *oikos* presented to the external world lay in its women: to survive, it had to produce new members in the male line, and this required the introduction of outsiders—women who would become the mothers of its sons. It was upon this service to the *oikos* as childbearers that women's lives were centered. At birth they were viewed as temporary and costly members of the household, for they were destined to leave it to become mothers in a rival *oikos*, carrying away with them a portion of the household's wealth in dowry. In the meantime, their vulnerability made them a constant threat to the honor of the house and they had to be continually guarded and watched. It is thus not surprising that there was little rejoicing at the birth of a girl.

Of course, a growing daughter could and probably did come to be loved and enjoyed by her parents; there were also practical ways in which she could be useful to her family, but these were tinged with negatives and were not traditionally reasons for celebration. For example, even in poorer families, daughters could be useful in creating new connections through marriage: wisely chosen in-laws possessed assets that complemented those of the bride's family, even if only extra hands to help out in emergencies. Again, a daughter could also serve as a valuable safety factor for the preservation of the *oikos* in the event that no sons were born or none survived. Such a daughter, on the death of her father, was designated an *epikleros*, a word usually, but somewhat misleadingly, translated "heiress." Unlike our concept of an heiress, the Greek term applied to poor as well as rich, and the *epikleros* did not herself inherit but was literally "attached to the *kleros*," or estate. The law required that her nearest agnatic male relative (usually her father's brother or his son) marry her, or arrange for her marriage to another; her sons by this marriage (called an *epidikasia*) would inherit the *oikos* of their grandfather.[5] Thus the institution of the *epikleros* served two purposes: it insured the marriage of fatherless girls, even poor girls, and it made possible the transmission of the *oikos* over a gap in the male line. But the birth of a son was a more direct

3

insurance for the survival of the line, and few new parents would have found the arrival of a potential *epikleros* an equal cause for rejoicing.

Two other benefits often provided by daughters in modern Greek families, care of parents in old age and companionship for mothers, were of less significance in ancient Greece. The early age of marriage meant that mothers could not enjoy their daughters as adult co-workers and companions. Moreover, it was sons, rather than daughters, who traditionally, and legally, were responsible for the care of aged parents. Thus female companionship, sharing of work, and physical care in old age would have been provided by the daughter-in-law. Nevertheless, the new daughter-in-law was welcomed with mixed feelings. Although bringing dowry and the promise of fertility, she came as an intruder, and her new family viewed her with mistrust as an alien element. Not only did the young wife as vulnerable female present one more threat to the honor of the house, in her role as official progenitor she could even threaten the continuity she was brought in to assure—"one mother, many fathers," as the Greek saying goes.

In this brief description, the *oikos* system may appear to be a rather unsatisfactory way of organizing the family, at least from the female point of view, but in fact it has been remarkably resilient, serving the needs of Greek villagers almost unchanged through the centuries. This description of the modern Greek village family, or *spiti* (literally, house), which Du Boulay visited and studied in 1966, could as well have been written about the *oikos* of classical Greece:

> The normative values of this society all contribute to the house being a sanctuary from the troubles which its members find in the outer community. . . . Whatever the relations within the house, the members of it do their best to conceal their differences and to close their ranks in the face of the wider community, and this solidarity is recognized in the fact that the "house" or "family" is treated by that community as a single social reality [6]

Even when modernization and economic changes began to transform Greek life, the system was not abandoned; rather, Greek families shifted and adapted it to suit new conditions.[7]

The structural similarity and the many striking parallels between classical and modern traditional Greek household/families have been much noted; in fact, almost all ethnographic studies cite parallels with the ancient evidence,[8] and classicists have used modern village studies to illuminate their investigations of ancient Greece.[9] Given the paucity of evidence about the ancient Greek family, comparative material is especially welcome. Of course this does not mean that we can automatically apply findings about modern Greece to the classical period, for there are very real, and very basic, differences between the two—religious, legal, and economic. But in comparative studies differences can often be as useful as likenesses, especially in raising questions. A good example is the case of the mother-in-law. In modern traditional Greek families the mother-in-law was a crucial figure in women's lives, the veritable matriarch of the family into which the young bride entered. In fact, the birth mother was sometimes referred to as the "temporary mother," and a daughter as a "guest," for she was destined to spend far more of her life with her mother-in-law than with her actual mother.[10] In classical Greece, in contrast, the mother-in-law is an almost invisible figure. The role of the mother-in-law in traditional Greece does not allow us to infer a similar role for her in antiquity, but it should lead us to ask whether this figure is missing or simply invisible, and what this might mean.

The Pattern of Female Life

BIRTH AND CHILDHOOD

In classical Greece the problems inherent in being female were believed to begin with conception. Females were held to be weaker, warmer, and more fluid than males, and thus to take longer to develop in the womb: one Hippocratic author gives forty-two days for the articulation of a female fetus, and thirty days for that of a male.[11] The period of the lochial flow, and thus the period during which the new mother was considered polluted and a threat to others, was calculated to correspond to the period required for articulation of the fetus: forty-two days for a female, thirty days for a male. Thus the mother who gave birth to a boy was able to resume her normal

5

life twelve days sooner than the mother of a girl.[12]

Since they were weaker and less active, and the child was believed to provide the motive force in the birth process, the birth of girls was considered to be more difficult for the mother.[13] Therefore it is perhaps not surprising that most of the cases of complications after childbirth described in the Hippocratic treatise *Epidemics* followed the birth of girls.[14]

At birth the guardian (*kyrios*) of a newborn infant, who was usually the father in the case of a child born to a citizen woman, had the right to decide whether to accept it into the *oikos* and raise it, or to expose it, but not to kill it outright.[15] Exposure put the child's fate in the hands of the gods and absolved the *oikos* of any blood guilt if it should die. A person taking in an exposed child could rear it as either free or slave, but the act of exposure did not break the legal tie between the child and its *kyrios*, and the child might later be reclaimed if it could be identified.[16] Did exposed children usually die? Were they expected to? How often were they "found" and saved, and for what purposes (as a free family member, as a slave, as a prostitute)?[17] We simply don't know the answers to these questions, but most scholars agree that the right of the *kyrios* to expose an infant was not purely formal.[18]

That girls were exposed more often than boys remains, as Golden puts it, "likely (though not beyond reasonable doubt)."[19] The literary and epigraphic evidence is fragmentary, mostly late, and inconclusive, and it unfortunately does not allow us to decide beyond that reasonable doubt.[20] It may be helpful, however, to consider attitudes in modern rural Greece, where newborn girls are often unwelcome arrivals (and where, of course, there is no legally sanctioned right of exposure). Sanders reports that men often do not count daughters when asked how many children they have (a practice that was common in antiquity as well and that complicates attempts to determine family size in the speeches of the Attic orators).[21] Among the modern Greek shepherd community of the Sarakatsani, when the husband visited his wife for the first time after the birth of a daughter she turned her head away from him in shame.[22] In a village in Euboea, according to Du Boulay, the birth of a girl often caused a man shame and aroused his anger at his wife.[23]

6

This devaluing of the female had its consequences. Blum and Blum report that in discussions with village women it was difficult to distinguish between abortions, "nine-month abortions," stillbirths, and infanticide. Female infants in particular were more likely to be candidates for "nine-month abortions." Although infanticide was abhorrent to the women, the belief that unbaptized babies were not yet fully human beings—and might even be demons—mitigated its impact.[24] Finally, Du Boulay reports two circumstantial stories of female infanticide: in one case, the mother, incited by her mother-in-law, threw her infant daughter into a ditch to die; in the other, a recent widow, who already had one young son, on the advice of others neglected her newborn female infant with the result that she died.[25]

In many cultures in which boys are more highly valued, sex selection takes place without conscious intention by comparative neglect in infant feeding and care.[26] Girls are weaned earlier than boys and thus are exposed to the risks of unsanitary food preparation and deprived of the immunological defenses that breast milk provides. In some modern cultures, ostensibly neutral or even positive reasons are given for early weaning of girls: girls are smaller and need less food, early weaning will ensure them an early menopause and an end to the burden of childbearing (Taiwan), breast milk transmits qualities of sexuality and aggression that are desirable in boys but undesirable in girls (Equador).[27]

There is no direct evidence for infant-feeding practices in classical Greece.[28] The fact that girls do not seem to have participated in Choes, the festival in which children marked the end of infancy and nursing, suggests that girls were weaned with less ceremony, and possibly earlier, than boys.[29] The prevalence of references to bladder stones in children, especially boys, in the Hippocratic treatises,[30] suggests that breast milk was often insufficient: bladder stones are rare in children except when breast feeding is supplemented with less nutritious substitutes, such as the barley gruel that was a favorite prescription of the Hippocratic doctor. But the prevalence of boys in these reports does not provide information about sex-differential feeding practices, for boys are anatomically more subject to bladder stones than girls. Moreover, barley gruel was viewed almost as a cure-all, and it might even have been given to boys as part of a preferential nursing regimen.

Although we cannot make definite statements about Greek nursing practices, there is some evidence that females in general were believed to require less food than males and that growing girls were fed less than boys (except in Sparta, which, in this as in many things, constituted an exception to general Greek practice in the treatment of women).[31] It is revealing that Xenophon's Ischomachus says admiringly that one of the few things his bride had been taught before her marriage was to control her appetite.[32] The situation in modern Greece appears to be much the same. Campbell reported that among the Sarakatsani, women ate the leftovers after the men had finished; no portion was set aside for them, and they often got very little.[33] Doumanis, in a study of mothering in a group of villages in Epirus (northwest Greece), describes the bride as standing by as the men eat, ready to wait on them; once her own household has been established, as a mother she eats at the table with her family when guests are not present, but she plays a coordinating role, eating less than anyone else and offering her share to whomever she judges to be in most need.[34] The result of a regimen of undernourishment must be to increase both infant and maternal mortality, and, in fact, one scholar has attributed the lower life expectancy of women in classical Greece to undernourishment rather than the hazards of childbirth.[35] This effect even extends into the second generation, for females who experience severe malnutrition during the first two trimesters of their own life in utero due to the undernourishment of their mothers have less favorable outcomes when they themselves become pregnant than do those whose uterine life was normal.[36]

Newborns who were not selected for exposure in classical Greece were officially accepted into the family in a ceremony called the *amphidromia*; it was held on the fifth or seventh day after birth and was restricted to members of the *oikos* and those who had been present at the birth,[37] although relatives and friends might send gifts. Families often named girls then as well, dispensing with the more elaborate and expensive second ceremony traditionally held on the tenth day, the *dekate*, at which friends and relatives were feasted and entertained.[38] It is unclear whether girls were introduced to the father's phratry, an occasion that marked the father's public acknowledgment of a son's legitimacy; if some girls were introduced, it was not a general practice.[39]

The names chosen for girls, as well as the way in which female names were used, reflected their subordinate status. Many girls' names were feminine forms of male names, or names embodying male military virtues, such as Lysistrata (loose the army); abstract nouns or adjectives expressing the qualities parents might hope for in a girl, such as Malthake (soft) or Makaria (happiness); or diminutives.[40] Girls' birth names were heard only within the family; girls were preferably not referred to in public at all, but if need arose, they were identified by the possessive case of the name of their father. Once married, the woman was similarly identified by her husband's name—women were thus linguistically defined as the possessions of men.[41] Similarly, in modern Greece among the Sarakatsani, women on marriage were referred to by a feminine form of their husband's name. The significance of this was made clear by Campbell:

> After her marriage a woman is never again addressed by her baptismal name except when she visits the home of her birth. She takes instead the christian name of her husband to which the suffix "-ina" is added . . . In this way there is expressed not only the severance of a woman from her family of origin and her subordination to the authority of her husband, but also the absolute quality of their union.[42]

In antiquity, the lives of free citizen girls as they grew up were centered in the *oikos* where they could be protected (again Sparta is cited in our sources as an exception: to encourage reproduction and for eugenic reasons, Spartan girls were required to exercise and to take part—unclothed—in public ceremonies with boys).[43] The girl was carefully watched and guarded to protect her honor—and that of the *oikos*—until she could be safely married off. Clearly, the less contact the young female had with the world outside the *oikos*, the less opportunity she had to jeopardize her own and its honor. Xenophon's Ischomachus says approvingly that his wife had been raised seeing, hearing, and saying as little as possible.[44] In modern

Greece, a bride is praised for being, "straight from her mother's arms," or "never going beyond the front door."[45]

In the home, girls learned to work wool and weave, spending much of their time on the production of items for their trousseaux.[46] Until recently, in modern Greek villages women and their mothers invested years of labor in producing the necessities for dressing a house: carpets, coverings for wall niches, wall hangings, curtains, and embroideries for every surface. These were displayed at the time of the wedding, and the girl's skill and diligence added to the honor of the house.[47]

Other activities of girls at home were also basically domestic. They learned child care by helping with younger siblings. Some may even have received informal instruction in the home in writing and reading, which would have been useful in household management.[48] Although cult activities provided opportunities for married women to venture outside the home, and a few girls from elite families filled prestigious civic cult roles,[49] it is unlikely that most girls took part in public religious ceremonies before their coming-of-age service to Artemis. As we noted, they seem not to have participated in Choes, the festival that marked the end of infancy. Girls, like Ischomachus's bride, were kept within the *oikos*, seeing, hearing, and saying as little as possible.

The main event in the life of a growing girl was menarche, for this signaled the time for marriage and her departure from the *oikos*. Traditionally menarche was reckoned as occurring at the age of fourteen, a number that probably had more to do with the concept of seven-year cycles of development than with actual physical maturation.[50] Thus girls literally laid aside their childhood toys when they dedicated them before their marriage to Artemis, the goddess who would soon determine their fate in childbirth.[51] Such haste in marrying off girls reflected concern lest their awakening sexuality bring dishonor on the household and make them less marriageable (requiring a larger dowry).[52] In Xenophon's *Oeconomicus*, Ischomachus's bride was a well-sheltered fourteen and Kritoboulos's was "a mere child" ($\pi\alpha\iota\delta\alpha\nu$ $\nu\dot{\epsilon}\alpha\nu$ $\mu\dot{\alpha}\lambda\iota\sigma\tau\alpha$);[53] Demosthenes' sister was betrothed at five, with marriage planned ten years later.[54] A woman in the *Epidemics* is reported to have died at about seventeen after giving birth to a firstborn son.[55] Evidence for a legal minimum age for marriage comes from Gortyn in Crete, where in mid-fifth century it was fixed at twelve for girls,[56] while a law from Thasos has been interpreted as mandating the provision of dowries to orphan girls at the age of fourteen.[57] Sparta again was an exception, decreeing on eugenic grounds that women should be fully grown before they married and bore children.[58] The early age of marriage in classical Greece is one of the noteworthy points of contrast with modern Greece, where women ordinarily marry in their mid-to-late twenties, and men (as in classical Greece) around the age of thirty.[59]

The approach of menarche was a time filled with anxiety for a girl and her family. For the girl, this was perhaps aggravated by participation in coming-of-age ceremonies such as "playing the bear" at the shrine of Artemis in Brauron, in which the previously sheltered girl took part in group activities, including games and races in the nude.[60] At this time the girl might first experience symptoms that the culture attributed to the womb: torpor, anxiety, suffocation, and suicidal and murderous impulses. In fact, so many girls were afflicted with this syndrome that the Hippocratic doctors devoted a special treatise to it, the *Parthenoi*, or *Illness of Maidens* (the treatise appears in translation with discussion in chapter 4). They diagnosed the illness either as blocked menses (i.e., delayed menarche) or as a wandering womb, an affliction that was destined to play a important role in the girl's subsequent life (see chapter 3).[61]

MARRIAGE AND MOTHERHOOD

Marriage was viewed as a practical business arrangement, not a love match. What mattered was the viability of the new family unit; affection might, or might not, come later. As in modern Greek families, preliminary inquiries about the suitability of prospective candidates were conducted surreptitiously to avoid the affront to the honor of the house that would be entailed by a public rejection. Once a match seemed possible, negotiations were carried on—still as secretly as possible—between the girl's father and the prospective groom,[62] who was probably in his early thirties.[63] The negotiations involved matters that would materially affect the girl's future living conditions: the prospective husband's inheritance and prospects, including the number of brothers who would share in the partible inheritance, any unmarried sisters (men ideally postponed their marriages until all of their sisters had been provided with dowries and married), the condition of the house in which the couple would live, and the amount and type of work the woman would have to do (in modern Greece farm work is avoided when possible, and premiums are paid in dowry to marry a girl into the town). All of these matters, as well as the character and personality of the candidates and the importance of their family connections, played roles in determining the dowry a girl's family might expect the prospective groom to accept.

Although the dowry was the focus of bargaining in marriage negotiations, this should not be seen simply as an expression of mercenary concerns. The dowry, which consisted of cash, movables, and sometimes houses, but not land,[64] was the woman's contribution to the joint household and a continuing source of protection for her.[65] Although managed by her *kyrios* (husband, father, son), it remained hers, going with her on the dissolution of the marriage by divorce (unless she had been unfaithful) or the death of her husband. Women were thus not financially dependent upon their husbands during the marriage, and they were assured of continuous support regardless of their marital status. And since the dowry was usually merged with the other household funds and might be difficult for the husband to repay, it offered a woman protection against frivolous divorce. It was a matter of family honor to dower a girl as well as possible, and speeches from the lawcourts suggest that well-to-do families provided from under 5 percent to nearly 20 percent of their resources.[66]

Girls whose families were too poor to provide a dowry ran the risk of remaining unmarried (which would have meant loss of status through life as a concubine, *hetaira*, or prostitute), although it seems that some way was usually found to provide a respectable life for the girl. A man might marry a girl with little or no dowry for the sake of friendship, or because of the honor attached to her family.[67] Providing a dowry for a poor relative was considered to be a significant act of piety, comparable with ransoming prisoners or providing funeral expenses for those unable to afford them.[68] The institution of the *epikleros* was also a way of providing for the marriage of girls who might otherwise lack a dowry.

There are strong parallels between dowry and marriage customs in classical and in modern Greek village life. Although dowry is no longer mandated by Greek law, it remains at the heart of marriage strategies.[69] Families work hard to provide daughters with dowries and take pride in the virtues and prestige of the husbands they are able to acquire for them. Village families are especially willing to sacrifice to enable girls to marry urban husbands, who can provide not only a better and easier life for the girl but also useful contacts in the city for the entire family. While Greek villagers find dowry burdensome, they also find it hard to understand how any society can do without it. (A clue might be provided by the Greek practice of considering an education beyond the state-mandated minimum as the equivalent of a share in the inheritance. Thus an American woman with a college degree or professional qualifications might be considered to be offering a dowry to a prospective spouse; in turn, she is likely to consider only men with similar or higher qualifications as prospective husbands. Nevertheless, such a "dowry" does not offer the protection of a Greek dowry, for the value of professional qualifications depends upon relatively uninterrupted employment, and on the dissolution of marriage American women who have opted to take time out from a career to raise a family often find themselves unable to return to career employment and thus in severe financial straits.)

Once the terms of the dowry were satisfactorily arranged, the contract was sealed by the *engye*, a ceremony in which the prospective husband pledged to the *kyrios* of the bride that he received her, "for the purpose of the plowing of legitimate children."[70] The *engye* was conducted between two males; the presence of the bride herself was not required, nor need she even be aware of the proceedings. Although the *engye* often functioned as the guarantee of a legitimate marriage in inheritance disputes, and was apparently the only legal requirement for an effective marriage, a separate and more public celebration with the bride present (the *gamos*) usually marked the actual transfer of the woman from her old to her new *oikos* and the consummation of the marriage (*synoikein*).[71] It was during the *gamos* that the bride, by her unveiling (*anakalypteria*), signaled her formal acceptance of the union.

Marriage, while much anticipated and desired, was nevertheless a traumatic affair for the bride. Not only was her new husband considerably older than she, she was unlikely to have had much, if any, contact with him, even though marriage between cousins was favored.[72] But at the heart of the trauma of marriage was departure from her own *oikos* and entrance into a new household that, even if it were composed of kin, still appeared, in the context of the *oikos* system, as part of the hostile external world and that, in fact, had its guard up against her as an intruder. When a daughter married, even if she continued to live in the same neighborhood, she became a member of a new household to which she was expected to give her primary loyalties.[73] The dramatic break with her old home is expressed in the traditional association of weddings with death and funerals, which can be traced from antiquity to modern Greece.[74] In Greek mythology the goddess Demeter's loss of her daughter Persephone through her rape/marriage by Hades, the god of the Underworld, is truly a marriage-death, and to celebrate marriage with Hades was a common metaphor for the deaths of unmarried girls.[75] In the tradition of Greek laments, which stretches back to antiquity and is still practiced in modern Greece, recognition that marriage and death both involve separation and loss is expressed by the use of almost identical laments for both:

> Now I have set out. Now I am
>   about to depart
> from my home and from my dear
>   brothers and sisters.
> [For a funeral: from the black and
>   cobwebbed earth]
> Everyone is driving me away,
>   everyone is telling me to leave.

14

Even my mother is driving me away.
   She doesn't want me.
And my father too, even he tells
   me to leave.
I am leaving with tears and with a
   heavy heart.[76]

Once the excitement of the wedding was over, the bride faced
life in a strange new household. As Euripides' Medea laments,
"coming to new customs, habits new, one need be a seer, to know
the thing unlearnt at home, what manner of man her mate shall
be."[77] Was she also, as a new member of the *oikos*, subject to the
control of her mother-in-law? This was the traditional pattern of
modern Greek village life (although today this is changing): young
married couples customarily lived with the husband's parents, and
the young wife was obedient to her in-laws.[78] It was the mother-in-
law who exercised the most notable control since it was she who
allocated resources and work within the household. This extended
household ideally endured until all the siblings had been married
and the youngest brother's children approached school age. At that
time the property was divided, each son establishing his own independent household. The parental home was allotted to the youngest son and his family, together with an extra share of the patrimony, so that he could care for the parents until their deaths.
Thus a woman had to survive an extended period of subservience
in a joint household under the control of her mother-in-law before
having a home of her own, but she could also look forward to several years during which she herself would be a virtual matriarch
ruling over her sons' wives (which must have made the birth of
sons especially welcome).

The mother-in-law is, however, almost invisible (as most
women are) in the ancient, male-oriented sources.[79] One catches
only occasional glimpses of her, as in Euphiletos's speech in Lysias
On the Murder of Eratosthenes:

When I decided to marry and had brought a wife home, at first my
attitude toward her was this: I did not wish to annoy her, but neither
was she to have too much of her own way I watched her as well as I

could, and kept an eye on her as was proper. But later, after my child had been born, I came to trust her, and I handed all my possessions over to her, believing that this was the greatest possible proof of affection. Well, members of the jury, in the beginning she was the best of women. She was a clever housewife, economical and exact in her management of everything. But then, my mother died. . . .[80]

Here Euphiletos, who has killed his wife's lover, in defending himself against a charge of murder emphasizes the care he took in watching over his wife so that no blame would fall on him for offering her an opportunity for adultery. Although the immediate connection between the death of his mother and the beginning of his wife's affair was that the lover saw her at the funeral, the coincidence of the two also suggests that it may have been the mother-in-law who had been the more important factor in keeping the young wife in line. Similarly, we might suspect a mother-in-law hidden behind Ischomachus's account of *his* training of his new bride in Xenophon's *Oeconomicus*, despite (or because of) his idealized picture of the process.

Mention of daughters-in-law may have been suppressed in our sources. Of thirteen cases in the Attic orators in which widows lived with adult sons, Hunter found only two in which son's wives were mentioned (or implied).[81] Lysias in [Demosthenes] 59.22 says that he did not bring prostitutes into the house out of respect for his wife and his aged mother who lived there. And Demosthenes 37.45 recounts an alleged intrusion into the women's quarters of a man's home in which his daughters and mother were residing (daughters presuppose a wife, at least at some time, but she is not mentioned in this passage). Of these thirteen men whose mothers lived with them, however, four were young, under the normal age for marriage of thirty, and Hunter judges that the evidence does not support Isager's inference of a marriage pattern in which sons of widows put off marriage until after the death of their mother.[82]

Other evidence is negative in nature, allowing us at most to infer the existence of mothers-in-law from the negative impression of their absence. Thus the speaker in [Demosthenes] 25.87–88 describes the way in which, in households containing father, sons, and even the children of sons, forbearance is exercised toward the inevitable differences in life-style between the generations, so that harmony prevails. He does not even mention the presence of women in such multigenerational households. Plato suggests that the forbearance described by [Demosthenes] often failed, for he recommends that newlyweds set up independent households (but on the paternal plot of land), in order to spare families from the irritations of too much togetherness.[83] It is unlikely that Plato would have recommended against the sharing of living quarters unless it was frequently done, and also unlikely that all these establishments were composed only of males.

Because these scattered bits of evidence are mainly negative in nature, and the mother-in-law is otherwise so invisible in our sources, we may suspect systematic suppression, on the principle that respectable women were not to be named in public.[84] Alternatively, the invisibility of the mother-in-law may in many cases be due to her actual absence. The average female age at death was probably about forty-five,[85] an age when a woman might expect to have an eldest son of no more than thirty. Golden estimates that only about 40 percent of mothers lived to see a son's child—and thus to spend much time in the role of mother-in-law.[86] When fewer than half of brides had mothers-in-law, it may be that the culture did not allot them an active matriarchal role in the new family structure, even if they continued to live in the household.

In order to establish her position in her new family, the bride had to produce a child, preferably a son. Only the birth of a child gave her full status as a *gyne*, woman-wife.[87] All eyes would therefore be upon her in the early days of the marriage. Corvisier estimates that 10 percent of Greek women (and 3 percent of men) were unable to conceive, which is about double the modern rate for women. He also calculates that appeals for cures of sterility at Epidauros amounted to 15.38 percent of all requests, topped only by eye troubles and blindness (17.94 percent).[88] Complicating matters for the young bride would have been the fact that many girls experience a period of postpubertal subfertility (problems might also be caused by the Greek misconception about the time of fertility, which was believed to occur just before or just after menstruation).[89] Any delay would naturally raise questions about the bride's fertility and might lead to the employment of fertility tests (if these had not already been performed as part of the marriage negotiations). Such tests figure prominently in the gynecological treatises; some involved sympathetic magic (give a fasting woman butter and the milk of a woman who is nursing a boy; if she belches, she will conceive), others employed the anatomical model of a woman's reproductive system as a tube extending from the mouth to the vagina (apply a pessary of a little bitter almond wrapped in wool to the vagina; if the odor of almond comes out of her mouth, the woman will conceive).[90]

If the girl passed the fertility tests, numerous treatments were available that were intended to foster conception. One of the more innocuous of these involved eating a sea polypus cooked over the fire until it was half-burnt, and then applying patties of ground Egyptian soda (nitron), coriander, and cumin to the genitals.[91] On the other hand, some treatments were quite harsh, even if not fatal:

> A woman who was healthy and stout was gripped by pain in the belly from a medication taken for the sake of conception; twisting in the intestines; she swelled up; breathing prominent, difficult, with pain. She did not vomit much. She was on the verge of dying for five days, so that she seemed to be dead. Vomiting cold water did not relieve either the pain coming upon her or the breathing. They poured about thirty amphorae of cold water over her body, and this alone seemed to help. Later she passed much bile from below, but when the pain gripped her, she was not able to. She lived.[92]

If the young wife survived to become pregnant, many obstacles still lay in her way before she became the successful mother of a living child. Aristotle explicitly warns that early childbearing produces small and weak infants and difficult and dangerous labor for the mother.[93] Years of undernourishment compromised the woman's chances of bearing a healthy child, and illnesses frequent among the general population posed special risks to her because of the suppression of cell-mediated immunity during pregnancy.[94] Women whose cases are recorded in the Hippocratic treatise *Epidemics* suffered from a wide variety of complications, which we will consider more closely in future chapters. Yet despite the problems that pregnancy entailed, the Greeks considered it as an optimum condition for women, rather than a state of illness.

No actual delivery is described in the cases in the *Epidemics*, and it is commonly accepted that normal births were handled by a midwife, with the doctor called in only if there were complications.[95] Two Hippocratic passages do, however, appear to imply that a (male) doctor was involved in deliveries: in the first,[96] the author includes childbirth and abortion among those situations in which the doctor must act at the opportune moment (καιρός); in the second,[97] he says that a doctor is blamed if he gives a pregnant woman a vomitive and she aborts, or if he gives a patient something to relieve the pain of childbirth and she worsens or dies. Both of these could, however, apply to the treatment of patients with complications.

The Hippocratic view of the mechanics of childbirth is outlined in the embryological treatise *Nature of the Child*. Its author explains that birth is initiated when the child, having exhausted the supply of food in the womb, becomes restless and moves about violently, breaking the membranes; the child then batters its own way out, like a chick out of an egg.[98] This view of the child as the active element in the birth process, initiating labor and making its way into the world by its own efforts, while the woman remains passive, is implicit in many other passages in the Hippocratic treatises. For example, *Nature of Woman* says that "the uterus becomes more open since the child is advancing through it and causing violence and pain [to the mother]."[99] This view was upheld despite the seemingly contradictory evidence of birth contractions, which were in fact noticed by the careful Hippocratic observers.[100] This provides an interesting example of the way in which preconceived assumptions and theories dictate perceptions: the Hippocratic physician, in keeping with the Greek view of women as passive, saw the pain and contractions of the woman as responses to the violent efforts of the infant.

Childbirth was not expected to be entirely "natural." Socrates in Plato's *Theatetus* says that midwives use drugs and incantations to bring on labor and to reduce the pain.[101] Among the medical texts, a passage in *Superfetation* prescribes the use of medications in the case of a dead fetus that presents difficulties in delivery: fumigations to moisten the womb are prescribed, and, if this is not effective, something (unspecified) to eat or drink to bring on pains is to be given.[102] (Many of the drugs listed in the gynecological treatises that have abortifacient properties may have been used more often to stimulate labor than to procure an abortion.)

Available pain-killers included the opium poppy, henbane, and the root of white mandrake; opium, of course, is a sedative, and the latter two plants yield hyoscine and hyoscyamine, which also have narcotic and sedative properties.[103] Helen King has argued, however, that the use of pain-killers was probably confined to complicated deliveries. She points out that the word *ponos*, which is regularly used for the normal pains of childbirth, was usually applied to the type of pain that was considered part of the necessary processes of living: it was used to describe pain that has a goal and that one is expected to bear, such as agricultural labor or strengthening exercises. In contrast, the term *odyne*, was used for sudden, sharp pain that pierced the body; this was the type of pain for which pain-relievers were considered appropriate.[104] Since the term *odyne* was sometimes applied to the pains of childbirth, it seems likely that medications were reserved for the excessive pain of complications.

How many pregnancies did the average wife undergo? By estimating the age of skeletal remains and analyzing pelvic scars, J. Lawrence Angel produced a set of well-known statistics: women in classical Greece underwent an average of 4.5 childbirths and their average age at death was thirty-five years, compared with an average age of death for men of slightly less than forty-five years.[105] But Angel's analysis is problematic. The data upon which it is based are very limited: the skeletal remains of thirty-four women and forty-four men from Corinth and Athens that have been dated between 650 and 350 B.C.[106] Moreover, determinations of the age of skeletons are characteristically low,[107] and it now seems likely that Angel underestimated the age of death for the females in his study by about ten years.[108] But the most serious challenge to Angel's figures are numerous recent investigations of the use of pubic bone scars as a means of determining parity. In these investigations "birth scars" sometimes appeared on the bones of women who had never given birth, while they were sometimes lacking on the bones of elderly women who had borne numerous children.[109] The conclusion of all these studies has been that no criteria exist that would allow a determination of parity on the basis of such scaring. Thus we must reject Angel's estimate of 4.5 births per woman, as well as his estimate of thirty-five as the average age of death of females.

Corvisier has taken another tack, making use of estimated rates of sterility and infant mortality to conclude that a simple replacement of population would have required each fertile woman to bear six children.[110] However, population seems to have been expanding in the fifth century, at least in Athens, if we are to judge by the Athenians' ability to cope with large losses of manpower successfully until the last years of the Peloponnesian War. This suggests that fertile Athenian women must have been bearing more than the six infants that would ensure mere population replacement. A similar conclusion is reached by considering references to a number of families in the Attic orators cited by Sallares; these include thirteen wives with twenty-nine sons and twenty-six daughters, and thus an average of 4.23 surviving children per wife.[111] These were admittedly wealthy families whose members could afford to raise more than the absolute minimum number of children and whose offspring may have had better chances of survival than those born to the poor; nonetheless, women in these families had access to no more effective birth control methods than did the poor, and the number of their surviving children suggests that they were undergoing more than six pregnancies in their lifetimes.[112] While women who reproduced at this rate probably succeeded in avoiding the problems of the wandering womb, which afflicted underutilized uteruses, they incurred the additional risks of multiple pregnancies: each pregnancy, with its associated suppression of cell-mediated immunity, exposes the woman to additional risks, and mortality rises sharply after three births.[113]

Although Euphiletos in Lysias's speech claimed to believe that bearing a child should strengthen the bonds between husband and wife, there is evidence to suggest that childbirth was an area of potential conflict between husband and wife. A woman who was eager for pregnancy when first married might become increasingly reluctant to undergo additional pregnancies as the number of her children increased, especially if her husband seemed likely to expose female offspring. He, in contrast, might still be interested in adding sons to the family. The evidence does suggest that it was women who took the initiative in seeking abortions (although that evidence is all from male sources). A Hippocratic author says that abortion is something women are "always doing," and another suspects that a patient who suffered an abortion might have done something to bring it on herself, withholding this information from both doctor and husband.[114] In the matter of abortion, Hippocratic doctors sided with the husband, disapproving it as dangerous and likely to result in sterility (a matter we discuss at greater length in chapter 3).[115] An even greater source of conflict between spouses than wives' propensity to resort to abortion, however, was the husband's suspicion that a wife who had not succeeded in producing a son would connive, perhaps with the assistance of a midwife, to exchange a female infant for a male substitute, or even feign pregnancy in order to introduce a suppositious child into the *oikos*.[116] Exchange would of course have been much easier than feigning pregnancy, and the male infants of slaves would have been available. Menander's *Perikeiromene* portrays an old woman who found twins and gave the boy to a woman who "needed" a child, keeping the girl for herself (twins were considered inauspicious and so were likely candidates for exposure).

Once a child was born, the mother's most urgent job was to keep it alive, for at least half of all newborns failed to survive until maturity.[117] The Hippocratic doctor offered her little help in the care of her newborn. Only one brief treatise, *Dentition*, is devoted to medical problems in infants, and that only in part.[118] We must assume that mothers relied on what they had learned themselves while growing up and helping to care for siblings, as well as on the advice of other women in the household, friends and neighbors, and especially the midwife. Here, again, information about the presence of the mother-in-law would be useful.

In addition to child care, the woman in the *oikos* managed the household, cleaned and maintained the house and courtyard, kept a kitchen garden, prepared meals, wove clothing for the family and items for the trousseaux of her daughters, or oversaw the activities of household slaves working at these tasks. Another important job that fell to the wife as housekeeper, the care of the sick, has generally been overlooked because the medical treatises are not explicit about who carried it out. But a passage in a speech attributed to Demosthenes suggests that women were active caretakers. Phrastor had repudiated his pregnant wife when he learned that she was not, as had been claimed, the daughter of an Athenian citizen. Then he fell very ill and, as he said, he had no one to care for him because he had quarreled with his relatives and was childless. His former wife and her mother came and took over, providing medicines appropriate to his illness as well as caring for him. Not incidentally, they also persuaded him to adopt the child the wife had subsequently borne. Regardless of the speaker's special interests in portraying this situation, it is significant for the traditional procedures of Greek medical care that he expected the jury to accept his helpless position as well as the role of the women in prescribing for his illness in addition to nursing him. Addressing the jury, the speaker comments, "You know of yourselves what value a woman has in the sick-room, when she waits upon a man who is ill."[119] (Nonetheless, the speaker's main point is the way in which the women took advantage of his helplessness to persuade him to adopt the child.) In their study of health conditions in modern Greek villages, the Blums found that 96 percent of the households reported that someone had been sick in the previous year, and that the earliest stage of advice seeking and care giving was within the family (followed by consultation with a neighboring "wise woman" noted for her healing skills).[120] Similarly, it is very likely that medical care and nursing filled a good part of the time of an ancient Greek wife.

Although a Greek woman's "place" was undoubtedly within the *oikos*, David Cohen has recently argued that this separateness of sphere did not mean a life of seclusion.[121] It is true that there were a number of occasions upon which women left their homes. They attended family rites of passage such as weddings and funerals; in cases of emergency they could be displayed in court to rouse sympathy, and they might visit male family members in prison; their assistance to neighboring women in childbirth probably was based on friendships that involved routine visiting, if only to borrow

23

household items. Women from poor families necessarily left their homes for practical purposes: lacking servants, they had to fetch water from the community fountain, where they would have met with other women, and they might even have worked as vendors in the market—but at a cost of social status.

Religious activities, especially those connected with their role as childbearers, perhaps offered women the most socially acceptable opportunities to venture outside the home. This participation began for most girls at puberty when initiation rites took the form of communal activities. For example, "playing the bear" for Artemis in the festival called the Arkteia took some Athenian girls as far afield as Brauron, where they stayed for an undetermined period of time; others celebrated the occasion closer to their homes.[122] The most widely celebrated of the occasions that allowed women a temporary respite from the routines of the *oikos* was the annual festival of Demeter, the Thesmophoria. This festival recalled the motherhood of Demeter and the loss of her daughter Persephone through rape/ marriage to Hades. During the celebrations, which lasted from three to ten days depending on the *polis*, married women left their homes and camped out together in a *polis* of women, while the operations of the male *polis* came to a halt. The women mourned Demeter's loss of her daughter, and, in most cities, they rejoiced in the festival of Beautiful Birth. The role reversal implicit in the creation of a *polis* of women, and the physical escape from the demands of the *oikos*, provided a safety valve for the tensions caused by the restrictions of daily life, while reinforcing community norms of marriage and childbearing.[123] A somewhat similar acculturating role is played in modern Greece by women's reverence for the Panayia (Mother of God), who, like Demeter, embodies the ideal values of motherhood in a woman's life.[124]

Some women from well-to-do families served as priestesses in the publicly celebrated cults of female divinities.[125] In Athens some forty such positions were available, as well as lesser offices, and there were similar opportunities in the local demes. Women in their roles as priestesses enjoyed an enhanced sociolegal position.[126] Some might even have expressed political opinions: Plutarch tells us that a priestess, Theano, defied a public decree to curse Alcibiades for profaning the Mysteries,[127] and, if the character of Lysistrata in Aristophanes' play is based upon the priestess of Athena Polias, Lysimache, the propeace stance of that comic character may reflect the publicly expressed opinions of her model.[128]

Women also visited shrines, sometimes at a distance from their homes, to request divine assistance.[129] In modern Greece, religious pilgrimages similarly offer women a means of escape from the confines of the *spiti* and a chance to socialize with other women. Visits to healing shrines are especially popular; men who otherwise are unwilling for their womenfolk to leave the house readily consent to these excursions in which the women act as the representatives of their households (few men participate themselves).[130]

Nevertheless, none of these various ways in which citizen women of childbearing age left the *oikos* and functioned in "public space" provided them with access to that space comparable with that of men. A man went daily and openly to socialize in the agora and the shops; none questioned his right to be there unless he was under judicial sentence of *atimia*. His wife, in contrast, went out only on special occasions or in emergencies. Moreover, to seek to find ways in which women functioned in public space, and to attribute a positive value to them, is basically anachronistic. In Greek terms, those women who were forced by circumstance or economic necessity to leave the home and play a role in the public life of the *polis* ran the risk of impairing their reputations and even of incurring charges of noncitizen status (which would also endanger the men of the *oikos*).[131] A Greek woman's relegation to the home may have been a fiction, but it was also a societal norm. Moreover, in determining just how much of a fiction it was, we should bear in mind Plato's reproaches against Greek society for allowing its women to cling to the known *oikos*, fearful and unwilling to venture into—and contribute to—the public world.[132]

Marriage in classical Greece was not necessarily "till death do us part." At least among the upper classes that we know best from our sources, a significant number of women were married more than once as a consequence not only of widowhood but also of divorce. In an analysis of the speeches of the orators, Thompson found fifty-three people who had at least two marriages; of these, thirty were women. Where it is possible to determined the cause of the termination of the first marriage, ten of the women were widows and seven were divorcées. Fifteen women are known to have borne children in a second or later marriage.[133] In some cases a woman's first husband arranged ahead of time for her remarriage in the event of his death, often to the man he chose as guardian of his children.[134] (Pericles arranged for the remarriage of his wife when he divorced her.)[135] If the husband had not made prior arrangements, a woman of childbearing age returned to her natal family, which arranged a new marriage for her.[136] The children often went with their mother to be raised by a stepfather or maternal uncle.[137] Women past childbearing age often stayed with their sons, whose obligation it was to support them, but a single life for a woman still capable of childbearing, whether as widow or divorcée, was considered pitiable. Moreover, community gossip was ever alert for widowly misbehavior. Thus Pericles advised the widows of men who fell in the Peloponnesian War to live so as not be talked about by men either for praise or for blame.[138] Medical theory reinforced the pressure for remarriage: women could avoid the problems caused by a wandering womb only by keeping that organ occupied. Among the cases described in the *Epidemics* are two that describe women who suffered virilization when they were abandoned by their husbands; both cases rapidly proved fatal.[139]

Modern Greece provides both a parallel and a contrast to classical attitudes to widowhood. Young widows are considered especially suspect. Hirschon says that in Kokkinia in the Piraeus "the position of a widow if she was under fifty was almost untenable. Her every action would be observed . . . and her behavior had to be extremely circumspect."[140] Nevertheless, in contrast to ancient Greece, remarriage is rare—only 1 percent of all marriages involve widows.[141] The difference apparently lies in the quite different religious orientations of pagan and Christian Greece. Faced with widowhood, the ancient wife clearly had the advantage: she was able to escape the social stigma of widowhood by remarriage, although she also ran the risk of continuing childbearing.

OLDER WOMEN

Once a woman had passed the age of childbearing her situation improved in some ways.[142] Her role in religious affairs probably increased, for a number of priesthoods were reserved for women past childbearing age.[143] Widows in particular often appear in the speeches of the orators as actively involved in the affairs of the *oikos*, with considerable knowledge about and input into the family's business.[144] Thus Lysias 32.12–18 describes a widow's defense of the interests of her children against their guardian (her own father) in a family council in which she cited records of bottomry loans, land mortgages, and wheat imports. Her presentation of a formal speech before an audience was a matter for apology (a common rhetorical device, however), but not her knowledge of the matter or her right to involve herself. The speaker in Demosthenes 36.14 claims that Apollodorus's mother had an accurate knowledge of the business at issue (leases), so that as long as she lived Apollodorus never made his (illegitimate) complaint. In both these cases, regardless of the truth of the claim, the speaker considered that the woman's involvement and influence in family affairs would be believable and acceptable to the jury. Similarly, the kinswoman of the Hippocratic author of *On the Nature of the Child*, who was the owner of a female slave who brought in money as a singer, appears to have been in active control of the slave, a valuable economic asset, and to have agreed to the singer's abortion in order to protect her income.[145]

Interestingly enough, some of the strongest evidence for the position of the older woman in Greece comes from comedy. Henderson has pointed out that the young women are consistently portrayed as flighty, weak, manipulative, and unable to control their passions, whereas the older women offer sensible advice and act as leaders.[146] The *Lysistrata, Thesmophoriazusae*, and *Ecclesiazusae* all portray older women offering advice and acting in the public sphere, albeit as rebels.

Although in real life older women surely did not have the degree of freedom and input into the affairs of the city that they possessed in comedy, they did enjoy a certain measure of freedom of movement outside the *oikos*.[147] This was the case, in large part, because the male community accorded them less value and interest once they had lost their childbearing capability; nevertheless, the newfound freedom must have been welcome. If they could not match the heroines of comedy in their influence on the *polis*, they did serve a useful role within the community of women, acting as messengers and intermediaries for younger, housebound women (not always to their advantage, however—it was an older woman serving as an agent for a younger woman who brought Euphiletos the message of his wife's infidelity).[148] Such women would have played a vital role in alleviating the isolation of younger women, offering advice as well as conveying gossip and news told from the female point of view.[149] Henderson notes that women in comedy display a solidarity across the generations that contrasts sharply with the generational conflict characteristic of relationships between older and younger men. The potential breach in the system of male control that these activities of older women involved perhaps helps to account for the very derogatory picture of them in some of our (male) literary sources.[150]

Evidence of the exercise of influence by women within the home has led to the argument that they held the "real" power in the society by virtue of their role within the household. Friedl in particular was influential in arguing this for the modern Greek village.[151] She claimed that the private sphere was the area of greatest importance for both sexes and that it was women who exercised power there, while men were confined to the mere appearance of power in the public sphere (prestige). For Friedl, the power women exercised in the home was based on the economic contribution that they made to the family in the form of dowry. Other scholars have applied the same argument to other cultures and added other means of influence, such as women's religious roles[152] and their manipulative abilities (nagging, playing one person off against another, withholding services).[153] In ancient Greece such informal means of influence as dowry, religious activity, and manipulative ruses were certainly available to women. Moreover, as we have seen, in the speeches of the orators some well-to-do older women appear as knowledgeable about the complex business affairs of their families and as respected and influential members of their *oikoi*. Nevertheless, to conclude from this that women had the real power in Greek society stretches the evidence. In the form in which Friedl presented it, the argument can be applied only at the village level, where the lack of an official life offers little scope for a significant male public role. It cannot be extended to the city or to the ancient *polis*, where the public arena, from which women are routinely excluded, involves or involved decisions of crucial importance to the individual as well as the community. Moreover, the interpretation overlooks the factor of age, and it overvalues the significance of the power women may hold within the home, failing to distinguish between informal power, which has no claim to legitimacy, and the legitimate exercise of authority, which is restricted to men.[154] Informal power is indeed "real," in the sense that it can get results, but it is everywhere the prerogative of the powerless.

As women grew older, sons became ever more important to them. Adult sons of widows acted as their mother's *kyrios* and managed their dowries, which they would eventually inherit. A son thus provided his mother with a public voice for the protection of her property and rights.[155] The law also required him to support his mother, which was crucial in a society in which there was no public system of old-age pensions. A view to the future undoubtedly figured in the family-planning strategies of both parents and contributed to a woman's joy at the birth of sons.

The Reproductive Lives of Less Privileged Women

The role of citizen wife in the *oikos* was the norm in terms of which the Greek view of childbirth and its management was structured. Most closely resembling this norm was probably the life of a legitimate wife of a well-to-do resident alien (metic) who engaged in business in the city.[156] Next in status and situation was the free concubine (παλλακή), with whom a man might live "for the bearing of free children."[157] (A man might also take a slave woman as a concubine, but her children had the status of slaves.)[158] The free concubine's offspring were *nothoi*, free but illegitimate and not cit-

izens; they did not share in the patrimony when there were legitimate sons, but the father was permitted to bequeath legacies to
them even in the presence of such sons.[159] Women who lived as
concubines were usually not citizens themselves and thus not eligi-
ble to enter a legitimate marriage (although nothing prevented a
man from giving his legitimate citizen daughter or sister to a man as
a concubine).[160] The most famous concubine was probably Aspasia, a resident alien from Miletus with whom Pericles lived; after
both his legitimate sons died, he successfully requested a special
dispensation from the *polis* to legitimatize his son by Aspasia as his
heir.[161] The usual fate of such children, however, appears in the case
of Phrastor that we discussed earlier. Phrastor married a woman
whom he later found out to be an alien, not a citizen. When he
discovered her true status, he sent her away, even though she was
pregnant. She then bore him a son, whom he later adopted, but
when he tried to introduce the boy to his phratry and gens as his
legitimate son, they refused to accept him.[162] Later when this liai-
son furnished his political enemies with the pretext for a legal challenge to his citizenship status, he portrayed the adoption as brought
about by his former wife's manipulation of him as he lay ill and
helpless.

Below concubines in status were *hetairai*, women with whom
men associated on a more casual basis for their sexual and conver-
sational abilities, especially at drinking parties.[163] Probably the
closest modern parallel would be the high-priced call girl. Still
lower in status were female slaves trained as entertainers—dancers, singers, or flute girls—who could be hired out and provide an
income to their owners, and who might also act as prostitutes.[164]
Lowest in status were common prostitutes. The lines were not
clearly drawn, however: a *hetaira*, or even a prostitute, might become a concubine if a man set up housekeeping with her.

Pregnancy would present serious threats to the livelihood of
hetairai, entertainers, and prostitutes, and (despite the suspicions
of husbands) it was probably such women who most often sought
abortions. One of the doctor-authors of the Hippocratic treatises
remarks that he has seen many fetuses aborted by prostitutes,[165]

and the abortion by an entertainer is described in *On the Nature of the Child*:

> A kinswoman of mine owned a very valuable singer, who used to go with men. It was important that this girl should not become pregnant and thereby lose her value. Now this girl had heard the sort of thing women say to each other—that when a woman is going to conceive, the seed remains inside her and does not fall out. She digested this information, and kept a watch. One day she noticed that the seed had not come out again. She told her mistress, and the story came to me. When I heard it, I told her to jump up and down, touching her buttocks with her heels at each leap. After she had done this no more than seven times, there was a noise, the seed fell out on the ground.[166]

It is interesting that the doctor is unconcerned about admitting that his kinswoman kept a prostitute; as Lonie remarks in his commentary on this passage, "There were brothels and brothels: some of them . . . were very select maisons."[167] Doctors in fact treated all sorts of women who suffered complications in pregnancy, without apparent differentiation between slave and free, respectable and otherwise.

Conclusion

The social system of the *oikos* was one whose patterns of marriage, inheritance, and support in old age clearly privileged the male at every stage of life. Females born into the *oikos* and destined for an early departure in marriage were deemed a poor investment in comparison with males, who required less watching as children, brought workers and dowries into the *oikos* upon marriage, and assured the support of aging parents and the continuity of the *oikos* itself. Marriage was viewed as the introduction into the *oikos* of an alien woman from a competing *oikos*, necessary but suspect. The birth of a son gave a woman an immediate increase in status and the potential (if he survived) of continued support throughout her lifetime. Given the *oikos* system, it is not surprising that mothers as well as fathers rejoiced more at the birth of sons than daughters and perhaps even expended more effort on their care.

Greek medical theory supported the androcentric bias of Greek society by providing a rational (or rationalized) basis for the belief in the weaker and inferior nature of women. It did this by creating a coherent (if imaginary) model of female function and dysfunction in which women were held to be weaker, moister, softer, more porous, and warmer than men. As inferior creatures, they were slower to develop in the womb but faster to age and decline in their lifetimes (an observation that in itself reveals much about the treatment of women in Greek society).[168] Moreover, female physiology was seen as essentially incomplete: without the moisture and weight provided by semen and the fetus, the womb would wander about the body causing alarming and dangerous symptoms. The wandering womb provided a handy catchall diagnosis for the illnesses of women, justifying early marriage, frequent childbearing, and the rapid remarriage of divorced or widowed women, all of which served the reproductive aims of the *oikos*.

In the chapters that follow we will look more closely at the experience of Greek women as childbearers. But before we turn to this investigation, it will be helpful to review briefly the medical system and the medical texts that provide much of our evidence, since these are not nearly as well known as the other types of evidence upon which we will draw.

Two

Hippocratic Medicine and the
Epidemics

B y the late fifth century, health had become almost an obsession in Greek society. Widespread general interest in medicine is reflected in medical treatises aimed at a lay audience,[1] as well as in numerous literary sources, such as the medically sophisticated description of the plague by Thucydides,[2] and the frequent appearance of medical themes and allusions in Attic comedy and tragedy.[3] Plato describes Hippocrates as well known in the *Protagoras*,[4] portrays the physician Eryximachus in society in the *Symposium*, and parodies Hippocratic theories of sex determination in that same dialogue.[5] In the *Republic* he complains about the popularity of time-consuming medical regimes:

> Is it not also disgraceful to need doctoring, not merely for a wound or an attack of some seasonal disorder, but because, through living in idleness and luxury, our bodies are infested with winds and humours, like marsh gas in a stagnant pool, so that the sons of Asclepius are put to inventing for diseases such ingenious names as flatulence and catarrh. . . . In the old days, until the time of Herodicus, the sons of Asclepius had no use for the modern coddling treatment of disease But Herodicus, who was a gymnastic master and lost his health, combined training and doctoring in such a way as to become a plague to himself

first and foremost and to many others after him.   . Surely there could be no worse hindrance than this excessive care of the body, over and above the exercise it needs to keep it in health It becomes a nuisance to anyone who has to manage a household or serve in the field or hold any office at home. . . . Asclepius recognized this and revealed the art of medicine for the benefit of people of sound constitution who normally led a healthy life, but had contracted some definite ailment. . . . But where the body was diseased through and through, he would not try, by nicely calculated evacuations and doses, to prolong a miserable existence and let his patient beget children who were likely to be as sickly as himself.[6]

The demands of this avid public were met by the numerous medical treatises aimed at a lay audience or its doctors that were produced from the end of the fifth through the fourth centuries. Despite the variety of medical theories that these treatises espoused and the mutual criticisms and contradictions that they contained, in late antiquity they were collected together and identified as the work of the physician Hippocrates. However, the real Hippocrates is an elusive character. Although he was almost an exact contemporary of Socrates and, unlike the philosopher, apparently committed his ideas to writing, we actually know little about his teachings The "Hippocratic" treatises are anonymous, and the ancient sources that refer to his methods are conflicting,[7] offering no firm clues for identifying those treatises that were truly his work.[8] Thus in calling these treatises, and the medical ideas that they embody, "Hippocratic," we are simply following the traditional way of referring to this material.

Hippocratic Medicine

Despite the varied nature of the works that make up the Hippocratic Corpus, it is possible to identify an essential core of medical thinking that characterizes "Hippocratic" medicine [9] In general the treatises follow an empirical approach, attributing illness to natural rather than supernatural causes and firmly rejecting the Homeric and Hesiodic idea that gods, daimons, or any other sort of supernatural beings cause illness. Nevertheless, some "natural" causes seem far more imaginative than strictly empirical. For example, they include postulated displacements of internal organs about which the Hippocratic doctor, who did not do dissections, could have had only limited knowledge, such as the movements of the womb to which the gynecological treatises frequently attribute women's symptoms. A number of treatises also depart from strict empiricism in their interpretation of illness in terms of the philosophical concepts of the day.[10] Thus they describe health as a balance in the basic elements that make up the body, an idea borrowed from the philosophers' attempts to identify the basic elements of the cosmos. But like the philosophers, the doctors did not agree on the number or identity of these elements. Thus the author of the treatise called *Ancient Medicine* followed the philosopher Alcmaeon in maintaining that the elements of the body were indefinite in number, whereas the author of *Regimen* I postulated only two basic elements, fire and water, as did the author of *Affections*, who chose the humors (fluids) bile and phlegm.[11] The author of *Breaths* even abandoned the notion of a balance of elements entirely in favor of a monistic theory of air borrowed from the philosophers Anaximander and Diogenes of Apollonia. The gynecological treatises make comparatively little use of humors, attributing many difficulties to mechanical causes such as blockages of menstrual or lochial bleeding or displacements of the uterus (wandering womb).

Of these many hypotheses, it was the theory of four humors— blood, phlegm, yellow bile, and black bile—that became almost canonical in later medicine. According to humoral theory, the imbalance that caused illness could have a number of (natural) causes. An individual might upset the balance of the humors by excessive indulgence in food, drink, or activity, or might have an innate tendency toward an imbalance (thus a person might be naturally phlegmatic or bilious).[12] The season or the climate in a particular locality might also augment certain humors. Humors could also migrate within the body, or transform themselves (*metastasis*), turning a slight symptom into a serious illness, or vice versa.

The Hippocratic doctor viewed recovery from illness or trauma as a natural process in which the forces of the body overcame the problem, a process that the doctor tried to assist. In treating patients, doctors therefore watched carefully for clues to the nature of any humoral imbalance (hence their reputation as excellent observers), and then sought to assist the body's efforts to restore balance by alterations in diet, purging, or bleeding. In cases with favorable outcomes the offending humor would be overcome by the body in a process called *pepsis* (ripening, cooking) and would then be isolated or excreted (*apostasis*) in various forms, such as blood (nosebleeds were considered especially beneficial), pus, urine, skin eruptions, or joint ailments.[13] When *apostasis* occurred, the illness had reached a decisive point, the crisis, after which the patient either died or recovered (although in some cases the crisis was incomplete and the illness dragged on in the same or another form). In fevers, the crisis was identified by decisive changes in the pattern of the fever, usually remission, but sometimes peaking. In cases with unfavorable outcomes *pepsis* and *apostasis* did not occur properly and the crisis was a turning not toward recovery but toward death.[14] In gynecological troubles attributed to displacements of the womb, it might be attracted or repulsed back into its normal position by fumigations and odor therapies, and kept there by the moisture provided by frequent intercourse or the weight of a developing fetus. Another remedy frequently prescribed for menstrual blockages was intercourse.

Doctors and Medical Practice

Most Hippocratic doctors lived itinerant lives, traveling from one town to another and setting up shop for several weeks or months at a time.[15] This gave them a special interest in the idiosyncrasies of particular places and their possible connection with particular health problems, and they paid close attention to environmental clues.[16] We see this especially in the *Epidemics*: in the case histories the patient's location and the season are often noted, and in passages summarizing the doctor's experiences over the course of the year (called "constitutions"), the writer draws generalizations about the climate and the prevalent illnesses in the locality.

Another consequence of doctors' itinerant practice was the continuing need they had to establish their reputations. There were no

medical boards to certify doctors and no prescribed course that
students were required to follow; anyone could set himself up as a
doctor, usually (but not necessarily) on the basis of an apprentice-
ship.[17] Thus the successful doctor had to be an accomplished sales-
man of his own skills. This need encouraged doctors to master the
art of public speaking and to express their medical theories in
terms of popular philosophical theories.[18] Doctors also worked to
perfect their skills at prognosis, for a good physician was expected
to be able to discern the past and future course of a patient's symptoms. (In modern Greece, the Blums report that confidence in a
doctor is based on his ability to make a correct prognosis, and that
his reputation is enhanced if he is able to diagnose an illness without taking the patient's history or making an examination.)[19] To
assist prognosis, doctors noted symptoms that seemed to foretell
the progress of an illness and drew generalizations from them, as in
this passage in *Regimen in Acute Diseases*:

> When speechlessness comes over a patient that has had fever for four-
> teen days, a swift resolution or relief from the disease is not likely to
> occur; on the contrary, this indicates chronicity in such a patient; for,
> whenever speechlessness appears on that day, it is present for a longer
> time. In a patient with fever, when on the fourth day the tongue be-
> comes confounded in speech, and the cavity passes watery bilious
> stools, such a patient is likely to rave.[20]

The interest in numbered days that appears in this passage is another consequence of the prognostic orientation of the Hippocratic
doctor. In addition to prognostic notes such as this one, complex
lists of days on which crises might be expected are also recorded in
the treatises,[21] and most case histories in the *Epidemics* note the
number of the day on which particular symptoms occurred. Attention to numbered days would have been especially useful for prognosis in cases of the periodic fevers of malaria, but number magic
and the concept of auspicious days probably also figured in its
popularity.

An Overview of the Hippocratic Epidemics

The treatise *Epidemics* consists of seven books that record the observations made by their doctor-authors during the course of their travels as itinerant physicians in northern Greece—Thessaly, Thrace, and the island of Thasos—at the end of the fifth and in the first half of the fourth centuries. The meaning of the title, "Epidemics," is ambiguous; it could mean either "of the people [*demos*]," or "sojourning in a place [*deme*]"; thus its subject could be either the illnesses occurring in a given place and time, or the doctor's visits in an area.[22] The non-Athenian context, in addition to the fact that these cases are, at least in origin, nonliterary texts, makes them especially valuable as sources for social history, since much of our other evidence is thoroughly Athenocentric and literary.[23]

In addition to the case histories, each book of the *Epidemics* contains two other types of material: constitutions (καταστάσεις) and generalizations (aphorisms, prognostic indications, lists of things to consider). The constitutions are summary accounts of the climatic conditions and the illnesses encountered by the doctor in a particular locality over a specific period of time, usually a year. These were probably derived by generalization from the doctor's notes in case histories, but only in a few instances can a patient named in a constitution be identified with one in a case history.[24] The constitutions are sometimes carefully crafted literary pieces, which suggests that they were intended for publication, either to students or to the general public. This impression is reinforced by their similarity to Thucydides' description of the plague in his history of the Peloponnesian War,[25] and by the presence in the Hippocratic collection of other treatises in which the doctor-author directs his efforts at a lay audience.

The first childbirth case referred to in the *Epidemics* occurs in one of the constitutions of Book 1 in a passage that gives a good general idea of the style of the constitutions:

> Though many women fell ill, they were fewer than the men and less frequently died. But the great majority had difficult childbirth, and after giving birth they would fall ill, and these especially died, as did the

daughter of Telebulus on the sixth day after delivery. Now menstruation appeared during the fevers in most cases, and with many maidens it occurred then for the first time. Some bled from the nose. Sometimes both epistaxis and menstruation appeared together; for example, the maiden daughter of Daitharses had her first menstruation during fever and also a violent discharge from the nose. I know of no woman who died if any of these symptoms showed themselves properly, but all to my knowledge had abortions if they chanced to fall ill when with child.[26]

The case histories that deal with pregnancy and childbirth are presented in Appendix B. There they are arranged in chronological order as determined by modern scholarship, but the reader should be warned that this order does not coincide with the traditional numbering, which I have preserved. Each book of the *Epidemics* has its own idiosyncratic character, and on the basis of these differences scholars have noted "family resemblances" between books that have allowed them to define and date three main groups of books: I and III, dated 410–400; II, IV, and VI, dated 400–375; and V and VI, dated 375/360–350. Thus the cases in the appendix are arranged in the order: I, III; II, IV, VI; V, VII.[27]

Books I and III of the *Epidemics* stand out from the other books in their polished form. They contain four complete and finished constitutions (three in Book I and one in Book III), whose conclusions contain the sole aphoristic material in these books. The case histories, of which Book I contains fourteen and Book III two sets of twelve and sixteen, are organized chronologically according to the days of the illness. They consist mostly of lists of symptoms; only rarely is allusion made to treatment, and then only when it elicits symptoms useful in prognosis. From antiquity I and III have been the most admired books of the *Epidemics*, and scholars agree that they form a single work that is the oldest part of the treatise, dating to circa 410–400. They appear as representative of the *Epidemics* in most modern selections from the Hippocratic treatises, yet, from the standpoint of narrative interest, as sources for social history, and as evidence for the development of medical thinking, the other books are an equally valuable resource.

Books II, IV, and VI were grouped together from antiquity and attributed to Thessalus, the son of Hippocrates, who was said to have edited and published them from notes made by his father.[28] Thus ancient scholars gave them the status of Hippocratic at one remove. Book II contains twenty-four brief cases that give the impression of being rough notes taken at the bedside; it also contains four fragmentary constitutions, none as thoroughly worked out as those of I and III. The main interest of the author seems to have been in medical theory and treatment, which he presents in the form of general statements that are not incorporated into either the constitutions or the cases. The book includes a miscellaneous chapter devoted to gynecological information as well as several other chapters dealing with gynecological conditions and the development of the fetus. It has the highest percentage of female patients (55 percent) of any of the books of the *Epidemics*.[29]

Book VI shares many characteristics with Book II. It too contains only a few case histories, nineteen in all, and, like Book II, it gives a good deal of attention to didactic theoretical expositions and to treatment. In contrast to Book II, however, only 32 percent of its patients are female, and there is only one pregnancy-related case. Book VI is probably best known for the constitution usually called "the Cough of Perinthus," which is the product of an accomplished literary writer.[30] The philosophical allusions that characterize this book suggest that its author was highly educated: some aphorisms bear a stylistic resemblance to the work of the philosopher Heraclitus,[31] while a methodological statement is reminiscent of the method of Collection and Division propounded by Plato, who was probably a contemporary of the author.[32] Nikitas, who has done a detailed study of II, IV, and VI, has suggested that the author of II and VI had a fundamentally didactic aim; these books might even have served as lecture notes for a medical course.[33] Smith stresses the author's active, invasive approach to treatment: if nature makes a mistake, the doctor must intervene.[34]

In contrast to Books II and VI, the third member of this middle group, Book IV, has few aphoristic or theoretical passages but reports on more than ninety cases, with many chapters including multiple cases. The book contains two constitutions that make numerous references to individual patients; neither is a polished literary piece. When theory appears in IV, it is modest and often placed within the case histories, a procedure unique to this book. In general, the book lacks the attention to therapy and diet, and the didactic tone, that are characteristic of Books II and VI.

The differences between Book IV and Books II and VI suggest that two authors were responsible.[35] Nikitas, who characterizes the author of II and VI as a well-educated medical theorist, probably a professor, assigns IV to a slightly later author.[36] He describes him as a practical, working physician who had long been active in the area and had many patients, some of whom he visited several times; in some families he seems to have functioned as a sort of "house physician."[37] Nikitas's study of the names and relationships of the patients involved in these three books demonstrates that they all belonged to a single generation, which he placed in the first quarter of the fourth century.

Books V and VII have also been grouped together since antiquity and their close interconnection is marked by considerable overlapping of material.[38] Even in antiquity these books were considered to be post-Hippocratic: Galen remarked that everyone agreed that VII was spurious (*nothos*).[39] Langholf has recognized three strata in V:[40] the first, A, consists of 31 case histories and appears to be the record of a doctor traveling from the Peloponnesus through Athens to Thessaly and Thrace; the second, B, consisting of chapters 32–50, is clearly different in content and style from A but similar to C, which consists of chapters 51–106. All of the chapters in part C, with the single exception of chapter 86, also appear in Book VII, but in a different order, sometimes with minor changes in language, and sometimes augmented. Deichgräber interpreted the changes in the material of C when it recurs in Book VII as editorial reworkings; Langholf, on the other hand, argued that the two versions of C derived independently from a common source, which he identified as the archives of the Hippocratic school on the island of Cos.[41] Whatever the solution to the puzzle of these parallel passages, modern scholars agree that V and VII are later than II, IV, and VI. Deichgräber dated them between 375 and 350; Grensemann more narrowly, between 360 and 350. In particular, the fact that three of the patients were identified as residents of Olynthus requires a date before 348, when that city was totally destroyed.[42]

Books V and VII both contain relatively large numbers of cases. Each of the fifty chapters included in V A–B describes a case. The chapters of V C contain, in addition to cases, a few general comments on treatment, and two miniconstitutions. Book VII contains eighty-two cases not included in Book V. Both V and VII pay special attention to treatment; prognosis appears to have fallen into the background, and numbered days have lost some of their fascination. On the other hand, narrative interest is higher in these books than in the earlier ones, and the writer is attracted to unusual cases. For example, V 86 (the only case in V C without a parallel in VII) recounts the illness of a young man who overindulged in wine, fell asleep on his back in a tent, found a snake in his mouth, bit it, and, seized with pain and convulsions, died. This case (except for its unfortunate conclusion) bears a striking resemblance to the procedure of dormition cure used in the temples of Asclepius: patients slept overnight in the temple and during their dreams they were visited by the god who either prescribed for them or treated them; sometimes the companions of the god, a snake or dog, healed the patient by licking. Was the story of V 86 perhaps intended to suggest that those who resorted to the god Asclepius and his snake for a cure might find death instead? Perhaps, but if we consider it in the context of some of the other cases in V and VII, it seems rather to be a case of inversion, possibly reflecting further influence of the philosopher Heraclitus, which we first noted in Book VI, where it was limited to aphoristic style.

The other cases that exhibit the trait of inversion follow a pattern in which the same object has opposite effects, as illustrated by the Heraclitean dictum: the bow is both life (βίos = life) and death (βιός = bow).[43] For example, in V 9, the case of the man who found a cure for itching in the baths at Melos and then died of hydropsy, the same element, water, was both life/cure and death; and in V 74/VII 36, the patient was a ship's cargo director for whom an anchor, an instrument of life/livelihood, became an instrument of death.

Still another of these odd cases seems to involve a mocking or inversion of taboos: VII 78, about a man who urinated into the sea as part of a cure. Among the numerous admonitions in Hesiod's *Works and Days* are two that involve the pollution of water by urination: one forbids urinating into a stream that flows into the sea, and the other forbids urinating into a spring.[44]

An interesting point is the number of cases in which baths are indicted as the cause of illness: VII 11, chill after a bath; VII 24, relapse after a bath; VII 50, fever after warming in a vapor bath; and v 9, the fatal baths of Melos. (On the other hand, in VII 102, a patient was saved because she vomited up a poisonous mushroom in the bath.) The author of *Sacred Disease*, in his condemnation of the religious charlatans who interpret epilepsy as divine possession, says that a prohibition on baths is part of their treatment.[45] It was also a Heraclitean dictum that it is death for the soul to become wet.[46] On a more pedestrian level, however, these cases documenting the deleterious effects of baths may simply indicate experience with malarial relapses brought on by a chill suffered during bathing.[47]

Finally, a possible incursion of magic appears in v 25, in which a woman, barren all her life, at the age of sixty suffered laborlike pains after eating raw leeks; she was cured when another woman extracted a stone from the mouth of her womb. While probably reflecting the results of dietary indiscretion, this odd story fits the pattern of shamanistic cure by the removal of a foreign object. Moreover, it typifies the womb-centered approach of the later books of the *Epidemics*, which will be discussed in the next chapter.[48]

An especially interesting feature of the case histories in the later two groups of books is the frequency with which medical mistakes are acknowledged.[49] This is most noteworthy in Book V, whose author reports overly strong or ill-timed purgatives, badly done cauterization, inadequate or late trepanning, and the application of irritating medicine to a wound. One of these unfortunate cases involved a pregnant woman who died as a result of an overdose of a purgative (v 18). Most of these references to mistakes appear in v A, although one occurs in v B, and one in v C, and thus also in Book

VII.[50] Robert has argued that these critical comments, some of which appear to refer to the acts of others, reveal that their author worked as a member of a medical team.[51] Similarly, the author of Book VI criticizes the treatment of a patient who was given an emetic when a steam bath was called for, and Smith sees this as evidence that he was working in a community of doctors.[52] Again, the author of II 1.7 criticizes the treatment given in IV 26 to the niece of Temenes, who had an insufficient *apostasis* to the thumb after suffering fever and a distended hypochondrium—the doctor did not know if she was also pregnant.

The Epidemics *and Statistical Analysis*

The cases described in the *Epidemics* are not representative of the general population in the area in which the doctor was working, or even of his own case load. For example, one of the more striking aspects of the childbirth cases in I and III is the relatively high mortality rate for these patients, both in terms of what one would anticipate even in a premodern medical situation, and in terms of the mortality rates of similar cases in the two later groups of books in the *Epidemics*. In Book I, three of the five patients died, while in Book III, all five cases proved fatal. Taking the two books together, this gives a mortality rate of 80 percent for cases associated with pregnancy. In comparison, nonpregnancy related cases in I and III had a death rate of 54 percent, and women among these had a rate of 50 percent. In contrast, in II, IV, and VI there are no deaths in the nineteen pregnancy-related cases, while in V and VII four of nine such patients died, or 44 percent. While mortality from childbirth must have been high (this will be discussed in chapter 4), the explanation for the unusually high mortality rate for pregnancy-related cases in I and III—or for the zero mortality in II, IV, and VI—should not be sought in actual mortality rates but in choices made by both doctor and patient.

The decision to use a male doctor for complications following birth rather than relying on the traditional help provided by female kin and neighbors was, like all significant decisions in the life of a Greek woman, in the hands of her male guardian; in most cases, this would have been her husband or, if she was a slave, her owner.[53] The doctor's fees may have been a factor,[54] for many identifiable patients, whether slave or free, were members of relatively affluent households.[55] Moreover, the guardian who chose the care of a doctor for his female dependents must have regarded himself as sophisticated in medical matters and been willing to make a nontraditional choice. Given the popularity of medical theory, use of a doctor was probably viewed as a mark of prestige (Friedl reports that the prestige associated with hospital care has been a major factor in the acceptance of hospitalization by modern Greek villagers).[56] Thus those choosing to utilize doctors were not a representative sample of the population of a Greek *polis*.

The doctor also exercised choice, both in the cases he accepted and in the cases he reported. He might turn down obviously hopeless cases. Such avoidance was considered professionally judicious if the doctor could avoid the appearance that his skills were inadequate to the task.[57] Moreover, no medical board required a doctor to record each case that he accepted and treated. We can often see a selective element at work when the writer notes that the case being described is similar to the case of another patient that he does not present, when he groups similar cases together, or when he juxtaposes similar cases with different outcomes.

An example of the editorial process at work in shaping the raw materials of bedside observations into case histories appears in the first two childbirth cases in Books I and III: 1 4 and 1 5. In these cases, which the author appears to have deliberately juxtaposed, we can see that he reinforced certain similarities in symptoms by using similar phrases and by the order of his reporting. The author first notes that both women underwent normal deliveries with proper lochial discharge, and that both bore daughters. He then reports the earliest symptoms in both cases as fever and chilling accompanied by pain in the *kardia* and genital area. In both cases, these pains were relieved by the application of a pessary, but pains remained in the head, neck, and hip; sleep was not possible, and little passed from the belly. On the sixth day both patients were delirious. Other common symptoms were bilious and strongly colored stools, thirst, and convulsions.

As the illnesses progressed, however, the symptoms diverged. The wife of Philinus apparently never vomited, and her urine did not form a sediment (evidence that *apostasis* was not occurring); quivering, raving, and then speechlessness preceded her death on the seventeenth day. In contrast, the wife of Epicrates suffered pains in her legs, deafness, and heaviness in the left side; she not only vomited, but her urine formed a sediment (signs of *pepsis* and *apostasis*). She suffered a multiplicity of symptoms before her illness came to a complete crisis on the eighteenth day. Most significant, however, is the note toward the end of the case history that she had had pain in the throat from the beginning, with redness and a drawn-back uvula, while a bitter salty flux lasted throughout the illness.

By omitting mention of the sore throat and flux suffered by the wife of Epicrates early in his account, in proper chronological order, but noting it only as an aside at the end of the case history, the physician-author has downplayed this difference and emphasized the similarities between these two cases.[58] In essence, by editorial means he has created a matched pair of cases, one with a positive and one with a negative outcome. Since only the application of a pessary is noted as treatment, and that early on and without apparent effect on the ultimate outcome of the cases, it cannot be that such a pair was meant to guide treatment. On the other hand, they could have assisted prognosis: they are composed in such a way as to allow the reader to compare symptoms and to detect those that signaled the different outcomes of these otherwise similar—as presented—cases.

This sort of rethinking and reformulation is one of the significant contributions of writing in the form of personal notes, as Goody remarks:

> A permanent record enables one to reread as well as record one's own thoughts and jottings. In this way one can review and reorganize one's own work, reclassify what one has already classified, rearrange words, sentences and paragraphs in a variety of ways . . . for recall and conceptual clarification.[59]

The Hippocratic texts stand at the beginning of the transformation of Greek culture from predominantly oral to literate,[60] and, as we see here, the *Epidemics* can be especially useful in revealing the changes that this shift made possible in the development of ideas about illness and cure. Although Plato deplores these developments—and also deplores the increasing reliance on written texts—it was this move from an oral to a literate culture that made possible the creation of *logoi*, or scientific accounts, of medical knowledge in various fields, including the creation of gynecology (the science of women's illnesses) from the raw materials of women's traditional lore.

Conclusion

We have seen that the books of the *Epidemics* form a series that covers the period between 410 and 350 and that they have at least three different authors, and probably more. The earlier books are more rigorously prognostic, with few indications of treatment and a strict concentration on the description of symptoms. In the later books the course of the illness is less often followed in detail and indications of treatment are more frequent. Interest in theory in the different books varies probably more in accordance with the interests of the individual authors than in accordance with any general shift in direction over time, but there does seem to be an increase in Heraclitean thinking and possibly even the appearance of shamanistic practices in the latest books. Given these differences, we can expect that the different books will also vary in their treatment of women, and that these variations may reflect changes in the thinking of the society as a whole over this period of time, as well as changes in medical thinking and practice.

Three

The Treatment of Female Patients in the *Epidemics*

> It requires much care and knowledge to carry and
> nurture the child in the womb and to bring it to birth.
> Hippocrates, *Diseases of Women* I 25

The cases in the *Epidemics* do not provide a basis for statistical analysis in the modern sense, but as we discussed in Chapter 2, some simple calculations are nonetheless revealing. They suggest the degree to which various doctors were involved in the treatment of women in general, and in cases of pregnancy and childbirth in particular. They also reveal changes over time in the percentage of female and pregnancy-related cases reported, in the degree to which these doctors interpreted women's illnesses as "female problems," in the apparent basis for selection of cases, and in the role of women as care givers in childbirth.

In *Epidemics* I and III, eleven of the thirty-eight patients mentioned in Book I were female (29 percent),[1] as were twelve of the twenty-eight cases in Book III (43 percent). Ten patients suffered from pregnancy-related illnesses: two from abortions, one from an illness in the third month of pregnancy, and seven from postpartum complications. Eight of these ten patients died.

In general, the descriptions of symptoms in women's illnesses in I and III do not differ significantly from those in men's illnesses. There is no suggestion that the physician involved himself less in the care of his female patients than in that of his male patients, or that he was less thorough in his reporting. He does not seem to have omitted, or put unusual emphasis upon, gynecological symptoms. There are, however, fewer female than male patients, which, if we assume that treatment was beneficial, would have had detrimental effects on the survival rate of females.

Another possible sign of gender bias has been noted in the predominance of female infants in the pregnancy cases: in the six cases in which sex is indicated, only one infant is male. Hanson suggested that this predominance of female infants may have been due to the Hippocratic belief that the birth of male infants was easier for the mother because boys are more active and better able to force their way out in delivery.[2] Thus the sex differential would be a case of fulfilled expectations. Another possibility is suggested by reports that in northern India, a culture that traditionally devalues the female, midwives are paid less when they deliver girls, a practice that might be expected to affect the quality of the postpartum care that both woman and child receive from the midwife.[3] Given the general preference for male offspring in Greece, the complications following the birth of female infants in the *Epidemics* might reflect less attentive postpartum care given to mothers of girls by midwives and other care givers, motivated by lower social support (financial or emotional) for such women.

Finally, in the search for gender bias we should look at cases of female patients who did not have problems related to pregnancy for signs of the womb-centered approach to the general treatment of women that is characteristic of the gynecological treatises. In *Epidemics* I and III there are eight such patients:

Book I case 14 (2.716.5–14 Li.)

> Melidia suffered from pain in the head, neck, and chest. Immediately acute fever seized her, and a slight menstrual flow appeared. After a crisis on the eleventh day, she recovered.

Book III case 6 (first set) (3.50.1–52.9 Li.)

> Fever seized the *parthenos* daughter of Euryanax. After a crisis on the seventh day she relapsed and eventually died on the sev-

enth day after the second attack. The doctor reports that "they said" the trouble was caused by eating grapes.

Book III case 7 (first set) (3.52.10–54.7 Li.)

The female patient had angina (sore throat). The illness began with indistinctness of speech and fever; she died on the fifth day.

Book III case 9 (first set) (3.58.1–8 Li.)

The woman who lay at the house of Tisamenos had a bowel obstruction with vomiting and pain; nothing they could do helped her, and she died.

Book III case 7 (second set) (3.122.1–18 Li.)

Fever of the *kausos* type seized the *parthenos* who lay sick on the Sacred Way; menarche; deafness, delirium, copious nosebleed on the seventeenth day; a slight nosebleed on the twentieth; crisis on the twenty-seventh day and recovery.

Book III case 11 (second set) (3.134.1–15 Li.)

In Thasos, a naturally bad-tempered woman after a grief with a cause became sleepless and lost her appetite; thirst and nausea, convulsions, raving, fever, coma, delirium. Near the crisis, she had copious menses; she recovered.

Book III case 12 (second set) (3.136.1–13 Li.)

In Larissa, an acute fever [*kausos*] seized a *parthenos*. On the sixth day, a violent nosebleed and crisis occurred; after the crisis, menarche. She recovered.

Book III case 15 (second set) (3.142.5–146.6 Li.)

In Thasos, a shivery fever seized a woman of Dealkes immediately after a grief. She wrapped herself up; groped about like a blind person, without a word; plucked, scratched, pulled her hair, wept, and then laughed. She had rambling speech, then was sensible again; a slight fever was present. She died.

In none of these cases is there any suggestion that the doctor saw the womb as the cause of the illness. In fact, in the case of the naturally irritable woman, the doctor took pains to characterize the grief as *prophasios*, "with a cause," that is, objectively problematic. Menses are reported in two cases, once in connection with crisis; and menarche in two cases, once in conjunction with crisis. One *parthenos* had a nosebleed followed by crisis and menarche; this nosebleed might have been construed as misdirected menses,[4] but the doctor provides no indication that he thought this. In one of the constitutions menstrual bleeding in fever is seen as analogous to nosebleeds in men, and thus as a favorable sign in terms of humoral theory.[5]

While the case histories of I and III reveal comparatively little evidence of gender bias, in the constitutions a more one-sided picture emerges. The patient throughout is assumed to be male; women are mentioned only six times, twice to note that they were affected in the same way as men,[6] and four times to note that they were differently affected. Of the four passages noting differences, one states simply that fewer women were affected,[7] another that, in women, pains in the womb accompanied other symptoms,[8] and a third that most women who had copious menstruation recovered (the exception was a woman who overate).[9] Nevertheless, the only passage in the constitutions that deals specifically with pregnancy and childbirth, while it focuses on gynecological problems, is not womb-centered in its interpretation of the illness (although menstruation was a saving factor, it operated *qua* bleeding).[10]

The books of the second group, II, (IV), and VI, differ significantly from I and III in the percentage of female patients, the outcome of the cases, and the interpretation of female illnesses not associated with pregnancy. Cases in this group are relatively brief; some that involve pregnancy amount to no more than a sentence, and they never exceed a short paragraph. Given this brevity, it is not surprising that in general they provide few indications of the exact days on which symptoms occurred. On the other hand, the writer's interest frequently extends temporally beyond the boundaries of the particular illness. For instance, we hear that the daughter of the *agoranomos* did not have menses for two years following childbirth, but had hemorrhoids in the winter (IV 24); and that the wife of Agasis, asthmatic from childhood, who suffered a severe pain in her right hip with an asthmatic attack after a difficult delivery, continued to have pain associated with asthmatic attacks, especially when she had worked with her right hand (VI 4.4). This expansion of the doctor's interest beyond the immediate illness is in sharp contrast to I and III, where the author confines his attention strictly to the specific illness.

In this group, Book II is noteworthy for its special focus on women. Eleven of its twenty-nine cases, or 37.9 percent, deal with pregnancy-related problems, and sixteen of its patients, or 55 percent, are female. None of the pregnancy-related cases was fatal. The book contains eight chapters dealing with individual gynecological problems (including five prescriptions), and one long chapter that is a miscellaneous collection of gynecological material. Its author attributes one out of four female illnesses that are not pregnancy-related to uterine problems. Among these are two cases of problems cured by pregnancy, as well as a wandering womb that (rather atypically) responded to venesection. Book II thus stands out in its attention to gynecological matters as well as in its high percentage of female patients.

In Book IV, only 9 of the 103 patients suffered pregnancy-related problems (8.7 percent), and 37 (35.7 percent) were female. (In two other cases, the doctor reports that he, or the patient, did not know if she was pregnant.) None of the pregnancy-related cases reports a fatal outcome. In nonpregnancy cases involving female patients, we find three instances of womb-centered diagnosis: pains in hips and legs relieved (albeit temporarily) by pregnancy and childbirth,[11] and menstrual hemorrhage that "turned into" asthma, then fever.[12] In only one instance did the doctor's attention extend beyond the immediate case history.

From the standpoint of the treatment of women, the most interesting characteristic of Book IV is its author's expressions of doubt about the reports of women. In the case of the wife of Achelous (IV 6), he doubts her claim that she had earlier aborted a twenty-day fetus.[13] In IV 20 he reports that the patient had aborted, *as she said*, a thirty-day male, and again at IV 22 he applies this same skeptical phrase to the patient's report that she had aborted a sixty-day female. In contrast, he does not hesitate to pronounce, apparently on his own authority, that the miscarriage in IV 25 was that of a seven-month female. Elsewhere in the *Epidemics* we find similar signs of distrust of women patients, such as a doctor's suspicion that a woman may have taken an abortifacient (V 53), as well as numerous descriptions of women as sullen, irritable, depressed, or uncooperative.[14]

An interesting fact revealed by the accounts in which the doctor doubts the woman is that women were carefully counting the days of their pregnancies. This suggests that they were familiar with medical theories about the development of the fetus, in which the number of days featured prominently. While these theories probably had their origin in traditional female lore about pregnancy, by the classical period medical theorists had incorporated them into more systematic presentations. In the late fifth century, such theories were widely known, as witnessed by the speech Plato put into the mouth of Aristophanes in the *Symposium*, which parodies Hippocratic-type theories of sex determination.[15] We cannot tell whether the patients in the *Epidemics* derived their counting practices from women's lore or from medical theory, directly or indirectly, but it is interesting that Grensemann has suggested that *Diseases of Women* I was written with a patient audience in mind.[16] This question of women and literacy is one to which we will return shortly.

Book VI begins with a womb-related problem: the author discusses the prognosis for women who, after abortion and swelling of the uterus, suffer heaviness in the head and other pains of uterine origin. This chapter is typical of Book VI, whose author throughout displays a strong tendency to interpret illness in women as uterine in origin. Six of the nineteen patients are female (32 percent). Two of these, whose husbands were absent, suffered a fatal virilism attributed to the suppression of the menses.[17] The only pregnancy-related case is that of the asthmatic woman who, after a difficult delivery, suffered chronic asthma aggravated by physical work and associated with hip pain; the physician recommended restrictions on her diet and activity (VI 4.4). The chronic problems described in this case reflect a theory of uterine causation, since they are closely paralleled by a passage in *Diseases of Women* in which uterine problems caused by physical stress are discussed and similar prescriptions are outlined.[18] Book VI also contains one chapter of miscellaneous gynecological material.[19]

Despite the smaller proportion of pregnancy-related cases and female cases in VI as compared with II, the approach to gynecological cases in these books is similar: both focus on unusual cases and are prone to interpret women's illnesses as "female problems." The author of VI demonstrates interest in gynecology in his opening chapter, as well as in a subsequent chapter of general gynecological material, and the one pregnancy case that he records has a parallel in *Diseases of Women*. On the basis of its treatment of women, there thus seems to be no reason to question the traditional assignment of Book VI to the same author as Book II. Perhaps these two books were put together for different "courses" in a teaching program.

Books V and VII contain large numbers of cases but proportionately fewer female patients and pregnancy-related cases than the other books of the *Epidemics*. Book V records 105 cases, 27 of which deal with women (25.7 percent); of these, 6 are pregnancy-related (5.7 percent). Book VII records 128 cases, 87 of which are unique to it. In these 87 cases, 22 patients are women (25 percent), and 3 of these suffered from pregnancy-related complaints (3.4 percent). Of the 9 patients with pregnancy-related problems, 4 died (44 percent). Although the absolute numbers of pregnancy-related cases are similar to those in the other books, owing to the large number of cases that these books contain, they have the lowest percentage of cases involving women of any of the books of the *Epidemics*. Book VII has the lowest percentage of childbirth cases, while V is second in this only to VI. Their author attributes a high proportion of female illnesses to gynecological causes. These include hysterical suffocation;[20] pains or death arising from suppressed menses;[21] and headaches caused by the womb.[22]

Books V and VII suggest that errors of treatment, or medical treatment itself, were what the mother-to-be had most to fear. Of the four fatal outcomes in a total of nine pregnancy-related cases in V and VII, three can be attributed to treatment, whether by the doctor or by another practitioner, and one to a fall. In one case the writer frankly admits that the woman had been given an overdose of a cathartic (v 18); another patient died after latent tuberculosis had been activated by the stresses of delivery, including succussion (v 103, suspension and dropping in order to dislodge the infant). In still another case the doctor suspects that the women who died had taken an abortifacient (v 53); obviously this was a treatment that he himself had not supplied.[23] The one bright spot is the recovery, following a harrowing succession of symptoms, of a woman who had taken a fertility drug.[24]

The Wandering Womb

Many of the ailments that the Hippocratic doctor attributed to the womb were explained in terms of that organ's state of deprivation or misbehavior. Hippocratic anatomy viewed the womb as free to wander about the body, causing mischief wherever it settled: liver, hypochondrium, head, *kardia* (heart or stomach), bladder, seat, side/hip/flank, midriff, or even out of the vagina (prolapse, perhaps the only "real" wandering). The symptoms suffered by the victim of a wandering womb varied according to the site to which it moved:[25] suffocation, chills and fever, headache, pains in various other locations, vomiting, loss of speech, strangury, and effects on consciousness ranging from lethargy to delirium. The doctors offered a mechanistic explanation: the womb, lacking the moisture and fullness supplied by intercourse and pregnancy, was attracted by sources of moisture. In contrast, Plato records an animistic interpretation that may have had more popular appeal:

> The same is the case with the so-called womb or matrix of women. The animal within them is desirous of procreating children, and when remaining unfruitful long beyond its proper time, gets discontented and angry, and wandering in every direction through the body, closes up the passages of the breath, and, by obstructing respiration, drives them to extremity, causing all varieties of disease, until at length the desire and love of the man and the woman bring them together.[26]

On either the mechanistic or the animistic interpretation, however, the cure prescribed was the same: intercourse and pregnancy to restore moisture and the "natural" condition of fullness in the womb. Thus for the girl suffering from the "illness of maidens" whose enlightened father called in a Hippocratic physician, the prescription was a speedy marriage. It is noteworthy, however, that the Hippocratic author complains that traditional healers, who were most often consulted by the women of the family, recommended a less drastic cure: dedications to the goddess Artemis.[27]

The wandering womb concept may have arrived in Greece from Egypt, for it was a well established part of Egyptian medical lore by at least the second millennium,[28] or it may have been an independent development in Greece.[29] A somewhat similar affliction, the "wandering navel," is found as a folk illness in modern Greece. Unlike the wandering womb, however, the wandering navel afflicts both men and women. Its symptoms include weakness, vomiting, thirst, and dizziness. It is treated by folk healers who "collect" the navel from various parts of the body into a specific location, such as a nerve in the armpit, which swells to the size of an egg when it is massaged; the patient is also given a hot drink and advised to eat well and avoid carrying heavy loads on his or her back until the symptoms subside.[30]

The idea of the wandering womb may have developed as an analogue of the phallus as an independent creature that Eva Keuls has documented in Greek visual images.[31] Plato in fact describes the activities of the womb as analogous to those of the male organ in the passage just preceding that quoted previously:

> And the seed, having life and becoming endowed with respiration, produces in that part in which it respires a lively desire of emission, and thus creates in us the love of procreation. Wherefore also in men the organ of generation becoming rebellious and masterful, like an animal disobedient to reason, and maddened with the sting of lust, seeks to gain absolute sway, and the same is the case with the so-called womb or matrix of women.[32]

But the rebellious phallus was a far less troublesome creature for its possessor than was the angry womb. Despite Plato's disapproval of sensual indulgence, Greek society provided and sanctioned ample sexual outlets for male citizens in homosexual relationships and extramarital heterosexual contacts with slaves, prostitutes, or *hetairai*. For women, in contrast, sexual outlets were strictly limited to marriage, and, to be truly effective in satisfying the womb, these had to result in pregnancy. Thus the risk of wandering womb entailed early marriage for girls and continuous pregnancies for married women.

Although the optimum cure for a wandering womb was intercourse and pregnancy, Hippocratic medicine also tried to influence the errant creature in other, less drastic ways. Fumigation "from below" with pleasant smelling agents might attract it back down, or it might be repelled and driven back to its proper place by fumigation with evil smelling materials "from above." Such treatment depended upon a view of the female reproductive organs as a tube connecting two "mouths"[33] (the same model was operative in fertility tests that depended upon odoriferous substances applied at one "mouth" subsequently appearing at the other, as we noted in chapter 1). Another model of female anatomy that appears in the gynecological treatises is that of the womb as upside-down jar.[34] It was believed that the mouth of the jar/uterus closed on the product of conception when a woman successfully conceived. The jar model also lay behind the use of succussion in cases of difficult delivery (shaking a woman up and down, or attaching her to a frame and dropping it repeatedly on the ground)—getting the baby out was viewed as similar to getting an olive out of a bottle.[35] In fact, the Hippocratic doctors, who did no dissections, had no direct knowledge of the nature and function of the reproductive organs of the human female, but drew their notions instead from animal analogies, "logic," and a rather vivid imagination.

Abortion

In one of the cases in V and VII the doctor suspects that the patient may have taken something to bring on the abortion:

> In the wife of Simon, abortion on the thirtieth day. This happened to her when she had drunk something [an abortifacient], or it was spontaneous. Pain; vomiting of much bile, pale, leek-green, when she drank;

she bit her tongue. Her tongue was big and black; the white in her eyes was red. Sleepless. On the fourth day in the night she died.[36]

It is significant that the doctor in this case is not privy to information about the cause of the abortion. What lies behind his suspicion? A clue is offered by a passage in *Diseases of Women* I that echoes his feelings on a more general level: abortion is something that "women always do."[37] The secret in this case as well is probably that of the woman, not that of the male-headed *oikos*. Nor was it one with which the doctor himself had much sympathy (this is not to say that he lacked sympathy with the patient herself, however). Like the author of the passage in *Diseases of Women* I, he probably had—rightly—strong reservations of a practical nature about abortion: it was always dangerous. In fact, it was far riskier than childbirth since all methods involved violence of some sort.[38]

A consideration of the evidence about abortion in the Hippocratic Corpus has led to the assumption that elective abortion in cases of apparently normal pregnancy was a normal practice of Hippocratic doctors, but this conclusion is by no means sure. First of all, we should consider the evidence for a distinction between the use of therapeutic abortion (cases of dead or defective fetuses or impeded delivery) and elective abortion. Then we need to consider who it was that was performing the abortions.

In *Diseases of Women* I, there are nine cases in which ἐκβάλλειν/ἐκβόλιον (cast out, terms also used for exposed infants) are used for a dead or damaged fetus,[39] and seventeen cases of "another," presumably for the same purpose. In *Nature of Woman*, there is one such case,[40] making a total of twenty-seven cases of explicitly therapeutic abortion. In addition, the brief treatise *Excision of the Fetus* gives instructions for the dismemberment and removal of a fetus in an abnormal (μὴ κατὰ τρόπον) pregnancy.

There are also many chapters in the gynecological treatises devoted to the causes of spontaneous abortion,[41] as well as recipes for emmenagogues.[42] Either type of information might prove useful to a person wishing to bring on an abortion, but the assumption that such indirection was intended seems unwarranted. Given the high rate of infant mortality and the significance of reproduction for both the *oikos* (continuity) and the wife (status), there must have been much concern about bringing pregnancies successfully to term and much interest in methods of preventing spontaneous abortion. Moreover, Hippocratic theories about the ill-effects of blocked menses would have provided a ready market for emmenagogues in and for themselves.

There are, however, a number of passages in which ἐκβόλιον or ἐκβάλλειν is used without further qualification and which therefore could refer to elective abortion. There are six such passages in *Diseases of Women* I,[43] and three in *Nature of Woman*,[44] although two of the former occur before or after discussions of the treatment of dead or defective fetuses and their immediate context may imply that the qualification extends to them as well.[45] The unqualified uses are followed by "another" recipe, presumably for the same purpose, in eighteen cases. Thus there are a total of twenty-seven instances in which these terms, either explicitly or implicitly, appear in unqualified form and could refer to an elective abortion. In addition, an apparently clear reference to such an abortion appears in the phrase ἔμβρυον ἡμίεργον ἕλκει (draw the half-formed embryo) in *Diseases of Women* I 78.[46] Nevertheless, this phrase occurs in a series with the expulsion of the chorion and bringing down the menses, and the same series appears earlier in the treatise with the term ἀπόπληκτον (crippled by a stroke, paralyzed) in place of ἡμίεργον.[47] As John Riddle says, this could be a substitution reflecting the medical writer's pronatalist position, but, "who can be certain?"[48]

The usage of ἐκβάλλειν/ἐκβόλιον is thus fairly well balanced: in four cases the terms are used without qualification; in two more they may be but their sense is unclear since their immediate context may imply that the qualification extends to them. There are eighteen cases of "another" following unqualified uses and therefore presumably also unqualified. Thus there are twenty-five to twenty-seven cases of unqualified usage in addition to twenty-seven cases in which the terms are explicitly used to refer to means of aborting dead or defective fetuses. The possibility thus remains that doctors were conducting elective abortions.

The fact that the gynecological treatises contain recipes for abortion of course does not in itself constitute firm evidence that doctors themselves actually performed abortions. John Riddle provides convincing arguments that the writer(s) of these passages were acting basically as compilers of the traditional lore of women.[49] As might be expected in such a compilation, the material is poorly presented: recipes are piled up in list form, and there are variations in section headings that point to the recording of an oral tradition. Confusions in terminology also suggest that the writer was unfamiliar with the material, as when the word used for the chaste tree is in one recipe λύγος, whereas in the recipe immediately following, ἄγνος is used. Riddle concludes that the compiler(s) "probably did not understand the data and merely recorded it without assimilating and reformulating the material."[50] Presumably the compiler(s) understood the possibility of using the information about abortion for elective abortions, even when they were unfamiliar with some of the ingredients used. But even this is an assumption; we can only say that the person(s) who compiled these treatises had no objections to passing this information on, certainly for therapeutic abortion, possibly for elective termination of pregnancy.

The information recorded in the gynecological treatises thus *could* have provided the doctor with knowledge useful to induce an abortion, if he had understood it and if that was his aim, and this is the interpretation of those who argue that Hippocratic doctors routinely performed elective abortions.[51] But in nearly every case this argument overreaches the evidence.[52] In the Hippocratic treatises there is only one passage in which a doctor reports that he himself made use of (what he believed to be) a cause of spontaneous abortion to end a pregnancy—and this is also the only passage that directly attests a doctor's intentional abortion of a (presumably) normal pregnancy.

In this case of doctor-induced abortion, which is recounted in *Nature of the Child*, the patient was a valuable slave who provided an income to her owner, a kinswoman of the doctor, by her singing (the passage is given in Chapter 1). Her pregnancy threatened this income, and the slave herself reported it to her mistress as soon as she was aware of it. The doctor reports that he instructed the woman to jump up and down so as to touch her heels to her buttocks, and after seven jumps the woman aborted.[53] The story has attracted attention especially because the doctor's participation in an abortion seems to conflict with the prohibition in the Hippocratic treatise *Oath* against procuring an abortion by giving a poisonous pessary to a woman.[54] One strategy intended to reconcile these two passages argues that the abortion was too early to count;[55] another focuses on the servile status of the woman.[56] Both hypotheses seem to be right to a degree.

While our distinction between viable and nonviable fetuses cannot be read into the Hippocratic evidence,[57] such an early "abortion" (it was one in the minds of the participants, if not in ours) utilized no invasive measures (no poisonous pessaries or potions, and no instruments) and involved a comparatively low level of shock to the body.[58] As far as slave status is concerned, there is nothing to suggest that Hippocratic doctors in general treated slaves any differently than free persons. On the other hand, the essential point in the story is the fact that the woman acted in accord with her *kyrios* (in this case, her owner): both wanted to end the pregnancy in order to have uninterrupted profit from the woman's professional activities. This brings us to what lay at the heart of the issue of abortion in Greece—the rights of the *kyrios*.

In most cases that might have involved inducing abortion in a free woman, the *kyrios* was the husband. In 1941 Crahay made the point that in abortion, the issue was not the sanctity of life or the rights of the fetus, but the rights of the (lawfully married) father—in other words, the rights of the *kyrios*.[59] This is suggested as well by the use for abortion of forms of the word ἐκβάλλω, which was also used of the right to expose a newborn infant. In the case of the married woman in v 53, the woman's silence on the cause of her problems must be linked to this. When wives, unwilling to complete a pregnancy, took things into their own hands, they were violating the rights of their husbands, not the rights of the fetus or some abstract moral code. Not unreasonably, they saw the male doctor as acting in the service of their male *kyrios* and did not take him into their confidence. On the other hand, a doctor acting as the agent of the husband/owner was not unwilling to carry out an abortion if the *kyrios* wanted it, as the story of the singer illustrates (although we cannot tell if he would have used the dangerous recipes included in the gynecological treatises), or if the fetus was dead or the pregnancy patently abnormal (here the risks of the abortifacients were justified by the certainty of death for the woman if action was not taken).[60] It is highly unlikely, however, that he would have assisted any woman in aborting a fetus against the will of her *kyrios*—or that many husbands who did not want more offspring would have chosen a risky abortion for their pregnant wives over the comparative safety of a normal delivery and exposure (which also allowed for sex selection).

It is well to keep in mind that the sharp distinction that we draw between contraception, abortion, and infanticide was not possible for the Greeks given their lack of information about female anatomy and physiology.[61] The situation found by the Blums among modern Greek villagers seems more relevant: as we noted in chapter 1, these women made little distinction between abortions, "nine-month abortions," stillbirths, and infanticide, considering infants before baptism as "creatures somewhat apart from the human family."[62] In other words, the sharp line of distinction was drawn at the point of formal acceptance into the community. In classical Greece, the ceremony of the *amphidromia* served, as did baptism for the Greek village women, to mark inclusion within the community, although in this case the right to reject a child before it was formally accepted had broad social as well as legal sanction.

The general suspicion of women's tendency to seek abortions that is expressed by the author of *Diseases of Women* I reflects the widespread general tension between women and men as it affected married couples. Despite all the ways in which Greek society acculturated girls and women to their role as childbearers, which will be discussed in the following chapters, many apparently still shrank from pregnancy and childbirth, especially after the requisite son had been produced. But in seeking relief from an unwanted pregnancy, they could not turn to the male Hippocratic doctor for assistance. As the author of *Diseases of Women* suggests, they turned instead to other women in a conspiracy of female silence.[63] Possibly it was this alliance among women that motivated some husbands to choose male doctors to treat their pregnant wives, especially when these doctors took care to utilize female helpers acting under their direction for actual examinations.[64]

Doctors and Midwives

Traditionally the care of women in pregnancy and childbirth was in the hands of women, who not only assisted in deliveries but also provided advice about fertility, abortion, contraception, and even (in imagination if not in reality) sex determination. None of the case histories of postpartum complications in the *Epidemics* gives us reason to doubt that women traditionally handled the birth itself, for none includes a detailed description of the events of the delivery, and the brief comments that the author sometimes does make about the conditions of delivery could easily have been relayed to him by the birth attendants when he took over treatment after the development of complications. Nevertheless, some passages in other books of the Corpus suggest that the doctor's absence at deliveries was not total,[65] and the cases in the *Epidemics* show doctors involved at every other stage of pregnancy and in the handling and treatment of a variety of ailments, many of specifically gynecological nature.

Probably the most compelling evidence that male doctors were very much concerned with the obstetrical and gynecological problems of women by the time that the Hippocratic treatises were being composed is the very creation of these treatises themselves. Grensemann noted that the major books, *Diseases of Women* I, II, and III (*Sterility*), *Nature of Woman*, and *Superfetation*, make up one-eighth of the corpus; in addition, there are the smaller books *Parthenoi* and *Excision of the Fetus*, as well as the embryological treatises *Seed* and *Nature of the Child*, and the treatises *Seven Months' Child* and *Eight Months' Child*.[66] In 1988, Rousselle suggested that these treatises, with their emphasis on treatment and long lists of remedies, incorporated a female oral tradition.[67] This is obviously a claim of the greatest importance to the interpretation of women's role in the history of medicine, but it has not found the reception it deserves. In the same year, Manuli took the apparently contrary position, stressing that the author of these books spoke with a male voice.[68] Lloyd noted the conflict but chose to bypass Rousselle's claim, referring only to "a male tradition," "male-oriented ideas," and "a masculine cultural bias."[69] Hanson praised Lloyd for his stance on this issue and herself portrayed the tradition as gender-less: "medical information belonging to the society at large," "soci-etal traditions and experiences familiar to anyone who cared to think on gynecological topics," "a tradition of home remedies."[70] Thus women's contribution to Hippocratic gynecology has essen-tially been denied. But we need to look further at this question.

Within this tradition Hanson pointed out certain concepts that can indeed be identified as male because they appear in the general literature as well as in the gynecological texts: the identification of women with their reproductive or sexual functions,[71] the image of woman as plowed field,[72] the belief that sterility was always at-tributable to the woman,[73] the prescription of sex as a cure-all for female illnesses,[74] and the analogy between the upper and the lower necks of the woman, implicit in the belief that one can tell when a woman loses her virginity: her (upper) neck enlarges in sympathy with the lower, thus lowering her voice.[75] In a modern context, these would indeed be classified as male assumptions—locker room lore, demeaning to women, but shared by doctors and laymen (and too often by women as well).

But, in fact, a choice between a male or a female tradition is both unnecessary and ill-suited to the data, for the evidence demon-strates that there were female as well as male components in the traditional lore about women's reproductive functions. The doctors themselves give us ample evidence that they consulted women,[76] and that there was much information about women's experience that was ordinarily confined to women—the sorts of things that you can talk about only to women, as the nurse in the *Hippolytus* advised Phaedra—and to which doctors could gain access only with difficulty.[77] Included in this female lore was the belief of "ex-perienced women" that they could perceive the womb closing in conception;[78] women's calculations of the timing of conception and the length of pregnancy;[79] and methods for dealing with various situations that might confront the midwife in delivery (for example, the material in *Excision*). But the most important element of female lore that is contained in these treatises consists in the practical therapeutic recipes that make up a large proportion of their contents, and which Riddle's recent detailed work has shown to have been transmitted by female tradition.[80]

A more accurate picture of the relationship between the Hippocratic author/compiler of a gynecological treatise and his material would be one that portrayed him as making use of the rich resources of women's lore, but as perceiving this raw material through the value-laden conceptual screen of traditional Greek male assumptions about female physiology. This "male slant" turned female lore into the male-filtered female (but hardly common) tradition of the male-authored treatises. Thus, in effect, both Manuli and Rouselle were right: the bulk of the material in the gynecological treatises consisted of midwives' or women's lore, but the doctors perceived that lore through the conceptual lens of the Greek male. Thus the treatises in which they recorded this lore did indeed speak with a male voice.

As doctors paid more attention to women's medical problems and entered more often into their care, they needed the continuing assistance of women and midwives. One practical reason for this lay in the problems that the male doctor faced in dealing with his female patients: even though husbands might be willing, or even anxious, to entrust their wives and daughters to a male doctor's care, the women themselves, brought up in seclusion and taught to be ashamed of their bodies, were often less than cooperative. As the author of *Diseases of Women* I explains:

> Many problems arise, especially in women who have not borne children, but they also often happen to those who have had children. And these are dangerous, as it's said, and generally acute and serious and difficult to understand, because women share [common] illnesses and sometimes they themselves don't know what they have, before they become experienced with menstrual problems and become older Then necessity and time teach them the cause of the illnesses, but often in those who don't know the cause of their problems the illness becomes

incurable before the doctor learns correctly from the patient what she is suffering. For they are ashamed to say, even if they know, and it seems shameful to them because of their inexperience and ignorance.[81]

In modern Greece, women also express shame and embarrassment in front of a male physician, and many women prefer to receive their medical care from female midwives.[82] It is not surprising, then, that we find the Hippocratic doctor enlisting the aid of midwives as assistants or instructing female patients to carry out self-examinations or treatments.

The midwives who assisted the Hippocratic doctor are shadowy figures whose presence must be inferred in the *Epidemics*, but more specific evidence about their role can be found in other Hippocratic treatises. Even this evidence, however, offers only hints at a female activity that in general was taken for granted. Thus *Fleshes* 19 speaks of ἀκεστρίδας (female healers) who attended births,[83] and in *Diseases of Women* 1 68, the author gives instructions for handling the delivery of a dead fetus that includes the statement that the female "who is doctoring" (τὴν ἰητρεύουσαν) will open the mouth of the womb gently and draw out the cord with the infant.[84] In the same treatise, chapter 46 refers to the woman who cuts the cord, and chapter 34 addresses the reader directly, telling her not to "do as the [male] doctors do" in treating cases of swelling of the uterus. Other passages instruct the doctor to have another woman (the midwife?) carry out a specific examination.[85]

These passages which allude to the midwife in various ways leave no doubt that women assisted, or were advised by, Hippocratic doctors in deliveries, both normal and abnormal. What is most significant, however, is the passage in which the doctor directly addresses the midwife, telling her not to do as male doctors do. As Grensemann noted, the author of *Diseases of Women* was addressing an audience that included midwives, and instructing them in the handling of problems both before and after delivery.[86] This presupposes that women were either auditors in a medical course in which he presented this material (these treatises are not rhetorical show pieces directed at a lay audience), or were expected to read it themselves.[87] Is it then possible that midwives were literate?

Recent studies of Greek literacy have concluded that at most 5 percent of women were literate (in a general population with literacy between 5 and 10 percent), and that these were women of the upper class or *hetairai*.[88] We would place in this upper-class 5 percent Ischomachus's young wife, whom Xenophon portrays as able to make lists of household items.[89] But what about midwives? Manuli, in a discussion of Hippocratic gynecology, claimed that midwives were deprived of writing and a proper literature,[90] and Harris assumed their illiteracy on the grounds that Soranus (second century A.D.) advised that they *should* be literate. But on the same grounds, we might infer that no midwives were mindful, industrious, and intelligent, other characteristics that Soranus recommended.[91] In the first centuries of literacy in Greece, the literacy of craftspeople was more significant and better established than literary literacy.[92] As Aristophanes' Sausage Seller shows, a knowledge of letters was unremarkable among the working poor.[93] Those people with a relatively high degree of basic (or crafts) literacy— poorer citizens and resident aliens engaged in crafts or trade— made up most of the pool from which midwives were drawn. There is, therefore, no a priori reason to assume that midwives were illiterate. And the very existence of gynecological treatises that address such women offers good evidence that they were expected to be able to read them.

Whether women were auditors in a medical course or read medical treatises themselves, in either case they shared the peripheries of a male profession.[94] The midwife who worked with the doctor would have become familiar with the Hippocratic theory in which the male doctor had framed the information that he adopted from women's lore, whether from association with the doctor or from attending lectures on, or even reading, the gynecological treatises (it is for such theoretical understanding that Soranus recommends that midwives be literate). Such women possessed a *techne*, or art, in much the same sense that male doctors did, as was recognized by Plato when in the *Republic* he matter-of-factly spoke of female doctors.[95]

The entry of the Hippocratic doctor into the care of parturient women probably elevated the status within the patriarchal value system of those women who became his assistants (although it may well have also lowered the status of traditional midwives who were not associated with doctors). Even though such status was still nowhere near that attainable by male doctors,[96] it could have provided a significant improvement in the lives of some women[97] in a society in which fitness had become a male passion and medical theories could be the topic of fashionable conversation at upper-class parties, as portrayed in Plato's *Symposium*. In a profession without licenses or established standards, this foot in the door could—and did—lead to a gradually widening sphere of female activity in the treatment of other women, and to women who would more and more lay claim to the title "woman doctor."[98] The first such woman attested in our sources was Phanostrate, whose grave monument in the mid-fourth century identified her as *maia* and *iatros* (see plate 12).[99]

But the most radical and long-lasting effect of the association between Hippocratic doctors and midwives was less favorable to women. This was the transformation of (female) lore about childbirth and women's reproductive problems into the (male) form of written treatises, and thus the creation of a *logos* of women's medical problems, literally, a gynecology. Foucault has pointed out the association between the creation of a discipline, in the form of a body of knowledge in written form, and the use of that knowledge as a mode of control and power,[100] and the Foucauldian model, although created for early modern France, finds confirmation in the Hippocratic situation. The doctor, in possession of his written treatises, assumed control over female lore and the reproductive capabilities of women.[101]

Why was control of female reproduction an issue? As we noted in the case of abortion, female control in the vital area of the production of heirs was something that concerned Athenian men a great deal.[102] That this concern was widespread can be seen by its appearance in comedy. In Aristophanes' *Thesmophoriazusae*, men's complaints about women include their skill with drugs (poisons and abortifacients), their propensity to take lovers, and—the greatest suspicion of all—their willingness to introduce supposititious children into the household.[103] In one passage the women condemn servants who expose wives who try to introduce such infants; in another passage men are said to sit beside their wives' beds in childbirth to prevent the introduction of a supposititious child; and in still another, the wife is said to have exchanged her baby girl for her maid's boy. The role that male imagination assigned to the traditional midwife in this female misbehavior is graphically portrayed by Aristophanes:

> I knew a woman who said she was ten days in childbirth, until she bought a child. Her husband ran all over buying helps to hasten the birth, but the old woman brought in a child in a pot, with its mouth stuffed with honeycomb so it wouldn't cry. And then when she signaled, straightaway the wife cried out, "Go away, go away, husband, I'm about to give birth," for the child kicked at the belly of the pot. And he, delighted, rushed out, while she drew the honeycomb out of the mouth of the child and it cried out. Then the miserable old woman, the very same one who had brought in the child, ran smiling to the husband and said, "A lion, a lion for you! Your very image in every way, even his little prick is like yours, crooked like a little pine cone."[104]

Little wonder then if some men sought to bring this sphere of their lives under the dictates and control of male doctors.

In his treatment of women, the Hippocratic doctor was able to assert control in ways that were particularly advantageous to the anxious Greek husband. He was in a good position to prevent the connivance of the midwife in the introduction of a supposititious infant, and possibly even to prevent unauthorized female resort to abortion. And he could rely upon his professional assessment of the risks of female sexual and reproductive abstinence in order to reinforce social norms of early marriage for adolescent daughters and the remarriage of divorcées and widows of childbearing age.

The entry of formal medicine into the arena of childbirth was a crucial point in women's history. Modern feminists have decried the "medicalization" of childbirth by male doctors and the subsequent loss of female autonomy and control, but, in fact, the male usurpation of control over female reproduction goes back to the Hippocratic doctors and had its ultimate root in the essentially dysfunctional construction of women's role by Greek culture. That beginning in the formative days of Western medicine and culture, in connection with the creation of the Hippocratic gynecological texts that would long be influential in medical practice, contributed significantly to the consolidation of male control over women's reproductive lives that has continued throughout Western history. While it also gave a few women an association with the male profession of medicine, they remained marginal until the late twentieth century (and remain so even now in some medical specialties).

Four

The Risks of Childbirth

lthough, as we have seen, the Hippocratic doctor was in a good position to exercise control over the reproductive lives of his female patients, in a strictly medical sense he was often far from being in control of the misadventures of childbirth. Lacking the basic tools and methods of modern biomedicine—antibiotics, blood transfusions, forceps, and cesarean sections—the Greek doctor was all but helpless in the face of obstetric emergencies that today's doctors meet successfully almost as a matter of routine. The situation as described for early modern Europe would apply to classical Greece as well:

> A whole variety of conditions, such as hemorrhage, pelvic deformity, disproportion between the sizes of the child's head and the pelvis, severe abnormal presentations such as transverse lies, eclampsia and uterine inertia early in labour, are likely to have posed problems which were beyond the capacities of those attending the birth to alleviate. . . . Furthermore, attempts to remove a dead child, especially by the old-fashioned hooks and crotchets in general use before the eighteenth century, probably severely threatened the mother's life.[1]

Records for modern developed countries before the 1930s, when maternal mortality began the steep decline associated with the introduction of antibiotics, show that 35 to 55 percent of maternal deaths were due to puerperal infection (an exception being the period of the early modern hospital when death rates in epidemics reached 80 to 90 percent), 20 percent to toxemia, 20 percent to hemorrhage, and the remainder to various causes, especially abortion.[2] Yet the argument persists that childbirth for women in preindustrial societies posed relatively few risks. Thus Calvin Wells attributed women's indisputably shorter life-span in such societies in comparison with that of men not to the risks of childbearing but to nutritional deficiencies resulting from the preferential feeding of males.[3] In particular, he maintained that women in preindustrial societies, not exposed to the conditions that gave rise to rampant puerperal fever in the early modern hospital—the unwashed hands of physicians and medical students—did not suffer from that scourge. Well's arguments seem to have gained considerable acceptance,[4] and, as the preceding figures attest, there is something to be said for his judgment on puerperal fever. Nevertheless, his overall assessment of childbirth risk is far too low—and too reminiscent of the old cultural stereotype that "natives" do not suffer in the same way that their modern Western observers do.

Two sorts of evidence that one would assume would help in determining childbirth risks, skeletal remains and epitaphs, are more promising in prospect than in fact. Skeletal remains in particular would seem likely to offer direct evidence of death in childbirth in the form of fetuses lodged in pelvic bones. In fact, the skeletal evidence is disappointing. One reason for this is that attention has only recently begun to be paid to this type of evidence, and relatively few studies are available for classical Greece. The redirection of the archaeological focus to these and other mundane finds may add somewhat to our information in the future, but the outlook is still not promising for several reasons. Problems with the age- and sex-determination of skeletal remains, and especially with the use of pelvic scars to estimate numbers of births, discussed in chapter 1,[5] will continue to limit the usefulness of skeletal material in the study of childbirth even when more attention is paid to it in excavations. Moreover, the nature of the Greek soil makes it highly unlikely that fetuses will be found actually lodged in the pelvises of female skeletons. In fact, there are remarkably few instances of this phenomenon from any area in antiquity: Calvin Wells reported only two cases from Egypt, one from early Saxon England, and two from medieval Europe, but none from Greece. Owsley and Bradtmiller in a study of native American burials in four well-preserved sites in South Dakota (A.D. 1600–1832) also found the phenomenon to be extremely rare, amounting to only two cases (0.9 percent of the burials), neither one of which provided evidence for cause of death.[6] An interesting example of the ambiguity of such skeletal material, where it does exist, is provided by the Anglo-Saxon burial of a mother and infant reported by Wells and Hawkes in 1975: they could not determine whether the infant was placed upon the mother's body after death or whether both died during an impeded delivery, perhaps as a result of "contraction ring," cord round the neck—or whether both mother and child were quickly dispatched when the infant's head emerged unpleasantly deformed as a result of placenta praevia.

Epitaphs are another form of evidence that one would think would be helpful, at least in providing demographic information. Unfortunately, Greek epitaphs seldom give age at death, and even the far more numerous Roman tombstones, which often do include this information and which might have offered at least an ancient parallel, reflect commemorative practices and economic realities more than actual death patterns. Thus widowers were more likely to commemorate spouses than were widows, who usually had fewer resources; parents were more likely to commemorate children than children parents, again, probably a matter of resources; and the very young are underrepresented while the very old are overrepresented.[7] One form of funerary memorial, the pictorial representations of women in labor on tombstones, can be useful in assessing community attitudes, but it does not help in determining the type or degree of risk of childbearing (and, as we shall argue in chapter 7, at least some of these monuments may not record childbirth deaths at all).

The childbirth cases in the *Epidemics* are thus left as the most promising form of evidence for assessing childbirth risks in Greece. In considering them, perhaps the most obvious question is the one upon which Wells focused: did these women suffer from childbed fever? Retrospective diagnosis is, of course, difficult. We cannot automatically use the categories of modern biomedicine to analyze and diagnose illnesses described in terms of the medical system of a premodern culture.[8] Nor can we assume that modern medicine has the "right" answers, and that we can fit the symptoms described by the Greek system into modern diagnostic patterns and come up with a "correct" diagnosis. The differences in diagnostic categories are such as to make an exact, one-to-one fit unlikely. Symptoms noted and described by a doctor who interpreted illness as an imbalance of humors, who saw the uterus as capable of wandering about the body causing trouble, and who lacked thermometers, instruments for measuring blood pressure, and other modern diagnostic tools are unlikely to fit neatly into the diagnostic categories devised by doctors who attribute illness to the actions of microorganisms and describe symptoms in terms of sophisticated modern laboratory tests. Nonetheless, attempts at retrospective diagnosis continue to compel interest, and scholars search for ways to overcome the bind created by the disparities in medical systems.[9]

A helpful strategy in dealing with this bind is offered by the distinction made by medical anthropology between illness and disease, and by the related concept of a culturally constructed illness. The term "disease" is used to refer to a specific physiological and/or psychological malfunction—an entity defined by the list of symptoms in the Merck Manual, if you will. It is what the doctor sees and diagnoses; it is viewed as some *thing* that a person *has,* like tuberculosis, and there is an assumption that it will be the same disease in any culture or society in which it appears. On the other hand, the term "illness" is used to apply to the disease as it is experienced by a particular patient in a particular cultural and social context; it encompasses the meaning that the disease has for the patient and for those around him, and the way he or she responds in seeking treatment.[10]

Intrinsic to the distinction between disease and illness is the concept of illness as a cultural construct:

> A given medical system in its socio-cultural context does considerably more than name, classify, and respond to illness. . . . In a real sense, it

structures the experience of illness and, in part, creates the form disease takes. Disease occurs as a natural process. It works upon biophysical reality and/or psychological processes, as the case may be But the experience of illness is a cultural or symbolic reality. . . . What is perceived as illness in one culture may not be so perceived in another. . . any disease . . . is in part a cultural construct.[11]

In terms of these concepts, we can identify puerperal infection as a *disease* defined by modern Western medicine as an infection of the genital track arising after childbirth; its definitive symptom is "a temperature of 35° C or above on any two successive days after the first 24 h postpartum and other causes are not apparent."[12] Other symptoms include chills, tenderness of the uterus, headache, malaise, and changes in lochial flow (diminished, or heavy and offensive). When this disease occurred in the specific cultural environment of the early modern hospital, in which male doctors and medical students moved from autopsies to deliveries without employing effective antiseptic procedures, the result was the *illness* of childbed fever in epidemic form. In these epidemics, often 80 to 90 percent of the patients died.[13] This illness was a true cultural construct in that a pathogen converged with a specific cultural complex—the early hospital, its program of medical training, and its doctors' ignorance of the sources and prevention of infection—to create an extremely dangerous culture-specific epidemic illness.

The tragic results of early hospital obstetric care have left a vivid impression of childbed fever as an illness of the premodern hospital, but the disease that is puerperal infection can and does occur at any time and in any situation in which women give birth, arising either from external contamination or from normal vaginal bacteria that become pathologic in such situations as anemia, preeclampsia, prolonged labor, repeated examinations, traumatic delivery, retention of placental fragments, or postpartum hemorrhage.[14] Greek women indeed did not suffer from the culture-specific illness that was childbed fever, but from this we cannot infer that they did not suffer from the disease, puerperal infection. In order to determine this, we need to consider the evidence further.

The evidence that is available consists of the case histories in the *Epidemics,* descriptions of postpartum complications in the gynecological treatises, the conceptual framework—the theory of disease—within which the Hippocratic cases were recorded, and the definitions and descriptions of modern medicine (since it is, after all, for people in our own culture that we want to classify the Greek experience). It will also be helpful for comparative purposes to consider modern descriptions of cases for the period before puerperal infection became a treatable illness. For this purpose, descriptions of cases of childbed fever are useful,[15] for, like the postpartum complications in the Hippocratic treatises, they developed without the intervention of antibiotics; moreover, they occurred in a medical system that still employed the basic conceptual framework of Hippocratic humoral medicine.[16]

A considerable literature from the eighteenth and nineteenth centuries on childbed fever exists, from which we will consider only two doctors' accounts. The first of these describes three cases that arose after home birth and were treated in the patient's home; the other provides a general description of a physician's experiences with epidemic childbed fever, including accounts of both home and hospital births. Both authors distinguished between two forms of puerperal fever: sporadic and epidemic.

In 1768 Thomas Denman, a physician, published *Essays on the Puerperal Fever, and on Puerperal Convulsions,*[17] in which he described the illness and provided accounts of three cases that he had treated. In describing these cases he followed the model of the *Epidemics,* and he argued for a Hippocratic treatment by evacuations (cathartics and emetics), for which he gave recipes. He listed the symptoms as an initial chill followed by fever, vomiting of green or yellow bitter matter, swelling and tenderness of the abdomen (the definitive sign), great pain in the back and hips, change or suppression of lochia, nausea, diarrhea, painful and scanty urination (the kidneys being affected), and anxiety. He states that the illness usually began two to five days after delivery, but notes as an exception Hippocrates' wife of Philinus, who became ill on the fourteenth day. He notes that the patient usually died on the eleventh day, and that those who recovered did not undergo a crisis but improved gradually. He reports that mortality was high but that the three patients whose case histories he presents survived as a result of his method of treatment. The first fell ill in 1766 three days after an uneventful delivery; she suffered chills, fever, vomiting, tenderness and swelling of the abdomen, alteration in the lochia, and delirium, but was able to stop treatment at twelve days. The second patient fell ill in 1767 three days after a safe but laborious delivery; she suffered shivering, pains, swelling, and fever, but was able to stop medication at fourteen days. The third fell ill in 1768 five days after a favorable delivery, with vomiting, pain, and fever; she was finally well after eighteen days.

In 1845, three years before Semmelweis's discoveries about the causes of childbed fever were announced in England, William Harris published *Lectures on Puerperal Fevers*.[18] He began his account with a history of the malady, reporting that it had been known from antiquity, calling attention to the case of the wife of Philinus and remarking (as had Denman) that it was unusual in beginning fourteen days after delivery. He then discussed etiology, attributing the illness to atmospheric conditions. But he also expressed strong suspicions that it was contagious, suggesting that it was carried by doctors, especially by their clothing, and noting that it frequently occurred when a doctor delivered a patient after participating in an autopsy or the delivery of another patient who had developed the fever. He even mentioned specific doctors who were contaminated and who had lost almost all of their patients to the fever while neighboring patients of other doctors escaped. Nevertheless, he also knew of cases in which patients escaped infection despite their doctors' prior participation in autopsies, and he refrained from drawing definite conclusions as to contagion.

Harris presented a vivid picture of epidemic childbed fever from his own experience, noting its high mortality and more frequent occurrence in hospital deliveries. He listed as the most prominent symptoms a shivering fit followed by a hot fever and profuse sweating; severe pain in hypogastric and iliac regions; and great tenderness of the abdomen. Other common symptoms included distension of the abdomen, difficulties in urination, diarrhea, nausea and vomiting (in the last stage, black vomit), delirium, lochia diminished or badly odorous, hurried respiration, a cough (when the disease was complicated with pleuritis, the most common concomitant). He stressed, however, that the illness took many forms, that its symptoms depended upon the organs that were involved, and that the fever was sometimes missing in cases that proved fatal.

If we now turn to the *Epidemics,* we find descriptions of illnesses with similar symptoms (as both Denman and Harris had already noted). The gynecological treatises, however, attribute these symptoms to two illnesses rather than one: disorders of the lochial flow (flows of blood were evidence of *apostasis*), and inflammation of the uterus. In *Diseases of Women* I, chapters 35–41 deal with disorders of lochial flow and are organized in accordance (too much, too little, none, and various patterns of flow); these are identified by Grmek as puerperal fever.[19] Symptoms common to these chapters include a swollen tender belly, pain in the hips and flanks, chills, fever, and headache. The writer's frequent comment that such complications are serious and often fatal demonstrates the reality of the risk they posed for Greek women in childbirth. Nevertheless, the statement in chapter 35 that some cases occurred without fever shows that a complete correlation between the conditions described and the modern definition of puerperal infection is not possible (although Harris recognized afebrile cases in 1845). *Diseases of Women* I 50–54 and 63 discuss inflammations of the uterus; the various chapters describe the symptoms in varying degrees of detail as an inflamed and swollen belly, fever, chills, thirst, anorexia, and headache. Again, however, fever is not seen as a necessary element in these illnesses: chapter 54 allows for both fever and lack of fever, and chapter 53 does not mention fever.

These passages in *Diseases of Women* I make it clear that Hippocratic doctors were quite familiar with postpartum complications whose symptoms were similar to those of childbed fever. These illnesses are diagnosable as puerperal infection in terms of modern biomedicine, although the Greek system of classification and conceptual framework differed from those of the early modern and modern doctor: the illnesses from which Greek women suffered were classified in Hippocratic terms either as disturbance of the lochial flow or as uterine inflammation. Thus one disease— puerperal infection—took the form of different illnesses in different historical conditions, its incidence, mortality, and even the course of its symptoms depending upon cultural conditions such as sanitary practices, the type of childbirth attendant, and the training methods of physicians who participated in deliveries.

Since the Hippocratic doctors observed the course of the illnesses that they reported in the case histories in terms of their own conceptual framework and recorded syndromes unmoderated by antibiotic treatment, retrospective diagnosis in particular cases is difficult. Thus, of the five cases that Grmek diagnosed as puerperal fever in Books I and III—Book I, cases 4, 5, and 11, and Book III, cases 2 and 14 (second series)—only one appears to be a clear-cut instance of puerperal infection.[20] This case, reported in I 4, involves the wife of Philinus, who had fever, pain in the genital area, and cessation of the lochia. The fact that her illness was recognized as puerperal fever, despite its atypically late onset,[21] by doctors in the eighteenth and nineteenth centuries who were thoroughly familiar with the disease in the form of childbed fever is very persuasive.

Less convincing is I 5, a case involving the wife of Epicrates, who began to have shivering two days *before* delivery, but whose fever is noted only after delivery. No change in the lochial flow is reported, but she had pain in the genital area. The doctor also reports that she suffered from a severe sore throat throughout the illness.[22] The illness seems beyond positive identification. We noted earlier that the doctor seems to have edited this case to make it resemble I 4 by relegating the sore throat to a postscript. This suggests that he did not view the sore throat as the primary problem, and, since I 4 is recognized as puerperal fever, it gives weight to a similar diagnosis in this case, complicated by tonsillitis. Nonetheless, a malarial attack beginning as usual with chills also seems to be a possibility.

In I 11, the wife of Dromeades developed a fever on the second day after giving birth; she had pain in the hypochondrium and delirium. The lochia were normal, and there is no mention of pain lower in the belly or of tenderness or swelling. The symptoms are typical of malignant tertian, or falciparum, malaria. The two cases that Grmek identifies in Book III are also more probably malaria and will be considered later. Three other cases identified as puerperal fever by Fasbender do not report changes in the lochial flow or pain in the belly.[23] From the later books, v 13 may be a case of puerperal fever; it involves a woman of Larissa, who gave birth at full term to a stillborn infant with a birth defect, although her apparent rapid recovery seems atypical: the afterbirth was retained for three days, and six days after delivery she developed a fever that lasted forty-eight hours and was accompanied by pains in the belly (but did she recover after the forty-eight hours or did the doctor assume that explicit mention of her death was unnecessary?).

We can recognize elements in the Hippocratic handling of childbirth which would have exposed women to enhanced risk of postpartum infection, despite their freedom from hospital care: autogenic conditions (anemia, preeclampsia, and retention of the placenta) and the introduction of bacteria through the use of pessaries and manual interference in delivery.[24] There is no evidence or reason to suggest that the resultant illness was epidemic, and, given the great difference in conditions of obstetric care between classical Greece and nineteenth-century Europe, we cannot identify it as childbed fever. Nevertheless, we cannot deny that Greek women suffered—and often died—from puerperal infections, which were diagnosed and treated according to Hippocratic categories as uterine inflammation or bad lochial flow.

Prior to the 1930s, 20 percent of modern maternal deaths were due to toxemia,[25] although today preeclampsia occurs in only 5 percent of pregnant women, and 0.5 percent of these develop into eclampsia.[26] Symptoms suggestive of toxemia (preeclampsia and eclampsia) do not appear frequently in the Hippocratic cases. The definitive symptoms of these conditions that could have been observed by the Greek doctor are swelling in the face or hands after the twentieth week of pregnancy through the first postpartum week and (progressing into eclampsia) convulsions.[27] Although these symptoms are not the focus of the description (swelling is not mentioned and convusions are only indirectly indicated), Malinas and Gourevitch have identified the condition of uterine suffocation during pregnancy described in *Diseases of Women* as eclampsia;[28] the symptoms noted by the Hippocratic doctor were sudden and violent suffocation, loss of voice, eyes rolled back into the head, and "everything that women suffer during uterine suffocation"— that is, chilling, hypersalivation, grinding of the teeth, and epileptic manifestations. In the *Epidemics,* only two cases report swelling soon after delivery,[29] and one reports it in a woman pregnant for four or five months.[30] None of these cases report convulsions, but convulsions are noted in four cases in which swelling is not mentioned.[31]

Hemorrhage, which caused 20 percent of maternal deaths prior to the 1930s,[32] does not appear in the Hippocratic cases. The explanation for this is probably that it was rapidly fatal and a doctor was thus not consulted (or did not choose to try to treat it). Another omission, which underlines the selective nature of these cases, is the absence of any cases in which forcible intervention was used, as described in *Excision of the Fetus,* or the woman died undelivered.[33]

In addition to the risks presented by these specific complications of pregnancy, pregnant women are also at greater risk in a number of diseases that affect the general population. This is a result of the suppression of cell-mediated immunity during pregnancy, a condition that apparently serves to prevent the immunological rejection of the fetus.[34]Aristotle noted the shorter life-span of women who had several pregnancies,[35] and the Hippocratic doctors were aware that certain illnesses had especially severe effects on pregnant women. Thus the author of *Diseases* 1 3 states that in pregnant women *phthisis* (in most cases identifiable as tuberculosis) is usually fatal, as are pneumonia, *kausos* (remittant fever characterized by intense sensations of heat), *phrenitis* (remittant fever with pain in hypochondrium and delirium), and erysipelas of the womb (puerperal fever?). The author of the third constitution of *Epidemics* I notes that pregnant women suffered especially severe effects from *kausos,*[36] and the woman in IV 25 aborted at seven months during the course of an epidemic that took the life of her husband.[37]

Malaria posed perhaps the most serious risk to women in childbirth. This was the result of the suppression of cell-mediated immunity in pregnancy, as Eugene Weinberg has established.[38] In areas in which nearly all the population is affected, malaria is the most common cause of maternal death. The incidence of stillbirth and prematurity is also much higher among pregnant women with malaria, apparently because the parasites infest the placenta, decreasing its efficiency in supplying oxygen to the fetus.

There is evidence that malaria underwent a marked resurgence in Greece in the fifth century.[39] Its presence is especially noteworthy in the Hippocratic treatises,[40] where it is reflected in the concern with critical days,[41] and in the important role assigned to black bile: black bile is the only humor that does not actually occur in the body under normal conditions, and the suggestion is persuasive that it was postulated on the basis of the black urine of blackwater fever.[42] Malaria comes to our attention in the very first pregnancy reported in the *Epidemics,* that of the daughter of Telebulus, who died six days after childbirth in a constitution marked by fever (*kausos*).[43] *Kausos* as a medical term does not correspond with any one disease in the modern definition, although it frequently indicates malaria.[44] In this case this sense is certain, however, since another patient included in the same disease constitution of *kausos*, Philiscus, is also the subject of the first case in *Epidemics* I and has been identified in a careful and detailed study by Grmek as a victim of the malarial complication blackwater fever.[45] The writer comments that most women who gave birth in this constitution died, and that all the women who fell ill while pregnant miscarried.

Because the effects of malaria are frequently attributed to puerperal fever, it will be helpful to describe its symptoms in some detail. It is characterized by periodic attacks of fever caused by the reaction of the body to the presence in the blood of parasites of the genus *Plasmodium* carried by the Anopheles mosquito.[46] In Greece in the classical period three species of *Plasmodium* were present, each with a characteristic reproductive cycle that determined the periodicity of the fever: *P. vivax,* the agent of benign tertian malaria (fever every third day, or at intervals of forty-eight hours); *P. falciparum,* the agent of malignant tertian malaria (longer lasting than the benign form, with a low-grade fever usually persisting between attacks, so that the patient always feels miserable; in untreated cases, the mortality rate is high);[47] and *P. malariae,* the agent of quartan malaria (fever every fourth day, or at intervals of seventy-two hours). Multiple infection is also possible; in such cases the cycles combine and the fever may occur daily, mock other fever patterns, or become continuous. In addition to the fever, chills and sweating occur in most forms of the disease, and secondary symptoms include headache, anorexia, nausea, abdominal pain, vomiting, enlargement of the spleen and liver, generalized swelling of the limbs, nosebleed, diarrhea, respiratory difficulties, jaundice, and pallor due to anemia. In untreated cases, if the body's defenses are successful the attack ends; subsequent attacks add to immunity, and eventually the attacks cease. Those with immunity, however, often develop a chronic condition marked by malaise, listlessness, headaches, anorexia, fatigue, and low fever. Complications, which are often fatal, include cerebral malaria, in which the small vessels in the brain are blocked by enormous numbers of parasites, and which is most common in infants, pregnant women, and the nonimmune; hyperpyrexia, in which the fever continues to rise until the patient dies; and blackwater fever (malaria hemoglobinuria), a complication of falciparum malaria whose distinguishing symptom is black-colored urine.[48]

The course of illness in untreated women after delivery was described in 1900 by F. H. Edmonds:

> I have seen young and healthy women pass to the last week of pregnancy in good condition, then fall off, become sallow-looking, owing to low remittent fever; during labour the temperature rises, the tongue gets thickly coated with a yellow fur, the patient becomes very restless, the pains weak and long drawn; after delivery there has usually been gushing of dark fluid blood, then an improvement for—usually—forty-eight hours, when a relapse (another paroxysm?) comes on with higher temperature, deeper jaundice, greater weakness and constipation, which, on relief being given by an enema, results in the passage of a large, black, stinking stool. After five or nine days' alternations—each marked by increasing weakness—the patient dies quietly, *with many appearances of puerperal fever, but having had her lochia of good colour, quantity, and odour, and having had no uterine pain or tenderness.* In these cases the child is frequently strong and healthy, but there is not a more dangerous condition for a woman than to be seized by a malarial remittent during her puerperium[49]

Today the complications caused by malaria in pregnancy can be countered to a great extent by prophylaxis or treatment (and by the avoidance of malarial areas), but the Greeks had no effective means of either prevention or treatment. There is evidence that the Hippocratic doctors were aware of the dangers that malaria posed for pregnant women. *Prognosis* 20 mentions recurrent periodic fever in women after childbirth that follows the same pattern as it does in men, and a general warning about malaria in pregnancy appears in *Aphorisms* v 55. That the risk was recognized in lay circles as well is attested by Sophocles' *Oedipus Tyrannus* 25: "the barren pangs of women, withal the Fever-god swooping down, is ravaging the city."[50]

We can recognize eight probable or possible cases of malaria in pregnant women in the *Epidemics*. We have already discussed I 11, which Grmek had diagnosed as puerperal fever. Among the other cases in I and III that Grmek identified as puerperal fever, two are good candidates for a diagnosis of blackwater fever.[51] In III case 14 (second set), a woman in Cyzicus had a fever that began on the first day after delivery; she did not have pain or swelling in the abdomen and her urine was black, which should at least raise suspicions of blackwater fever. The second case (second set) in III, involving the woman who lay sick beside the cold water, is, however, the strongest in its suggestion of blackwater fever. The author notes that she had been feverish for a long time *before* the birth and that her urine was black throughout her long illness. She had pain in the hips, but not in the belly, nor is any change in the lochial flow noted. Moreover, she suffered from despondency and her mind was "melancholic," a mental condition frequently associated with malaria in the Hippocratic treatises.[52] Finally, the author notes that she was lying beside the cold water, perhaps a standing pool or a swampy place that provided a haven for malarial mosquitoes.

In addition to fevers involving black urine, other fevers may have been malarial, but in the absence of evidence of periodicity there is no clear indication.[53] We can, however, at least rule out puerperal infection when the illness preceded delivery or abortion. Thus in I 13, a woman three months pregnant was afflicted with a fever, pain in the hypochondrium, and delirium—symptoms characteristic of pernicious tertian malaria. She recovered, and there is no indication that she aborted (malaria is most dangerous in the later stages of pregnancy). Again in IV 6 a woman aborted on the sixth day of an attack marked by nausea, chills, and sweating that came to a crisis on the fourteenth day; no fever is noted, but the brevity of the account, and the likelihood that chills and sweating imply fever, make it tempting to assume its presence. The case in I 5, in which shivering began before birth and fever after, and in which the lochia were normal, was discussed earlier; its parallelism with I 4 may indicate puerperal infection. In other cases, a lack of specific symptoms pointing to puerperal infection (changes in lochial flow, pain in belly) may suggest malaria. For instance, in III case 12 (first set), fever arose after birth and shivering was pronounced throughout; no changes in the lochial flow are reported, and only slight pain in the *kardia* early in the illness.[54] Similarly the patient in III 11 (first set) suffered a fever after abortion; she had pain in the hip, but there is no indication of change in the lochia or pain or tenderness in the belly.

The role of malaria in pregnancy and childbirth in classical Greece has been all but ignored by modern scholars. Grmek does not even consider the subject when he discusses malaria, identifying, as we have seen, most cases of fever in the postpartum period as puerperal infection, even those in which the fever preceded delivery or in which black urine was a prominent symptom. Jones, however, writing in 1909, provided the most striking illustration of the way in which cultural values can shape perception. He realized full well the dangers the disease posed for pregnant women, for, in commenting on the passage about the Fever-god in the *Oedipus Tyrannus*, he said that the reference to childbirth was strongly suggestive of malaria, and he cited the article by Edmonds that contains the case quoted earlier.[55] Nevertheless, in his chapter on the effects of malaria on the general population he did not mention women; he even omitted women in discussing the reduction of population due to malaria and the effects of the disease on the newborn. In an appendix, however, he suggested that the role of women as nurses during malarial attacks increased Greek men's appreciation of their wives. Thus for Jones the noteworthy effect of malaria on Greek women was not miscarriage or death, but their service to men, which provided "a new ideal of womanhood."[56]

Phthisis is one of the most frequently used terms in the Hippocratic Corpus.[57] In most cases it can be identified as tuberculosis, although the wasting that defined the condition for the Greeks occurred in other illnesses as well.[58] It was recognized as especially dangerous in pregnancy: the author of *Airs, Waters, Places* says that it was frequent after childbirth because of the violence suffered by women.[59] The wife of Simus (v 103), who died six months after being shaken in childbirth (succussion), provides a good, if rather extreme, example. Her symptoms were typical of tuberculosis: fever, wasting, pain in the chest, pus-filled sputum, with diarrhea at the end. The use of succussion was (as far as we can tell) not typical of normal deliveries, being used mainly in emergencies involving the death of the fetus.[60] As Grmek points out,[61] the succussion did not cause the consumption, but pregnancy and the stressed birth aggravated the patient's latent tuberculosis.

While we will never have exact statistics, the evidence of the Hippocratic treatises leads us to conclude that Greek women who were attended by Hippocratic doctors, or by midwives following Hippocratic methods, faced all the risks of childbirth inherent in a premodern culture that lacks the resources of modern medicine. In addition, some of the practices of Hippocratic medicine—for example, the use of cathartics, succussion, and manual interference in delivery—were themselves the cause of (or contributed to) complications that sometimes proved fatal. There is ample evidence that women did in fact suffer from puerperal infection. Moreover, tuberculosis and malaria posed special risks for them, again augmented by the lack of modern prophylactics and treatment. There was every reason for Greek women facing pregnancy and childbirth to seize upon whatever promise of help that their culture and religion might offer, in addition to seeking the most up-to-date medical care.

Five

Appeal to the Gods

Awoman facing childbirth probably looked first to the gods for assistance, for they played a key role in traditional Greek conceptions of illness and healing. For Homer and Hesiod it was the arrows of Apollo and Artemis, and a host of unnamed daimons and spirits, that brought illness, while their appeasement could bring cure. These ideas continued to be powerful even in the enlightenment of fifth-century Athens—and despite the opposition of the doctors to some (but not all) religious healing. Even today in rural Greece belief persists that God may send illness as a test, or that daimons and other "exotika," or the evil eye, cause sickness;[1] for the cure of such illnesses many modern Greeks turn to folk healers: "wise women," magicians, priests.[2] The saints are especially popular as divine healers: Saint John the Baptist is invoked for the shivering fits of fever, Saint Paraskevi for eye diseases, and Saint Pantleon by cripples and invalids, while the celebration of the Dormition of the Virgin Mary on Tinos annually attracts thousands of pilgrims from Greece and the Middle East in search of miraculous cures.[3]

A Greek votive stele from the last quarter of the fifth century illustrates in the ambiguity of its modern interpretation the two divine helpers to whom women turned for assistance in childbirth.[4] The stele portrays a scene following a successful childbirth: in the center a woman sits slumped on a chair; to the right and behind her a female figure stands holding a swaddled infant in her left arm while she touches the head of the seated woman with her right hand; on the left stand two divine figures, both more than life-size. One of the divine figures, a female holding a torch in her raised left hand, looks down on the human pair. Behind her stands another figure of similar size, of which only a hand with a portion of a torch is preserved. Richter identified the divine pair as Hygeia and Asclepius, while Mitropoulou saw them as Eileithyia and Artemis Lochia. Because the figures hold torches, Mitropoulou's identification seems most likely, but, in fact, either pair of divinities might have been deemed responsible for the happy outcome.

Artemis and Eileithyia

Tradition gave the midwife divine helpers in the goddess Artemis and other, specialized childbirth divinities whom she often assimilated, such as Eileithyia or Lochia. Artemis was a goddess with whom young women were familiar and comfortable, for her worship had played an important role in their lives during childhood. She watched over young children, and it was she whom girls served in puberty rites and to whom they made sacrifices if they fell victim to the "illness of maidens." When they married, girls dedicated their childhood toys to her, and they continued to appeal to her for fertility and for successful delivery. Traditionally, the arrows of Artemis also brought death to women in childbirth,[5] but in the fifth century, at least at her shrine at Brauron in Attica, the goddess's baleful activities were relegated to a subsidiary divinity, Iphigeneia, to whom the clothing of women who died in childbirth was dedicated.[6]

Numerous epigrams in the *Anthology* attest to women's invocation of Artemis, Eileithyia, or other specialized divine helpers in childbirth.[7] For example, a late epigram by Callimachus thanks Eileithyia for the safe delivery of a daughter and promises still another gift if the woman should bear a son.[8] Archaeology also provides abundant evidence of appeal to these divinities in the form of dedications made at various shrines.[9] These range from humble terra-cotta figures to comparatively expensive relief sculptures such as the votive plaque illustrated in plate 1, indicating that women of all classes sought the assistance of the goddess. Most dedicatory inscriptions are simple in form and do not specify the favor granted; others explicitly thank the goddess for successful delivery or for a son. Some of the offerings are graphic, including two votives found in the sanctuary of Artemis Eileithyia on Mount Kynthos on Delos, the goddess' own birthplace,[10] that portray the suppliant woman as pregnant.[11] Numerous three-dimensional scenes in clay or stone portraying the moment of birth have been found in Cyprus.[12] A bas relief of a couple appealing to the goddess for offspring was found at the sanctuary of Artemis Kalliste in Athens, as were two vulvae and a pair of breasts (breasts offered as thank offerings for childbirth are attested by inscription).[13] Numerous statues of male infants and children found at the shrine of Artemis at Brauron were probably dedicated in the hope of obtaining the goddess's protection for a child, but statues of male infants may also have been intended as thank offerings for the birth of a boy.[14]

An especially significant site is the sanctuary of Artemis on Thasos, the location of much of the activity by the physicians of the *Epidemics*. There an inscription records the restoration of the temple of Artemis by a woman serving as her priestess. It is dated to early Imperial times,[15] but thousands of terra-cotta dedications to Artemis dating from the seventh century through the Hellenistic period were found at the shrine, attesting its continuing existence and popularity from the archaic through the Hippocratic era.[16] Yet in the Hippocratic treatises the shrine is mentioned only once, and then only as an address: in a case in the *Epidemics* it is said that a Parian man lay sick "beyond the Artemision."[17]

Perhaps the most important epigraphical evidence for appeal to Artemis by women consists in the temple inventories listing dedications made to the goddess at Brauron and found on the Acropolis in Athens as well as in Brauron itself. Tullia Linders has published a study of the Athenian lists (at this time the lists from Brauron itself, of which the Athenian lists are ancient copies, remain unpublished).[18] Although bronze objects (including numerous mirrors) as well as gold and silver are listed, most of the offerings were garments. These were displayed in open boxes or used to clothe the cult statues of the goddess. Some of these garments are described as having inwoven inscriptions and figures;[19] most, however, had been worn and appear to have been normal pieces of everyday dress. Some are even described as ῥάκος, "rags," a term about which there has been considerable controversy. Mommsen argued that it referred to cloths used as sanitary napkins in menarche.[20] Linders, however, made a good case against this interpretation. She pointed out that there are no parallels for such offerings in ancient sources, that Mommsen based his argument not on cult practices but on apotropaic and superstitious practices in agriculture, and that some items designated as "rags" appear in earlier lists without that designation, suggesting that the term referred to cloth that had deteriorated over time.[21]

Because these lists were copies of records at Brauron, Osborne's prosopographical analysis provides valuable information about the women who dedicated to Artemis at that shrine.[22] Of 125 names, 16 include the demotic of the husband or father and are thus traceable. Seven of these are from families known otherwise through inscriptions. Two of the families are known to have been wealthy, and all were of high status. All lived at a considerable distance from Brauron, which suggests that these were not casual offerings or offerings made by the women acting independently of their families. Of particular interest is a dedication made by the wife of Epeukhes, who was probably himself a doctor and certainly came from a family of doctors.[23] Thus membership in a family of doctors did not preclude a woman's appeal to Artemis for divine assistance.

It is likely that many of the offerings listed in the inventory of Artemis Braurion found in Athens were given in thanksgiving for successful childbirth,[24] although some may have been dedicated at marriage, and Kondis suggested that some might have been the chitons of girls who served the goddess as Bears in the coming-of-age ceremonies to be discussed in chapter 6.[25] It is unlikely that the garments included the clothing of women who died in childbirth since their recipient was Iphigeneia, not Artemis. Some might, however, have been offered in cases of the suffocating illness of maidens, which will be discussed later. The lists thus provide an intimate, if fragmentary, glimpse into the actual practices of women making offerings to the goddess.

Asclepius and Childbirth

Women facing childbirth also invoked gods whose sphere of activity was not specifically childbirth; some that are attested are Amphiarios, Aphrodite, Zeus Hypsistos on the Pynx, and Demeter.[26] But the best known, and best attested, of these more general helpers was Asclepius.[27] Asclepius appears in Homer only as the physician-father of Machaon and Podaleiros, but by the classical period he had become the preeminent healing divinity in Greece, replacing his father Apollo in that role, and his sanctuaries spread throughout Greece from the late fifth century. The offerings made to him, and the inscriptions describing cures that he effected, offer important evidence about religious healing.

Asclepius dealt with all sorts of health problems and was popular with women.[28] Numerous dedications, mostly of breasts, found in the god's sanctuaries served as thank offerings for a happy outcome to a pregnancy or as appeals for fertility or a good milk supply.[29] The Asclepieion at Corinth has yielded the largest number of offerings of this sort, all made of terra cotta and dating from the last quarter of the fifth to the end of the fourth centuries. The dedications listed in the catalogue of the excavation report (which records only the well-preserved objects) include eleven breasts or pairs of breasts and one (possible) uterus.[30] One breast votive from the classical period was found in the Athenian Asclepieion, and thirteen are included in the inventory lists from that sanctuary (ten singles and three pairs, extending through the third century B.C.).[31] One breast dedication was found in the Asclepieion in Cos,[32] as well as (in a questionable collection) a uterus,[33] and a model of a swollen abdomen, which could portray either pregnancy or dropsy.[34]

The most interesting evidence for the healing activities of Asclepius consists, however, in the cure records that were displayed in his temples.[35] Of forty-three cures recorded on two stelai found at the shrine of Asclepius at Epidaurus (dated to the second half of the fourth century), seven involved pregnancy.[36] In four cases fertility was the sole issue: the women, desirous of offspring, slept in the temple and saw dreams; they then conceived and delivered offspring (like modern fertility cures, those by Asclepius sometimes produced multiple births, in one case, twins, in another, five children—although the five were possibly the products of successive pregnancies).[37]

Folk elements stand out in these stories: one involves choice of sex, and two feature snakes, one of which is explicitly reported to have had intercourse with the woman. On the other hand, in a cure for infertility recorded at the shrine of Asclepius at Lebena, a medical instrument, the cupping glass, was used.[38] The cupping glass is recommended in the Hippocratic treatises as a method of stopping the menses;[39] although it plays no role in the cures at Epidaurus, it appears on the coins of Epidaurus from mid-fourth century.[40] Its migration into the religious sphere reflects the influence that rational medicine had upon religious healing. This influence was exerted not by the actual practice of doctors in the temples, but by widespread awareness of the types of treatments used by doctors, which provided (along with fantasy and folklore) the conceptual structure in which patients experienced divine cures.[41]

The intermixture of medical knowledge, folklore, and fantasy is especially striking in the Epidaurian cases of dream surgery. In these the belly was cut open in order to remove worms, or the head was removed and the patient suspended upside down in order to cure dropsy (succussion). In one such case Sostrata of Pherai is reported to have been "pregnant" (ἐκύησε) and delivered by cesarean section two washtubs of worms.[42] Such radical surgery as the opening of the abdomen was not attempted by rational medicine until Praxagoras at the end of the fourth century; in the classical period cesarean sections were limited to divine births such as that of Dionysus. Herzog accordingly attributed the fantasizing of such cures to experience with animals and awareness of Egyptian embalming practices, although he noted that the upside-down suspension of the dropsy patient reflected the use of succussion by Greek doctors. Another reflection of medical influence may be found in the concern with exact measures—the two tubs of worms —for an interest in measurement characterizes the later books of the *Epidemics*.[43]

In addition to infertility, Asclepius also treated abnormally extended pregnancies; in fact, two such cases head the list of cures on the stele. In the first case, Kleo, who had been pregnant for five years, came as a suppliant and slept in the temple; immediately on leaving the precinct in the morning she gave birth to a boy. The child had continued to develop in the womb during the extended pregnancy and, newly delivered, washed himself at a fountain and walked about the precinct with his mother.

In the second case of extended pregnancy, Ithmonike of Pellene asked to become pregnant with a girl, but she neglected to request the birth of the child, even when the god asked her if she did not need something else. It was only three years later when, still pregnant, she turned to the god again for help, that she finally realized that it was necessary to ask for the child's birth as well. When this request was explicitly addressed to him, Asclepius provided help and, as in the case of Sostrata, Ithmonike gave birth to the child she wanted immediately after she left the precinct.

These cures also have connections with rational medicine, although they seem at first consideration to be completely miraculous.[44] In the case of Kleo, Herzog points out the probable parallel with the case of the wife of Gorgias in *Epidemics* v 11, which the Hippocratic author interpreted as four years of suspended menses, followed by a pregnancy, and then a second pregnancy (superfetation); a child was born (in the fifth year of "pregnancy"), and then forty days later, the woman delivered the superfetation. Herzog therefore interpreted the "pregnancy" of Kleo as a mole (a condition that *Diseases of Women* 1 71 says may continue for two or three years), with a normal pregnancy supervening. Fantasy entered to embellish the case by attributing continued development to the child in the womb. In the case of Ithmonike, again a false pregnancy with true pregnancy supervening provides a rational explanation and one in keeping with Hippocratic ideas; only the timing of the birth during the woman's second consultation at the Asclepieion is "miraculous." Nevertheless, the story is built upon the folktale motif of the wish that has untoward consequences because of its imperfect wording. Possibly it also reflects gender valuation: a woman too dense to ask for delivery as well as pregnancy, even when the god prompted her, would also have been dense enough to ask for a daughter.

"Extended pregnancy" appears to have been a more frequent complaint than we might suppose, for the Hippocratic doctor offered a counterexplanation in terms of natural processes. In this he carefully directed his criticism at the women themselves and not at the god, however:

> But those women who imagine that they have been pregnant longer than ten months—a thing I have heard them say more than once—are quite mistaken. This is how their mistake arises: it can happen that the womb becomes inflated and swells as the result of flatulence from the stomach, and the woman of course thinks that she is pregnant. And if besides her menses do not flow but collect in the womb . . . then she is especially likely to imagine she is pregnant. After all, her menstruation has ceased and her belly is swollen. Then it sometimes happens that the menses break forth . . . spontaneously. . . . Now if they have intercourse with their husbands then, they conceive on the same day or a few days afterwards. Women who are inexperienced in these facts and their reasons then reckon their pregnancy to include the time when their menses did not flow and their wombs were swollen.[45]

As we shall see, this hint of competition between doctors and temple healers is subdued by comparison with the polemical attacks of the physicians on other types of religious healers.

Doctors and Charlatans

Doctors coexisted comfortably with the temple medicine of Asclepius, although they did not practice medicine in the temples. They viewed Asclepius as the patron god of medicine and from an early time identified themselves professionally as Sons of Asclepius (*Asclepiadai*).[46] Evidence for their veneration of Asclepius comes from a variety of sources.[47] Dedications by doctors to the god have been found, including medical instruments,[48] and a classical gemstone portrays Asclepius observing as a doctor examines a patient.[49] Even the great Hippocratic doctor Galen, in the second century A.D., claimed to have been cured of a deadly abscess by the god.[50] In return, as we have seen, the methods of treatment practiced by Asclepius in his dream cures often followed the model of Hippocratic theory and practice.

Doctors were also active in the worship of other major gods: Asclepiadai of Cos and Cnidus were assigned special privileges at Apollo's shrine at Delphi,[51] and sacred laws at Cos describe the role of doctors as a guild in the worship of Zeus Polieus[52] and also of Demeter.[53] And, as we saw earlier, a woman from a noted family of doctors, who was probably the wife of a doctor, is listed among those who made dedications to Artemis at Brauron.[54]

But if doctors venerated Asclepius and other establishment gods, they were vociferous in their complaints about marginal religious healers.[55] Thus the Hippocratic author of *Sacred Disease* directed his polemic against those who maintained that epilepsy was caused by a daimon and could be cured only by purifications, calling them impostors and charlatans.[56] And the author of the brief treatise *Parthenoi*, which discusses the odd illness of maidens that afflicted premenarchal girls, contrasts his own no-nonsense approach to the treatment of this disorder (quick marriage) with that of *manteis* who deluded women into making expensive dedications to Artemis. These religious practitioners continued to use the interpretation of illness espoused by Hesiod, attributing illness to the attacks of daimons and *keres*.

The *Parthenoi* is one of the most important pieces of evidence about these marginal religious healers, and it is also informative about the psychological state of young girls approaching marriage, which will be discussed in the next chapter. I quote it here in full:

> The beginning of medicine in my opinion is the constitution [ζυνθέσιος] of the ever-existing. For it is not possible to know the nature of diseases, which indeed it is [the aim] of the art to discover, if you do not know the beginning in the undivided [ἀμερεῖ], from which it is divided out.

First about the so-called sacred disease, and about those who are stricken, and about terrors, all that men fear exceedingly so as to be out of their minds and to seem to have seen certain daimons hostile to them, either in the night or in the day or at both times. For from such a vision many already are strangled [ἀπηγχονίσθησαν], more women than men; for the female nature is more fainthearted and lesser. But *parthenoi*, for whom it is the time of marriage, remaining unmarried, suffer this more at the time of the going down of the menses. Earlier they do not suffer these distresses, for it is later that the blood is collected in the womb so as to flow away. Whenever then the mouth of the exit is not opened for it, and more blood flows in because of nourishment and the growth of the body, at this time the blood, not having an outlet, bursts forth by reason of its magnitude into the *kardia* and diaphragm. Whenever these are filled, the *kardia* becomes sluggish; then from sluggishness comes torpor; then from torpor, madness [παράνοια]. It is just as when someone sits for a long time, the blood from the hips and thighs, pressed out to the lower legs and feet, causes torpor, and from the torpor the feet become powerless for walking until the blood runs back to its own place; and it runs back quickest whenever, standing in cold water, you moisten the part up to the ankles. This torpor is not serious, for the blood quickly runs back on account of the straightness of the veins, and the part of the body is not critical. But from the *kardia* and the *phrenes* it runs back slowly, for the veins are at an angle, and the part is critical and disposed for derangement and mania. And whenever these parts are filled, shivering [φρίκη] with fever starts up quickly; they call these fevers wandering [πλανήτας τοὺς πυρετούς]. But when these things are thus, she is driven mad [μαίνεται] by the violent inflammation, and she is made murderous by the putrefaction, and she is fearful and anxious by reason of the gloom, and strangulations [ἀγχόνας] result from the pressure around the *kardia*, and the spirit [θυμός], distraught and anguished by reason of the badness of the blood, is drawn toward evil. And another thing, she addresses by name fearful things, and they order her to jump about [ἄλλεσθαι] and to fall down into wells and to be strangled, as if it were better and had every sort of advantage. And whenever they are without visions, there is a kind of pleasure that makes her desire death as if it were some sort of good. But when the woman [ἄνθρωπος] returns to reason, women dedicate [καθιεροῦσαι] both many other things and the most expensive feminine clothing to Artemis, being utterly deceived, the soothsayers [μάντεων] ordering it. Her deliverance [is] whenever nothing hinders the outflow of blood. But I myself bid *par-thenoi*, whenever they suffer such things, to cohabit with men as quickly as possible, for if they conceive they become healthy. But if not, either immediately in the prime of youth, or a little later, she will be seized [ἀλώσεται] [by this illness], if not by some other illness. And of married women, those who are sterile suffer this more often.[57]

The statement in the introductory paragraph of this treatise that medical knowledge must begin with the nature of the whole of things occurs frequently in the Hippocratic treatises and is, in fact, cited by Plato as the characteristic mark of Hippocratic method.[58] It connects this treatise with the revolution in Ionian philosophy that replaced mythological explanation of the cosmos with explanation in terms of the actions of basic physical elements: water or air in their various forms, an undifferentiated substance (the Apeiron), "seeds" of different qualities, or atoms in motion.[59] The reference to the so-called sacred disease, by making an explicit connection with the Hippocratic treatise *Sacred Disease*, also alludes to the non-sacral intention of the author: he is signaling his audience that he will interpret a syndrome commonly held to be of divine origin and in need of a divine cure as a purely physical illness that is open to cure by human means, just as epilepsy is treated in *Sacred Disease*. After a detailed description of the illness, he offers his own prescription for its treatment. Women who rely on *manteis* for assistance and, at their direction, make dedications to Artemis, are deceived: what the woman needs is to become pregnant. The interpretation that the doctor offers of this illness as natural and explicable in natural terms amounts to a revolutionary correction of the traditional (women's) view; it also promised a revolution in the lives of the patients suffering from this illness—marriage.

The etiology of the illness in *Parthenoi* does not employ the most notable explanation for such female problems, the wandering womb. Rather, the explanation that is offered by its author, blockage of the passageways of the menses, is analogous to the explanation of epilepsy offered by the author of *Sacred Disease*: blockage of the passageways of phlegm. Our author was, in fact, unlikely to have agreed with an explanation of the illness as wandering womb, especially since he reported that the ailment affected both men and women (however, he does not offer a cure for men). Nevertheless, the author of the brief gynecological treatise *Superfetation* made the connection:

> Whenever in a *parthenos* the menses do not occur, she is full of black bile, feverish, suffers pain, is thirsty and hungry, vomits, and is out of her mind and then reasonable again: her womb is in motion. Whenever it turns toward the innards she vomits and is feverish and out of her mind; whenever it goes back, she suffers hunger and thirst and shivering fever [ἠπίαλος] holds her.[60]

The suffocating illness of *parthenoi*, explained by the author of *Superfetation* as a case of the wandering womb, was one of the family of illnesses that Greek popular tradition persisted in attributing to divine causes. The author of *Parthenoi* alludes briefly to other members of this family: the sacred disease (epilepsy), and a suffocating illness that affected men. More information about the suffocating illness of men is provided by a passage in the parabasis of Aristophanes' *Wasps*. There the poet, addressing the audience, says of himself:

> For you he fought, and for you he fights:
>> and then last year with adventurous hand
> He grappled besides with the Spectral Shapes,
>> the Agues [ἠπιάλοις] and Fevers [πυρετοῖσιν] that plagued our land;
> That loved in the darksome hours of night
>> to throttle [ἦγχος] fathers, and grandsires choke [ἀπέπνιγον],
> That laid them down on their restless beds,
>> and against your quiet and peaceable folk
> Kept welding together proofs and writs
>> and oath against oath, till many a man
> Sprang up, distracted with wild affright [ἀναπηδᾶν δειμαίνοντας],
>> and off in haste to the Polemarch ran.
> Yet although such a champion [ἀλεξίκακον] as this ye had found,
>> to purge [καθαρτήν] your land from sorrow and shame . . .[61]

Here we find, applied to older males (fathers and grandfathers), the same complex of terms and concepts that appear as the illness of unmarried girls in *Parthenoi*:[62]

Wasps	*Parthenoi*
ἠπίαλοις . . . πυρετοῖσιν	φρίκη[63] πλανήτας τούς πυρετούς
ἦγχον, ἀπέπνιγον	ἄγχεσθαι, ἀγχόνας, ἀπηγχονίσθησαν
ἀναπηδᾶν	ἄλλεσθαι
δειμαίνοντας	μαίνεται . . . φοβέεται καί δέδοικεν,
ἀλεζίκακον . . . καθαρτήν	καθιεροῦσι . . . κελευόντων τῶν μάντεων

The characteristic symptoms of such illnesses were choking/ strangling and mental disturbances that resulted in "seizure-behavior."[64] These symptoms may often have been brought on by high fever or epileptic attacks. Other symptoms included loss of consciousness, frenzied and violent activity including murderous or suicidal impulses, hallucinations, and extreme anxiety. The explanation in terms of an external agent was "rational" in the sense that patients did and said things they otherwise would not have (hence some external being must be acting through them), and they seemed to be actually seeing, hearing, and responding to beings outside themselves that had somehow seized control of them. (Even today epileptic attacks are popularly referred to as seizures.) This interpretation was also reinforced by the cultural sanction that such explanations enjoyed: daimons appear as the causes of illness in Homer and Hesiod, and in the fifth century tragedy still gave them dramatic portrayal.[65] Even Herodotus refused to choose between a divine and a natural explanation (alcoholism) for the madness of the Spartan king Cleomenes.[66] Finally, a ready supply of healers was at hand prepared to diagnose such maladies as divine seizures and to cure them with impressive displays—for example, purification by blood, which must have been a rather messy and memorable experience.

Who were these religious healers? In *Sacred Disease* they are identified as μάγοι, καθάρται, ἀγύρται, ἀλαζόνες, all pejorative terms that signal their marginal status within Greek society.[67] Although the term employed in *Parthenoi*, μάντις, itself lacks the implication of trickery contained in the terms used in *Sacred Disease*, the author explicitly adds the element of deception. It is apparent in *Sacred Disease* that such healers imitated the practices of the doctors in many ways. Like the doctors, they were concerned to provide a *logos*, or plausible explanation, for illnesses. They diagnosed by symptoms, a method employed by the authors of treatises on internal medicine and gynecology. And they prohibited the eating of many foods that were also proscribed by Hippocratic dietetic theory. But despite such similarities, the explanations of illness and the treatments offered by religious healers were fundamentally different from those of the doctors, being derived from, and acting upon, the spirit world, not the natural physical world. The religious healers attributed illnesses to gods, spirits, and daimons, and they employed as treatment a catharsis of the spirit that contrasted with the Hippocratic physical catharsis, as well as charms, spells, and taboos based on magical association of ideas (against wearing black, the color of death; against any employment of products from goats, an animal believed to suffer very frequently from epilepsy; against magical binding, "putting foot on foot, or hand on hand").

The claims of the *kathartai* also extended to magical control of the environment: the author of *Sacred Disease* says they claimed to be able to cause eclipses, change the weather, and render the earth barren.[68] In this there is a clear parallel with the philosopher Empedocles, who, in addition to a treatise on natural philosophy, also wrote one called *Katharmoi*. He claimed to be able to control the weather as well as to possess healing powers, skill with drugs, and even the power to raise the dead.[69] Similar control over physical phenomena was attributed to female figures as well: Thessalian witches were believed able to draw down the moon,[70] as was Medea, whose skill with drugs was notorious.[71]

Religion was the one public arena in which women were allowed to function, and, as these traditional figures attest, we cannot assume that they did so only in the celebration of mainstream religion. The author of *Parthenoi* uses the word *mantis* for those who misled women in cases of the illness of maidens. The term can denote either a male or a female, and a female *mantis* could act as a healer. Plato in the *Symposium* attributes to the wise woman Diotima of Mantinea (Μαντινικῆς, a play on the word *mantis*) a ten-year postponement of the plague as a result of a sacrifice,[72] and in the *Theatetus* he says that midwives use incantations as well as drugs, thus putting them into the *mantis* category.[73] Much later, but probably reflecting the same tradition, Plutarch speaks of purifiers as women.[74] Because they persuaded women in matters concerning "female problems," it seems likely that the *manteis* who treated young girls suffering from the illness of maidens were often, like the traditional midwives, women. Thus when Phaedra in Euripides' *Hippolytus* suffers from a condition suspiciously like wandering womb (and, in fact, imposed by a god), her nurse advises her to seek the help of women if her illness is a "delicate" one, but to resort to doctors if it is something "that can be told to men."[75]

The other side of the coin of the vociferous protest of the doctors against the charlatans was the widespread popularity of magico-religious methods of healing.[76] These were remnants of an old tradition that was still very much alive. In the sources that we have considered, the broad appeal of such healing methods is best illustrated by the fact that Aristophanes, in the parabasis of the *Wasps* where he is appealing to the audience for victory, uses the terms ἀλεξίκακον and καθαρτήν of himself, likening himself to an agent of Heracles in providing purification from the suffocating sickness. Making such a connection would have been counterproductive unless the audience was generally sympathetic to the methods of religious purifiers. We may, therefore, conclude that women, confronted with crises in their reproductive lives, frequently employed older, traditional explanations of illness and made use of marginal healers, and that here, too, women helped women.

Six

Acculturation to Early Childbearing

W hile most of the risks that pregnancy and childbirth presented to women in classical Greece
could not have been prevented or effectively
dealt with before the advances made by modern
medicine, there was one risk that was well
within the control of the society: that posed by early pregnancy and
childbirth. Even under the best of modern conditions, women who
give birth before the age of seventeen have a higher mortality rate
than older women. The closer a woman is to menarche, the greater
the risk to both mother and child, as well as to the mother's future
childbearing capabilities, for the reproductive system has not completely matured when ovulation begins.[1]

Critics of early marriage were not wanting among the Greeks.
Hesiod suggested marriage in the fifth year after puberty, or age
nineteen;[2] Plato in the *Laws* mandated from sixteen to twenty years
of age, and in the *Republic* he gave the age as twenty.[3] Aristotle specifically warned against early childbearing for women as a cause of
small and weak infants and difficult and dangerous labor for the
mother,[4] and the Spartans avoided it for just those reasons.[5] Nevertheless, Greek culture in general favored early childbearing. The
reasons usually offered by modern scholars in explanation of this

counterproductive custom were that it served to safeguard the honor of the *oikos* by ensuring the virginity of the bride and that it fostered the authority of the husband, who stood as a mature man of experience and independence in contrast to his sheltered, inexperienced, and dependent bride, who was, as Xenophon's Socrates described Kritoboulos's wife, a mere child.[6] Whether more lay behind the practice than this is a question that we will examine later; for the present we will focus on the more immediate experience of the women themselves.

Women, both mothers and daughters, probably offered some resistance to early marriage; in fact, the ancient evidence shows that fear and apprehension were traits that men valued in their brides.[7] It is, therefore, worth considering some of the more overt ways in which the culture worked to reconcile women to the practice. These included some of the most significant moments in the lives of girls and women: the dramatic suffocating illness of maidens that was common at menarche; the coming-of-age ceremony for girls (in Attica, the Arkteia); and the principal festival of married women, the annual Thesmophoria.

The Wandering Womb Syndrome as Acculturation

From the medical point of view, the transition from girlhood to menarche/marriage was problematic. As we have seen, at this dangerous stage in their lives girls were subject to a variety of rather dramatic and potentially fatal symptoms: shivering and fever, hallucinations, homicidal and suicidal frenzies, pain, vomiting, strangling suffocation. The syndrome was attributed either to blockage of the menses or to movements of the womb, which, suffering from dryness or desirous of pregnancy, had a tendency to wander about in search of moisture.

Since Littré in his edition of the Hippocratic treatises applied the label "hystérie" to a number of chapter headings in the gynecological treatises, transforming the Greek diagnostic label "having to do with the uterus" into a modern psychoneurosis,[8] hysteria has been the most widely accepted modern diagnosis of the wandering womb syndrome. While some scholars have been critical of this retroactive diagnosis,[9] the work of Veith and Simon has been influential in spreading this interpretation.[10]

In her history of hysteria, Veith began with the Greeks,[11] and moved through history to reach hysteria in its modern sense:

> A form of psychoneurosis in which, according to Freud, a repressed emotional conflict finds external expression in sensory and motor dysfunction such as loss of sensation over parts of the body, temporary blindness, paralysis of limbs, loss or impairment of speech or hearing, or even convulsions. . . . The term conversion hysteria is used to describe a situation in which a patient's inability to cope with reality is converted into a physical affliction, thereby becoming socially acceptable; the symptom is then said to carry a "secondary" gain, that is avoidance of the original problem causing the stress.[12]

Veith's book illustrates the fact that hysteria, when considered as a single entity across history has a protean character: its symptoms have varied over time and space in accord with fashions in illnesses. For example, in the Victorian period an outstanding symptom was fainting, yet, as Veith said, "Unacceptable today would be the fainting ladies of the Victorian period."[13] In fact, Veith claimed that hysteria is infrequent today, since "somatic expressions of hysteria have become suspect among the more sophisticated classes."[14] But these cultural variations were not Veith's main interest; her goal was a diagnosis in terms of a single modern diagnostic entity. In the case of the wandering womb, this approach involved ignoring the prominence of the symptoms of chills and fever in the Hippocratic descriptions and identifying hysterical suffocation with *globus hystericus*, or the feeling of a lump in the throat (the Hippocratic description involves the collision of the uterus with the diaphragm, not its migration into the throat; since the womb was theoretically free to wander anywhere, the Hippocratic writers could easily have assigned its choking function to the throat had a lump there been the form the symptom took).

Simon followed Veith in diagnosing the wandering womb as hysteria, and this approach also led him to a description of the symptoms that drew more upon modern definitions of hysteria than it did upon the Hippocratic descriptions of the affliction.

Thus he identified the classic symptoms of hysterical conversion as "paralysis of a limb, blindness, and anesthesia of one side of the body . . . the sensation of a lump in the throat (*globus hystericus*) and certain forms of headache," and stated categorically that, "When the term 'hysteria' appears in medical literature from antiquity down to the early twentieth century, it refers to these symptoms."[15] Yet paralysis, blindness, and anesthesia were not symptoms of the wandering womb, as Simon himself may have recognized when he identified the illness described in *Parthenoi* as a combination of hysteria and melancholy.[16]

At this point it will be useful to invoke an extension of the concept of illness as a cultural construct, that of the culture-bound or folk illness.[17] A folk illness is an illness affecting members of a particular group that is diagnosed and treated by that group but that does not fit into the diagnostic categories of modern biomedicine.[18] Folk illnesses often have a symbolic meaning and serve to express, and sometimes alleviate, moral, social, or psychological conflicts or disharmonies. Numerous folk illnesses have been described in the anthropological literature, including arctic hysteria,[19] "heart distress" in Iran,[20] and *'uzr* in Egypt.[21] Perhaps the best-known and best-documented such illness is *susto* (fright), which occurs widely among Hispanic Americans.[22] Its symptoms are listlessness, debilitation, depression, restless sleep, and indifference to food, dress, and personal hygiene. *Susto* is attributed by both sufferers and healers to a loss of soul after a frightening experience in which the victim perceives himself or herself as helpless (although a time gap of months or years may intervene between the frightening experience and the onset of symptoms). Treatment is by magical soul retrieval. Men and women, adults and children, all suffer from *susto*, but it is most frequent among adult women. The syndrome has defied diagnosis in the categories of modern biomedicine, but functionally it serves to give respite in situations in which the victim is too overwhelmed to carry out the obligations of his or her social role.

The wandering womb clearly fits the model of a folk illness. Recognizing it as such frees us from concern about finding a retrospective diagnosis in terms of modern medicine and enables us to focus upon the specific historical and cultural context of the condition.[23] Since Simon's interpretation of the adaptive advantages of the wandering womb syndrome for females in Greek culture has been widely accepted, it provides a good place to start. Simon stressed the difficulties posed for women by a society that devalued the female and repressed female sexual activity while emphasizing phallic sexuality. He suggested that the wandering womb syndrome provided a socially acceptable means for a woman to cope: he saw it as making her the center of attention in the household, giving her respite from household duties, putting pressure on the male members of the family to arrange a marriage for her, and providing treatments by the doctor, such as physical examination, fumigation, and massage, that offered immediate relief from sexual frustrations both physically and emotionally. In all of this Simon expresses a male perspective: what the girl really wanted was attention, respite from work, a quick marriage, and sex. He overlooks the possibility that the illness resulted from *fear* of the approaching changes rather than desire for them. And his suggestion that the Hippocratic doctor was "well placed to be seen as a caring and loving father"[24] is probably overoptimistic.

Other scholars have been less sanguine about the adaptive value of the wandering womb syndrome from the woman's perspective, pointing out the definite advantages that it offered to the males involved. Thus, according to Manuli, the syndrome, "sancisce nella superiore obiettività ed autorità che competono ad una scienza, il ricatto igienico a cui la femmina viene sottoposta."[25] The advantages of the illness of maidens and the wandering womb from the Greek male's point of view are fairly clear. For fathers, the illness of maidens provided a persuasive argument in favor of early marriage; in fact, they could argue that marriage was best contracted *before* menarche, since the "delay" in menarche might really be dangerously suppressed menses. (In contrast, the cure offered by the socially marginal *manteis* simply returned the girl to the status quo.) For doctors, the wandering womb provided a concept in terms of which practically any illness in a female could be explained and treated "rationally." By bringing treatment of these female problems into the sphere of Hippocratic medicine, the doctor effectively asserted control over illnesses previously dealt with by women and soothsayers (and, perhaps not incidentally, cut down on the channeling of wealth outside the household by women). Viewed in this way, the medicalization of the illness of maidens is related to the process of extension of male control over midwives which we discussed in chapter 3. Both were part of a general trend toward increased control over women through the medicalization of their reproductive lives.

Artemis and Coming of Age

We have seen that the advocates of Artemis who competed with the Hippocratic doctors in the treatment of the illness of *parthenoi* operated on the fringes of Greek religious tradition and that some were possibly even female. But the goddess was also invoked by the mainstream, male-oriented religious tradition in official coming-of-age ceremonies for girls. Of these, the one best known to us is the Attic Arkteia, or Bear Festival, of Artemis, in which girls "played the bear" as a prerequisite for marriage. The animal itself may be significant in emphasizing the connections with motherhood: Perlman has pointed out that in antiquity the bear was noted for its mothering skills, and she suggests that by "playing the bear" the girls were "transformed, at least ritually, from maiden to mother."[26]

The Arkteia was celebrated at the goddess's shrine at Brauron on the east coast of Attica, as well as at several other Attic sites.[27] The *aition* for the festival at Brauron related the story of a young girl who was scratched by a bear; her brothers came to her assistance and shot the animal, thus offending Artemis (and, in one version, bringing down a plague upon the land); retribution was demanded by Artemis (or decreed by the *polis*) in the form of a requirement that all young girls serve the goddess before marriage by "acting the bear."[28]

A rather cryptic allusion to girls' participation in this festival by the chorus in the parabasis of Aristophanes' *Lysistrata* has insured a lively debate over many aspects of the ritual:

> For we, all you citizens, are setting out to offer useful advice to the *polis*.
> This is only natural, since the *polis* brought me up to live in splendid

luxury: for at seven years I was *arrhephoroi* [supervisor of the weaving of the peplos of Athena]; and then at ten *aletris* [corn grinder] for the *Archegete* [Athena]; and then wearing the *krokotos* [saffron-colored robe] I was a bear at the Brauronion festival; and another time I was a *kanephoros* [basket bearer], being a beautiful girl with a cluster of figs.[29]

Even though the chorus of women here makes a general claim to a share in the *polis* by virtue of these roles, this series of contributions was by no means a *cursus honorum* followed by every citizen girl. There were only two *arrhephoroi* each year, girls between seven and eleven years of age chosen from the most distinguished families.[30] This passage is the only mention of corn grinders, but the scholiast claims that the office was prestigious (perhaps guessing from the context). *Kanephoroi*, or basket carriers, participated in many processions, but this seems to be a reference to the Panathenaia, in which a few girls of marriageable age (around fifteen) from distinguished families served in this role.[31] In fact, a deliberate focus upon wealth is suggested by the conditions in which the speaker claims to have been raised: χλιδῶσαν ἀγλαῶς (splendid luxury).

What sort of evidence about the Arkteia does this passage provide? In considering this question, it is of course important to keep in mind that Aristophanes' aim in composing it was not to provide accurate information about Athenian cult to future scholars, but to make a point, or a joke, within the context of the play. His emphasis on the luxurious upbringing of the women does not imply that he takes their claim to serve as advisers to the city seriously. On the contrary, he seems to be saying that the best that they can offer to parallel the education and training in warfare and citizenship given to young males is a series of aristocratic cult roles focused on female domestic duties: weaving, grinding corn, bearing burdens, and serving as sex objects (figs were symbols of sexuality). Nevertheless, we can assume that he did not have any reason deliberately to misrepresent the offices he lists and that, in fact, misrepresentations of customs well known to his audience would have undermined his comic purpose. For this reason, it seems that we can take the ages seriously: in the fifth century, being a bear was something one did, or at least could do, after the age of ten.

A second contemporary source of evidence for the Arkteia is

provided by large numbers of small black-figure krater-shaped vases with conical bases (*krateriskoi*) that have been found almost exclusively in connection with shrines of Artemis.[32] On some of these vases girls of various sizes and stages of sexual development are shown in processions, dancing, and racing; some hold torches or bunches of twigs; they wear various types of clothing and some are naked. Women appear in a few scenes, apparently assisting the girls. Altars, palm trees, and garlands make the connection with Artemis and her festival. The vases date from the Persian War period to the end of the fifth century and have been found not only at the Brauronion but also at other sites (the sanctuaries of Artemis Mounychia in the Piraeus, Artemis Aristobule near the agora, and Artemis at Halai; the grotto of Pan and the Nymphs at Eleusis; and in the Athenian agora and acropolis). Fragments of two larger red-figure vases of similar shape and iconography, but of unknown provenience, show more detail, including part of a bear and particularly clear indications of differences in size and physical development among the participants.[33]

Other evidence from later sources is collected by Brelich,[34] and we will refer to it as we discuss various aspects of the Arkteia. These late sources in fact raise most of the problems in the interpretation of the festival and have generated an abundant literature. A full discussion of all the problems involved in the evidence is not necessary for our purposes, but a consideration of selected aspects of the Arkteia will be useful in helping us to understand the impact of this and similar coming-of-age rites on their participants. The points that are important to note are that:

1. Girls of different ages and stages of development participated.
2. Participation (of some sort) was required before a citizen girl could be married.
3. The rites were communal and "public."

The age of the girls who participated has been perhaps the most contested point in the evidence about the Arkteia. The passage in the *Lysistrata*, while specific about the age of some activities, simply puts being a bear after being *aletris* at age ten. Although the list does not describe a democratic career pattern followed by all young girls, it does offer a series of occasions for female service to the *polis*, arranged in chronological sequence; therefore, even though no age is connected to the participation in the Arkteia, the period between ten and a "marriageable" age—that is, after menarche at age fourteen—is implied for that service. This age range would suit the evidence that the festival was penteteric (celebrated every fifth year, as the Greater Panathenaic Festival),[35] for it would provide sufficient opportunity for the obligatory service to be accomplished by all girls before marriage in their fifteenth year.

But ancient sources rarely make life simple for the scholar, and this case is no exception, for two scholia to the passage in the *Lysistrata* give the ages of bears as from five to ten years.[36] A number of modern scholars prefer the scholiasts' interpretation, perhaps because it seems unlikely to have been derived from the text itself.[37] The most fervent exponent of the younger age range cited by the scholiasts has been Sourvinou-Inwood, who has proposed acceptance of the reading of the Ravenna manuscript, καταχέυσα ταν κροκωτόν (stripping off the *krokotos*), rather than the standard reading, κἀτ' ἔχουσα (*and then* [after being an *aletris* at age ten] *wearing the krokotos*), which explicitly makes ten-plus the age at which the speaker was a bear. She has sought to support this reading by determining Greek iconographical conventions of representing age and then "reading" the evidence of the vases on this basis.[38] Her attempt to determine the age of the bears portrayed on the *krateriskoi* by iconographical conventions presents several problems, however.[39] Perhaps the most serious is the network of questionable assumptions upon which she bases her determination of the absolute ages of the various iconographical categories. Thus, if the *kanephoros* category must be postmenarchal,[40] why pick an "earliest known" age of menarche of twelve years for its beginning when the Greeks themselves placed menarche at fourteen? (The iconographical justification that Sourvinou-Inwood offered is that some full-breasted girls are portrayed as shorter than full adult height, but such variations in height never occur on a pair of girls on the same vase so that we cannot be sure that an age range is intended). But even if we were to accept the ages of *kanephoroi* as twelve to fifteen, why then place the upper limit of the next category (bears) at ten rather than twelve? Since she rejects biological reality as an interpretative tool,[41] there is no need for Sourvinou-Inwood to allow a full two years (ten to twelve) for the "budding breasts" of bears to grow into the "full breasts" of the *kanephoroi*. Moreover, ages ten to twelve, a vital transitional period between the end of childhood and the arrival of menarche, turn out to have no office assigned to them and no iconographical type. These are serious obstacles to the establishment of a convincing system of iconographical conventions of age representation. If, however, we discount these questionable determinations of the absolute ages in Sourvinou-Inwood's chronological categories and place full-breasted *kanephoroi* at ages fourteen to fifteen, we have support for Aristophanes' placement of service as a bear after age ten and before service as a *kanephoros*. This agrees with Kahil's estimation of the ages of bears as eight to thirteen, which was intuitively derived from study of the portrayals on the vases.[42]

It is truly a *lectio difficilior* to prefer the scholiasts to Aristophanes. Error on their part is far more likely than a chronological mistake by Aristophanes in reporting the ages customary for these cult offices to an audience in his own time. On the other hand, convincing explanations for error by the scholiast are not difficult to find. Brelich has suggested that over time, as the initiation rites lost much of their original significance, the age requirement dropped, as commonly occurs in such situations.[43] Confusion with other ceremonies is also possible; in particular, a large number of portrait statues of young children, mostly boys, from babies to about age ten, have been found at Brauron,[44] dedicated to the goddess in her role as *kourotrophos*, and a later scholiast may well have confused the ages portrayed in these statues with that of the bears. Confusion over the details of rituals would have been even easier after the sanctuary at Brauron was engulfed by mud and abandoned in the late fourth century.[45] All things considered, the contemporary evidence—the portrayal of developing girls on the *krateriskoi*, and Aristophanes' specification of the Arkteia as taking place after service as an *aletris* at age ten—outweighs the evidence of the scholiasts and provides compelling reason to favor an age range that would include the age of eleven for bears in the classical period. Thus Mommsen and Wernicke estimated eleven to fourteen,[46] Kahil eight to thirteen,[47] and Perlman ten to fourteen.[48]

In regard to the second point, the ancient sources are almost unanimous in their report that participation was required of all girls before marriage, even citing *pseuphisma* to this effect.[49] The evidence of the *krateriskoi* also supports widespread participation: they have been found in large numbers, in various locations, and are of poor quality; in other words, these were not fine vases dedicated only by a few girls from wealthy families.[50] On the other hand, participation limited to a few elite seems to be suggested by the passage in the *Lysistrata* with its emphasis on luxury and its inclusion of other exclusive offices such as *arrhephoros* and *kanephoros*.[51] A clue to a reconciliation of this apparent conflict in the sources may be found in the reference to Brauron in the passage in *Lysistrata*. This is the only office for which a location is specified, and there is reason to believe that its inclusion lent an air of luxury and elitism to playing the bear. As the various findspots of the *krateriskoi* show, it was not necessary to travel to Brauron to observe the Arkteia; many girls who lived in the city fulfilled their service to Artemis close to home. We have already seen that the records of dedications to Artemis at Brauron included a number from women who were members of wealthy and prestigious families living at some distance from the sanctuary; if married women from elite families made a point of traveling to Brauron to make their dedications to the goddess, the celebration of the Arkteia by girls *at Brauron* may also have been considered a mark of prestige.[52]

Regardless of whether participation was universal or representative, the evidence that the Arkteia was required by the *polis* is significant. As coming-of-age rites, these celebrations must have long predated the formalization of the *polis*, but in the form in which we see them they have been brought within its structure and control. In exerting this control, the male *polis* began to "tame" the natural, "wild" reproductive capacities of the female at their earliest manifestation—by service to Artemis, little bears were transformed into potential citizen mothers.

Finally, the rites were communal. The portrayals on the vases leave no doubt that "playing the bear" involved taking part in group activities such as races and processions in company with other girls of varying sizes and stages of development.[53]

In discussing the Arkteia, we have been considering a specifically Attic ritual, but communal female coming-of-age ceremonies similar to the Arkteia were celebrated throughout Greece. Hamilton stresses the parallels with Alkman and cites other similar rituals, including those for Hera in Elis and Dionysus Kolonatas in Sparta.[54] Middle Corinthian vases portray women and children participating in dances and other cult activities in honor of Artemis,[55] and laws explicitly requiring a sacrifice to Artemis before marriage are recorded in an inscription from Cyrene. At Cyrene pregnant women were also obliged to sacrifice to the goddess and to honor a priestess called *arko* (possibly related to the *arktoi*, the Attic bears).[56] Thus it is justifiable to extend the Attic female coming-of-age experience to girls throughout Greece.

If we consider these three aspects of the Arkteia together—it involved a range of ages and developmental stages, was required of all citizen girls, and was communal—we can make a reasonable assessment of its potential psychological effect on participants. If the age at which the Greeks believed menarche occurred (fourteen) represented the usual experience,[57] most participants would not yet have reached that crucial milepost (on any determination of their ages); the younger girls would be in various stages of development, and some would not yet have begun to develop. Yet as bears they were already officially preparing for marriage. The issue of menarche and development as a woman was stressed by the purpose of the ceremony itself, and even more by the girls' participation naked in a number of activities.

If we now return to the characterization of the illness of maidens as a folk illness, it will be apparent that it has considerable explanatory force here. Folk illnesses usually serve a socially adaptive purpose; based upon his study of *susto* in Hispanic American cultures, Rubel suggested that such illnesses could be understood "as a complex interaction between an individual's state of health and the role expectations which his society provides."[58] In the case of *susto*, he found that people usually associated the beginning of their illnesses with incidents in which they were unable to meet the expectations of roles in which they had been socialized.

In the lives of young female children raised within the confines of the *oikos*, there were probably few occasions that put them at risk of publicly failing to meet the expectations of their gender roles—until they reached the Arkteia (or its equivalent). The first strong message imposing extrafamilial gender-role expectations was probably sent by participation in such coming-of-age rites. Running naked in races, as girls are portrayed on the *krateriskoi*, many girls undergoing puberty rites would have found themselves physically wanting. Such a situation would be tailor-made to raise anxieties. We must also add to this the social pressure arising from the *oikos*: as was the case with the sister of Demosthenes, many girls were probably promised in early childhood for marriage in their fifteenth year. If the girl reached her service as a bear without reaching menarche or displaying the signs of approaching womanhood (which, given the age range and probable nutritional deficits, would not have been unusual), what was the matter? Were the menses being obstructed? If the girl suffered any sort of feverish illness, this would be the obvious diagnosis, and the symptoms would be structured for both the patient and her concerned family in accordance with the expected pattern—the result would be another case of illness of maidens.[59]

The Thesmophoria: Becoming Persephone and Becoming Demeter

A good attack of the illness of maidens would have turned the mind of a Greek father who subscribed to Hippocratic theory to the remedy of a quick marriage. On the other hand, the women in the family were more likely to resort to a *mantis*, whose conservative treatments may have reflected the mother's resistance to an early marriage. Nevertheless, there was a cultural force that spoke to the condition of the mother who resisted the marriage of her young daughter,[60] the festival of Demeter Thesmophoros.

The Thesmophoria, which was the principal Greek festival for married women and was celebrated throughout the Greek world, contained in its central myth of Demeter and Persephone a powerful message of reconciliation to female losses in marriage. The story, which was reenacted by the women during the festival, is told in its most accessible form in the Homeric *Hymn to Demeter* (an early hymn, perhaps dating to the seventh century B.C.).[61] According to the hymn, the god of the Underworld, Hades, carried off Persephone (Kore), the daughter of the grain goddess Demeter, as she picked flowers in a meadow, symbolic of the innocence of childhood pursuits. The rape/marriage was carried out with the permission of Zeus, the girl's father. In anger and mourning for the loss of her daughter, Demeter withdrew from the world, causing the death of the crops and threatening the survival of all life. This primeval strike finally forced Zeus to arrange for the restoration of the girl; however, while in the Underworld Persephone had eaten one pomegranate seed and thus she had become irrevocably the wife of Hades. Therefore, her return could be only temporary: she was allowed to visit her mother in the upper world for a portion of each year.

Fifth-century evidence for the Thesmophoria is provided by Aristophanes' play, the *Thesmophoriazusae*, a Euripidean parody for which the festival provides the comic setting and whose plot hinges upon the exclusion of men from the celebration. Aristophanes portrays the women during the festival as constituting an assembly and as participating in hymns and dances (and engaged in compromising behavior that reflects male stereotypes of women—secret tippling and revelations of sexual infidelities), but, unfortunately for the historian, Aristophanes reveals none of the secrets of the women's ritual activities. We are, therefore, dependent for much of our information upon less direct and later sources.[62]

The celebration of the Thesmophoria had many local variants,[63] but common to all was the creation of the *polis* of women that is portrayed in the *Thesmophoriazusae*. The women were required to leave their homes and "camp out" together for an extended period of time (in Athens three days, in Syracuse, ten). They had to maintain celibacy, and the presence of men was strictly forbidden. In Athens, Thebes, and some other cities the women took over the central place of government; in other cities the place of the women's assembly was outside the city walls.[64] In either case, the women created a "*polis* of women" that was outside the framework of the normal male *polis* and, in a sense, temporarily supplanted it; they elected their own officials, deme by deme, just as the men did. This civic significance was reinforced by the fact that their husbands were legally obliged to allow them to participate and to pay their expenses.[65] Despite the numerous other religious cults and ceremonies in which women participated, the Thesmophoria must have been the high spot of the year for married women, for it was the only time that they were given official leave—in fact, required—to be absent from their homes overnight.[66]

In Athens, on the first day of the festival, called *Anodos* (the Going Up), the women climbed up to the acropolis, carrying the necessities for their ritual activities and their three-day stay. It may have been on that evening or night that they brought up the decayed remains of piglets that had been thrown into a chasm at some earlier time, mixed them with seed grain, and placed them on altars,[67] thus enriching the seed to ensure a good harvest. The second day, *Nesteia* (Fast), was given over to fasting and mourning for Demeter's loss of her daughter. On the third day, which in many cities was celebrated as *Kallegeneia* (Beautiful Birth), the women engaged in feasts that included indulging in the meat of sacrificial pigs,[68] sacrificing cakes in the shapes of phalli and pudenda, and eating pomegranates. Recalling the pomegranate seed eaten by Persephone, which sealed her fate as a permanent, if part-year, resident/wife in Hades, the eating of the pomegranate may have represented the women's recommitment to marriage (yet the fruit's main use in women's lore was as a contraceptive).[69] The women also engaged in *aischrologia*: ribald joking, insults, and obscenities, which were characteristic of many fertility rites.

What was the meaning of the Thesmophoria? Traditionally, interpreters have viewed it from the male point of view, stressing the importance to the *polis* of the fertility of the crops and of the women, both of which were to be assured by the ritual activities of the festival.[70] But any living ritual is multivalent, able to give expression to the differing experiences of various individuals within the culture, while reflecting the concerns and interests of the modern interpreter as well.[71] In the case of the Thesmophoria, a festival in which participation was restricted to women, the recent interpretations of Winkler and Zeitlin are particularly important because they attempt to see its significance from the point of view of its female participants.[72]

Winkler in his discussion of the festival focused on the element of *aischrologia* and asked, "What were the women laughing at?"[73] Linking the Thesmophoria with the Adonia, in which women planted seeds in pots (gardens of Adonis) only to let them wither and die once they had sprouted up, he suggested that their laughter was directed at the sexual inadequacy of men in a sort of visual pun, "a small gleam of misandric humor about men's sexuality as a thing which disappears so suddenly."[74] But he suggested that the women in their laughter had a more serious point as well: it was a commentary on the brevity and relative insignificance of the male contribution to reproduction in contrast to their own much greater contribution in nine months of pregnancy, the sufferings of childbirth, and the effort and energy required in the nursing and rearing of a child. For Winkler, the women's realization of this contrast, and their recognition of their own much greater input, was evidence that Greek women had primary control and relative independence in reproduction. This, however, is analogous to arguing that the worker who actually produces the product that the company president decides will be produced is, by reason of the greater time and effort that he puts into the product, in control and independent. Moreover, in (male) Greek terms, as Aristotle put it, the male contributes form, which is a higher element in the hierarchy of being, whereas the female contributes only matter, the lowest element.[75] It is quality, not quantity, that counts.

This is not to say that the women were not disdainful of the male contribution or did not value their own. In fact, it seems very reasonable to suggest, as Winkler does, that the laughter of the participants in the Thesmophoria was aimed at least in part at the absurdity of the situation that the male culture imposed upon them: little reward for great value given. Aristophanes' female characters in fact make that very complaint as they celebrate the Thesmophoria.[76] Nevertheless, the "power" to laugh at the perceived absurdity of an

117

oppressive system, which is often granted by the system itself, cannot be equated with the legitimate power (authority) of the system to repress, or with the power to effect a permanent change for the better. The ability to laugh at the oppressor is not real power, but a safety valve that allows the system—and the oppression—to continue. The opportunity that the Thesmophoria provided Greek women to vent their frustration with their situation was granted to them to enable them to return to that situation, irrational as it was from their point of view. This is the crucial point grasped by Zeitlin in her analysis of the festival.

Zeitlin saw the Thesmophoria as a temporary release for women from the dissatisfactions and constraints of their daily lives.[77] Within the context of the festival women expressed their resistance to social norms through such elements of "disorder" as removal from the home and daily routines, refraining from sex, assuming male "political" roles in a city of women, eating sacrificial meat that was usually reserved for men, and indulging in lewd talk. It was through such open and public expressions of rebellion that women were enabled to return to the situation that had given rise to their emotional resistance in the first place: in the course of the festival, women moved, "from an original refusal to abrogate feminine power to an acceptance of the limitations placed upon it."[78] Thus the festival served annually to allow women to vent their frustration at social norms, while at the same time it reinforced these norms and reasserted male control.

A modern celebration that is somewhat similar to the Thesmophoria is held in Macedonia on Saint Dominique's Day, or Midwives' Day. Only married women of childbearing age are permitted to take part. They visit the midwife, bringing her gifts useful to her profession while she sits adorned with decorations of vegetables, fruits, and flowers on a throne. Each woman pours out water for the midwife to wash her hands and then kisses the *schema*, a phallic-shaped object made from a large leek or sausage. A banquet follows, with much drinking, and then the women lead the midwife in a carriage through the village, singing and telling obscene jokes, until they reach the fountain, where she is sprinkled with water. Men stay indoors, giving the village over to the women for the day.[79]

The function of the celebration as sanctioned rebellion seems clear.

It is significant that a functional interpretation similar to that offered for the Thesmophoria has been made for women's participation in the worship of Dionysus and other orgiastic cults in the classical period: the rites "offered a way of expressing and redressing serious social and psychological imbalance between the sexes."[80] Although the worship of Dionysus was not restricted to women as was the Thesmophoria, it was they who traditionally— and mythically as *maenads*—served the god in rites of ecstatic possession. In Dionysiac celebrations, however, the women's relief was provided not by taking over male roles in the *polis*, and thus moving closer to civilization with its rules and restrictions, but by escaping to the wild, where they could cut loose entirely from all civilized restraint. Greek women's need for such multiple and varied opportunities to vent their frustrations suggests the extent to which the feminine gender role was dysfunctional for women themselves, regardless of its utility for the culture as a whole.

A ritual that acts as a safety valve is, while crucial to the continuing viability of a repressive society, nevertheless essentially negative. It provides participants with a temporary release from the tensions of the situation that confines them, and this enables them to return to the status quo for another stretch of time, but it does nothing to change basic attitudes. In contrast, a positive mode of acculturation acts to change consciousness, to reveal value in a situation. This the Thesmophoria also did by offering women a positive view of the problematic separation of mother and daughter made necessary by marriage.[81] In its rituals women annually reenacted Demeter's loss, her grief, her anger at the girl's father, and her eventual reconciliation. In doing this, they also reenacted, or rehearsed, two crucial moments in their own lives: their early separation from their own mothers as they left their *oikos* in marriage, and their own later loss of daughters, still children, to another *oikos* in marriage. The ritual demonstrated dramatically that all married women were participants in a cycle of experience: they entered it as daughters newly married (as Persephone), but marriage soon made them mothers themselves of marrying daughters (Demeter). Thus the generations merged in an endless cycle, and that cycle was es-

sential for the continuation of life. The message of the Thesmophoria to women as mothers and daughters was clear: if Demeter
and Persephone endured the suffering of separation entailed by
marriage, so can you.

In conclusion, we should return to the important point of the
political structuring of the festival. Whatever psychological value
the Thesmophoria had for its female participants, the festival itself
was cast within the civic framework in revealing ways. Female
leaders were elected and governed a "*polis* of women," which was
often even situated in the locus of male authority, and the women's
polis temporarily superseded that of the men. That this framework
of civilization had enveloped the primitive mysteries of rotting pig
flesh and phallic cookies illustrates perhaps better than anything
else the determination of the male *polis* to extend its control over
the fertility of its women. This was not the least message of the festival to the women who celebrated it.

Seven

The Attitudes of the *Polis* to Childbirth: Putting Women into the Grid

> I would rather stand three times in the front of
> battle than bear one child
> Euripides, *Medea* 250–51 (trans. Rex Warner)

One of the messages of the Thesmophoria was that the continuity of the *polis* depended upon the cycle of female life: after risking death in childbirth themselves, women must soon give up their daughters to a similar fate. If childbirth was a mortal peril—and we have seen that it was—it was a peril that women had to undergo so that the community might live on. Was Medea's complaint not then justified? Is it not reasonable to assume that the *polis* honored women's contribution equally with that of men who risked their lives in battle?

In fact, modern scholars have enthusiastically embraced Medea's words as evidence that the Greeks did regard death in childbirth as heroic and the equivalent of male death in battle.[1] Supporting evidence has been found in Plutarch's statement (as emended) that the Spartans allowed the name of the deceased to be inscribed on tombstones only for men who had died in battle and women who had died in childbirth.[2] Although the emendation is rather daring (τῶν ἱερῶν to ἐν λέχῳ), appropriately inscribed tombstones have been found in Laconia that appear to support it.[3] Moreover, other funerary monuments have also been adduced as evidence. These consist of a group of Attic and atticizing monuments portraying women in labor.[4] Supporters of the equation argue that these were the memorials of women who died in childbirth and that they parallel tombstones honoring men who died in battle;[5] thus they are offered as evidence that both types of death were equally honored.

Aside from these tombstones depicting labor scenes, the case for this interpretation is by no means a compelling one. Euripides' *Medea* says nothing about anyone actually granting childbearing women honor equal to that accorded to warriors; on the contrary, her point is that they do not. And she is not alone. Female characters in the comedies of Aristophanes similarly complain about the lack of appreciation for their contribution of sons to the *polis*.[6] The evidence of Plutarch is also less than conclusive, depending upon a radical textual emendation that is supported by Laconian—but not necessarily Spartan—tombstones. And even if the stones are accepted as evidence for Sparta, the idiosyncrasies of the Spartan life-style cast doubt upon an extension of the equation to other Greek poleis. As Loraux stated, in Athens, at least on the civic level at which the Spartan practice operated, "the Spartan parallel between war and reproduction (dead *en polemoi* / dead *lecho*) would be unthinkable."[7] But Loraux also argued that the parallel did exist in Athens on the *private* level, calling upon the evidence of the scenes portraying women in labor and those commemorating warriors fallen in battle on Attic funerary monuments.[8] Given the weakness in the other evidence offered in support of this piece of received opinion, we thus need to look more closely at these funerary monuments.

The scenes appear on two types of monument, stelai and lekythoi (a vase type rendered in stone).[9] They depict a seated woman who is visibly distressed or collapsing, usually with hair and clothing loosened. She is physically supported by a woman who stands behind her. In some scenes a third female figure approaches her to offer assistance; in others another figure, male or female, stands nearby in an attitude of mourning. This type scene was identified as a representation of labor by Wolters in 1885; he relied upon the woman's sinking posture and, more specifically, her loosened hair and clothing, which serve as signs of childbirth in ancient texts.[10] Most scholars have agreed with this identification,[11] and it seems to be confirmed both by those few examples that are graphic in their physical depiction of pregnancy, and by the appearance of a woman in the "sinking posture" on a fifth-century votive relief in New York, where the childbirth context is made explicit by the presence of a swaddled infant (plate 1).[12] Since Wolter's identification, other stones have been added to the group. In 1905, Michon suggested the parallel with warrior monuments; Loraux took up the idea in 1981, and, in 1988, when the German scholar Ursula Vedder published the labor scenes as a group, she adopted this interpretation of them as portrayals of heroic female deaths.[13]

In the following descriptive summary of the monuments I omit fragmentary and damaged pieces and consider only those stones that show the relationship between the various figures in the scene:[14]

1. The lekythos for Theophante in Athens, dated circa 340–330 (plate 2).[15] A female figure sits with hair and clothing loosened and stares downward into space; her arms are limp. A man standing to the right supports her left hand and raises his right hand to his head. On the left a female figure supports her with a hand under her arm.

2. The lekythos for Pheidestrate and Mnesagora in the National Archaeological Museum in Athens, dated circa 370/360 (plate 3).[16] The names stand over the figures. The seated woman, labeled Pheidestrate, stares off into space. She is supported at the waist by a short female figure on the right. A third female figure, labeled Mnesagora, stands to the left and places her hand to her bowed head.

   Both these scenes portray a seated woman with supporting and mourning figures. The other scenes include an additional, active helping figure:

3. A lekythos for Killaron in the Louvre, dated circa 370/360 (plate 4).[17] A woman with loosened hair and clothing sits

on a chair staring into space; her arms hang inertly. She is supported on the right by a less than full-sized female figure, while another female figure standing to the left reaches out to touch her and supports her right arm with her right hand.

4. A stele at Harvard in the Sackler Museum, dated circa 340 (plate 5).[18] The seated woman is supported by a smaller figure on the right. She clasps the hand of a man standing before her, to whom she looks; his left hand is held palm up near her face. An inscription suggests that he is her father; however, this male figure has been reworked; originally the figure was a female.[19] A third female figure, only partially preserved, stands behind the reworked figure. This stone could function as a bridge between the first two, which portray only supporting and mourning figures, and the others in the group that include an active helping figure: in its original form it depicted an active female helper, but in its later form this figure has been reworked to portray a typical farewell handshake gesture: now a man, the figure bids the woman goodbye rather than offering her assistance.

5. The grave stele for Plangon and Tolmides in Athens, circa 320s, found at Oropus in the border territory between Attica and Boeotia (plate 6).[20] The seated woman is more obviously afflicted than the seated women in the other monuments: she is physically contorted and out of control, with her right leg awkwardly swung upward. She is supported by a slightly shorter woman on the right, and on the left another female figure moves toward her, supporting her right hand with her own right hand and holding out her left hand to her. A man (Tolmides) stands on the extreme left, holding his head in his hand.

6. The stele for Nikomeneia in the Kerameikos Museum, dated in the 320s (plate 7).[21] A second name is incomplete; it could read either "Stephane" (female) or "of Stephanios" (male). The seated woman is supported by a female figure on the right, and her right arm rests on the

shoulder of another female figure on the left, at whom she looks and who offers her something, possibly in a bowl.

7. A lekythos in Copenhagen, dated in the 320s (plate 8).[22] The seated woman is supported on the right by a female figure who holds her left hand and in whose direction she looks. The woman's hair is not loosened. To the right another smaller female figure reaches out to touch the right hand of the seated woman with her right hand, thus covering her own face with her arm (a gesture of mourning or of helping?). In this case, it is the supporting figure on the right who seems to be the primary helper; she is larger than the figure on the left and more actively involved with the seated woman.

8. The stele for Malthake in the Piraeus Museum, dated circa 300 (plate 9).[23] A woman is seated on a couch leaning on pillows; her hair is done neatly in braids; her left arm hangs down and her right is on the shoulder of the only other figure, a woman who stands behind the couch and touches the seated woman's chin with her right hand. The inscription reads, "Malthake: Magadidos, Chreste." Clairmont suggests that Malthake is not the woman on the couch but the standing figure, and that she was a midwife (midwives were often called "Chreste,"[24] and the name "Magadis" is foreign,[25] thus fitting the context of midwifery). If this is the case, Malthake is depicted in her lifetime activity, and the funerary relief belongs to a group of reliefs that portray professional activity rather than death in childbirth.[26]

9. One of two similar relief stelai in Alexandria, early Hellenistic (plate 10).[27] The second stele is less well preserved. The seated woman is visibly pregnant and physically contorted. The supporting figure on the right is child-sized; a second female figure on the left holds out something in a bowl to the seated woman. A third-century painted limestone stele from Hadra in the vicinity of Alexandria, now in the Metropolitan Museum in New York, portrays a similar scene in a different medium.[28]

10. A stele from Rhodes, third century (plate 11).[29] The woman sits on a couch staring into space. A small female figure on the right places her hand on the woman's shoulder, while a full-sized female figure on the left touches the head and arm of the seated woman.

In contrast to these labor scenes, another and more frequently found type scene appears to have been used to commemorate death in childbirth: it depicts a seated woman with an attendant who holds an infant; in most cases the seated woman appears oblivious to the infant.[30] The late painted stele of Hediste in the Volos Museum, which is usually included in the labor group, perhaps better fits this second type, and its inscription offers a clue about the message intended by those who dedicated such memorials.[31] It is the best preserved of several in the museum that bear the same motif: the deceased woman lies prostrate on a bed; a man sits beside her with his head in his hands, and in the background a female figure appears in a doorway holding a swaddled infant. An epitaph conveys the sense of pathos considered appropriate to such a situation:

> The Fates spun on their spindles then for Hediste their painful thread, when the bride went to meet the pains of labor. Miserable one! She will not embrace her infant, or wet the lips of her baby with her breast, for one light [of day] looked down on both, and then Fortune coming to both alike carried the two away to one tomb.[32]

That not all scenes portraying a woman and an infant were intended to be seen as mother and child by those who chose them is, however, demonstrated by the well-known stele of Ampharete in the Kerameikos Museum.[33] On Ampharete's monument, an inscription identifies the "mother-child" pair as grandmother and grandchild. Unexpected iconographical traps thus may lie in wait, and cautious skepticism about the "obvious" meaning is always in order in interpreting the significance of scenes on tombstones In order to use the labor scenes to reveal Greek attitudes about childbirth, we should try to eliminate modern assumptions and see the scenes as much as possible in terms of Greek iconographical conventions. In this we are following and extending the method adopted by Wolters in his original identification of them as labor scenes, in which he relied on motifs of loosening associated with childbirth in ancient texts. We need especially to look for similar recurrent themes that are significant in terms of otherwise-attested Greek values but that may have been overlooked in modern interpretation.[34]

The principal iconographical elements in the labor scenes appear to be posture (seated, standing, collapsing), relative size, type of clothing (typical of slaves or free persons), state of clothing and hair (loosened or normal), mode (active or passive), and activity (suffering, helping, supporting, mourning). Of these, the active-passive dichotomy especially deserves our attention because, although it was important in defining Greek gender roles,[35] it bears less significance in our value system and has received little attention in modern interpretations.

The Greek application of the active-passive pair to gender roles was somewhat more complex than this dichotomous expression suggests, however. While in general the Greeks allotted the active role to the male and the passive to the female,[36] the situation was not a straightforward association of active-male-good. The sphere of operation was also relevant: women could be active within the home, where the busy and competent household manager was valued, although she was barred from activity in the public sphere of the *polis*. Thus active-female-*oikos* was viewed as desirable, but active-female-*polis* was firmly rejected.

Attic comedy provides still another dimension of value in the application of this dichotomy in its distinction between women according to age (or, rather, childbearing capacity). In comedy, it is *young* women in particular who are portrayed as passive, as "weak, prone to passion and standing in need of constant supervision . . . frivolous, naive and unreliable, unable to speak sensibly about any matter of interest to the city . . . their weapons are intrigue, guile and sexual manipulation."[37] In contrast, *older* women play an active role in comedy: it is they who serve as spokespersons, offer useful advice to the city, directly confront the men, and keep the younger women in line. Similarly, we have seen that in real life a degree of activity was tolerated for older women (especially mothers) who were past the age of childbearing: they were free to move about in public and could in some circumstances even confront men directly in the affairs of the *oikos*. Thus we have the value judgments that female-childbearing-active (outside the *oikos*) is bad, but female-postmenopausal-active (in the community) is at least acceptable in some cases. Because of such complexities, Greek values are better thought of as a multidimensional grid rather than as a simple dichotomy.

Viewing the labor scenes through our own perceptual screen, we see the pregnant woman as the focus of the scene because she is central both spatially and by virtue of being the center of attention, both important clues in our iconographical system. Another sign— size as an indicator of importance—is also caught by our perceptual net: we generally recognize that the smaller size of the second female helper signals her ancillary position (and possibly younger age), an interpretation that is confirmed in some cases by clothing that indicates servile status. But the active-passive dichotomy is not of great significance from our iconographical viewpoint, and therefore we fail to focus upon it as an important element in the scenes.

In Greek terms, however, the passivity of the seated figure is readily comprehensible. In the first place, she is young—still of childbearing age. Thus passivity is appropriate for her. Moreover, since, as we have seen, the Hippocratics viewed women's role in childbirth as passive,[38] in this way, too, passivity is appropriate for her. By failing to register this aspect of the scenes, we not only underestimate the importance of the seated woman's passivity, but we also fail to appreciate the significance of the central helping figure who provides the active focus on a number of the monuments.

We should now turn to the tombstones commemorating men who died in battle. If the Greeks did equate death in childbirth with death in battle, we should be able to see similar iconographical signs on monuments for both types of deaths.

Most warrior tombstones portray a standing male figure, often shown shaking hands with another figure in a typical funerary farewell scene.[39] The man is identifiable as a warrior by his clothing and war gear. In such quiet scenes, while the men are not shown in military action, they are portrayed as self-composed and in control of the situation, active in taking the first step toward the warfare that will lead to their deaths.[40] There is no hint of pathos either in the scenes themselves or in epitaphs. They offer a parallel with the swaddled-infant type scenes on women's monuments, but without the element of pathos that is central in the women's scenes, signaled by the epitaph for Hediste.

This difference becomes even more striking when we compare the iconographic elements in the labor scenes with those employed in the scenes of warriors portrayed in military action, of which there are about a dozen.[41] In these, male figures are shown charging into battle with shield and drawn sword,[42] or in actual battle and overcoming an enemy. The portrayal of battle scenes on these monuments is not gruesome in its realism, but idealized; only defeated enemies are depicted as wounded or dying, never the honored warrior himself.[43] Again, as in the case of the quiet warrior scenes, there is no hint of suffering or pathos.

As we have seen, in Greek terms, the active-passive dichotomy applied to people in their prime was a significant value indicator. Taking it into consideration allows us to see that, far from supporting the view that the classical Athenians accorded equal honor to death in childbirth and death in battle, the funerary monuments reflect and reinforce the role traditionally assigned to women of childbearing age in the grid of Greek values: as childbearers, they were passive while men were active; they could display patience and submission, but not an active courage to match that of the warrior.[44] They elicited pity, while warriors inspired admiration and emulation.[45]

This is not to deny that the Greeks saw a sort of similarity between these two types of deaths. But the funerary monuments locate this similarity in the Greek grid according to age and gender, making it iconographically clear that the women who are memorialized are passive and worthy of pity, whereas the men are active and heroic. The monuments thus register an important distinction between men and women who died "for the *polis*," rather than establishing an equivalence between the two. For the Greeks, the

129

sexes were separate and unequal, and the funerary monuments faithfully express and communicate this by attributing to the one passivity and pathos, to the other, activity and glory.[46]

Postscript to the Monuments

An interesting question is raised by Christoph Clairmont's identification of the stele of Malthake as the memorial of a midwife. Could it be that we have also mistaken the memorial intention of other labor-scene monuments? Might not at least some of the other monuments have been the memorials of midwives as well?

We have already seen, in the stele of Ampharete, one example of the use of scenes in ways that are, to us at least, unexpected. When we consider the context of the purchase of a funerary monument, as well as the evidence for the use of particular scenes, we find conditions that made such flexibility possible. Most monuments were selected from ready-made stock or from pattern books;[47] some, such as the Sackler stele, were even secondhand and reused.[48] In all these cases, scenes could be customized to some degree (again, as the Sackler stele was), or an epitaph could be employed to assure a correct interpretation (as in the case of the stele of Ampharete and her grandchild).[49] Although a few families went beyond such relatively simple customization to commission a unique work representing a special characteristic of the deceased, most extant monuments utilized type scenes, as did the labor scenes. As a result, the Greeks "read" the scenes on funerary monuments with a degree of flexibility that we tend to overlook. This is illustrated by a fourth-century epigram attributed to Perses and cited by Wolters and Michon, which has a special pertinence to the interpretation of the labor scenes:

> Unhappy Mnasylla, why does it stand on thy tomb, this picture of thy daughter Neotima whom thou lamentest, her whose life was taken from her by the pangs of labour? She lies in her dear mother's arms, as if a heavy cloud had gathered on her eyelids and, alas, not far away her father Aristoteles rests his head in his right hand O most miserable pair, not even in death have ye forgotten your grief.[50]

This epigram in fact describes a scene very like that portrayed on Theophante's memorial (plate 2). It should alert us to the fact that such scenes were capable of expressing a variety of meanings for those who employed them. It is only the epigram that reveals that the principal deceased is not the woman portrayed in childbirth but her mother, who helped her in her fatal labor and mourned for her. (Incidentally, this adds to the evidence for the privileging of the active mode in the Greek conceptual grid, for it is the activity of the older woman that is commemorated.) Thus the same scene might have been used to memorialize the woman who died in childbirth or her mother—or possibly both. Sometimes, as in the case of the Sackler stele, a stone was reworked to be more appropriate, but the rarity of reworked stones suggests that this was not a common occurrence. More often an epitaph served to make the intention clear; unfortunately, in the series of labor scenes no epitaphs are preserved, unless we include the late and anomalous stele of Hediste, which we suggested above better fit the swaddled-infant type.

Lacking an epitaph, how can we know who the honored deceased was? Sometimes figures are labeled, but labels were used to identify other figures in the scenes, such as mourners, as well as the deceased (perhaps the dedicator of the monument—or possibly such scenes were used as memorials for more than one person, the second to die appearing as a mourner for the first). In the labor scenes the seated aspect of the figure has been assumed to identify the one being memorialized, but that this is not a safe assumption is shown by the epigram for Mnasylla. This conclusion is also reinforced by a number of other stelai whose inscriptions attest that the seated figure is not the deceased (one, that of a midwife and female doctor, will be considered later).[51]

Thus we cannot assume that the figure portrayed in labor is the deceased because she is seated, centrally placed, or labeled. But a consideration of the active-passive value system and the positive value given by the Greeks to the active in the case of males and older women should direct our attention to the active helping figure in these scenes, as the epigram for Mnasylla also suggests. In order to appreciate the significance of these figures, it will be helpful to review the changes that we have seen taking place in the care of women in childbirth during the classical period.

Traditionally childbirth had been entrusted to the informal care of female kin and neighbors. Some of these women became known for their skills and were accorded the title of *maia* or midwife; as they worked, they accumulated lore about many aspects of women's reproductive lives. In the fifth century Greek doctors began to collect and commit this material to writing in the form that we have it in the Hippocratic gynecological treatises. Male doctors also began to participate in the treatment of complications in pregnancy and childbirth, using female helpers. The gynecological treatises leave no doubt that women served as assistants to doctors in the care of women patients; in other words, we can see in them the faint traces of the birth of the professional midwife (the midwife recognized by the male doctor) as women moved from the folk to the professional sector.

This Hippocratic attention to women's reproductive problems cannot be attributed to a disinterested concern for increasing the professional opportunities of women, however. As we have seen in earlier chapters, female control over reproduction worried Greek men a good deal. They were concerned about what they saw as women's propensity to abort prospective heirs and to introduce supposititious infants into the household. In this misbehavior of wives the Greek male often saw—or imagined he saw—the hand of the midwife, who was, of course, a potential source of information about the poisons used as abortifacients and in an excellent position to find and smuggle changlings into the birth room. As a consequence of this perceived vulnerability, men welcomed the extension of the sphere of the Hippocratic doctor into gynecology and obstetrics and his assumption of control over the midwives who worked with him. But inadvertently such practices also changed and improved the status of the women who became assistants to male doctors: they entered the professional sector. Early in the fourth century Plato refers to women doctors as a matter of course,[52] and a midcentury grave monument of a woman named Phanostrate identified her as *maia* and *iatros*[53] (plate 12). This monument bears consideration both for itself and for what it can contribute to our understanding of Greek iconographical conventions.

In the scene on Phanostrate's monument we see a seated woman on the right. This is another example of a seated figure who is not the deceased: she is identified by inscription as the dedicator of this monument (who is also named Phanostrate).[54] Standing facing her we see the deceased, Phanostrate the *maia* and *iatros*. Four small children also appear; they may be the offspring of her patron, whom Phanostrate delivered and cared for, but at any rate, in the scene on the tombstone they serve as attributes of her profession, the recipients of her care.

If we reconsider the labor scenes in which a principal female helper provides the active focus in the context of these changes in the role of the midwife, we are led to an obvious question: might not the deceased be, in at least some cases, not the seated, passive, and suffering woman after all, but rather the active helping figure, who is to be identified as a midwife, as Clairmont has suggested for Malthake? The use of funerary monuments, even those with reliefs, by poorer residents, including metics and slaves, is well attested, and there is no reason to exclude midwives.[55] In fact, most of the labor scenes are small and not very skillfully done, suggesting that they were inexpensive and used by people of limited means.[56] Scenes of labor in which the midwife was the central figure would have been chosen as memorials for such women in order to define their professional role, just as the death in childbirth of Mnasylla's daughter was chosen for portrayal on her monument as the defining moment in her life. The laboring woman may have been a relative or friend: in one scene both she and the helper are identified by the placement of the names in the inscription. Nevertheless, iconographically she could also serve simply as an attribute to indicate the woman's profession, just as, in the case of Phanostrate, the children serve as professional attributes.[57] A parallel can be seen in the more explicit scene on the tombstone of a Roman midwife.[58]

In the case of our stelai, those of Plangon, Nikomeneia, and the stele in Alexandria would be good candidates for identification as the monuments of midwives because of the emphasis they put on the active helping figures. In any case, Malthake seems certain. On the other hand, there is no active helping figure in the scene memorializing Theophante; nevertheless, the scene fits the epigram of Mnasylla, and the honored deceased might therefore have been the mourner, who was the mother or other relative of the woman in labor. But even if we cannot identify the midwife as the deceased, her prominent presence in these scenes of crisis attests her increasing status and importance in the care of women in childbirth. Thus scenes that were created to place childbirth firmly within the grid of Greek values as subsidiary and subordinate were sometimes transformed in use into celebrations of the new recognition within the male *polis* of the achievements of women as midwives.

Control and the Metaphor of Male Pregnancy

Putting women into the grid iconographically was a way of putting them under male control. Perhaps the best way to exercise control, however, is to usurp the function itself. Hippolytus in Euripides' tragedy *Hippolytus* offers such a fantasy solution to the dilemma that women's childbearing presented to men:

> Zeus! Why did you let women settle in this world of light, a curse and a snare to men? If you wished to propagate the human race you should have arranged it without women. Men might have deposited in your temples gold or iron or a weight of copper to purchase offspring, each to the value of the price he paid, and so lived in free houses, relieved of womankind.[59]

While mortal Greek men never figured out an effective means of male surrogate parentage, they attributed it to their gods, and the metaphor of male pregnancy was an especially productive one in Greek thought. It is as old as our earliest evidence, for Homer knew Zeus as the birthing parent of Athena.[60] Hesiod's account of the tale put it squarely in the context of the maintenance of male control and authority: Zeus, warned that Metis would give birth to a god greater than himself, swallowed her and subsequently gave birth to Athena from his head.[61] Zeus also took over Semele's pregnancy after he blasted her with a thunderbolt when she unwisely asked him to appear to her in his true form; nurturing the infant in his thigh, he gave birth to Dionysus.[62] In both cases, the father of the gods maintained control by usurping the female role of childbearing.

These fantasies were facilitated by popular notions of the roles of the sexes in reproduction that reduced the female role to little more than a mere incubator. Thus in the *Oresteia* of Aeschylus in 458 Apollo proclaimed the father to be the true parent, the mother only a nursemaid, a stranger feeding a stranger (τροφός . . . ξένῳ ξένη).[63] This low valuation of the role of the female reappears in our sources in the lament of Euripides' Hippolytus just quoted,[64] and the poet expressed a similar notion in the *Orestes* when he identified the mother as the field that receives the fertile seed.[65] In fact, the metaphor of woman as plowed field was deeply embedded in Greek culture, as shown by the wording of the *engye*, in which the future husband agreed to take the woman, "for the plowing of legitimate children."[66] The idea that the woman supplied only nourishment was given philosophical sanction when Aristotle assigned to the female the role of supplying only lowly matter, whereas the male provided the vital element of form, thus determining the child's rational (and therefore human) nature.[67]

It is perhaps not surprising that a society in which wet-nursing by slave or poor free women was a practical expedient in infant care did not consider the provision of nourishment as contributing a significant formative element to the development of the child. What is most interesting in the light of this consistent devaluing of the female role in reproduction, however, is the fact that most Hippocratic writers did not adopt the "incubator" theory. Observation of inherited characteristics in offspring perhaps spoke too strongly against it, and most Hippocratic authors held that the woman contributed significantly to the nature of the child.

In the late fifth century Socrates adapted the metaphor of male pregnancy to the service of his own philosophy. In the *Theatetus* Plato portrays him assuming the role of midwife of ideas for young men:

> My art of midwifery is in general like theirs; the only difference is that my patients are men, not women, and my concern is not with the body but with the soul that is in travail of birth. . . . The many admirable truths [my patients] bring to birth have been discovered by themselves from within But the delivery is heaven's work and mine. . . . those who seek my company have the same experience as a woman with

135

child; they suffer the pains of labor and, by night and day, are full of distress far greater than a woman's.[68]

That this self-identification as a midwife of ideas was truly a Socratic expression and not a Platonic invention, and that it was not confined to a narrow circle of Socratic disciples, are shown by Aristophanes' employment of it in the *Clouds* to establish the identity of his character: one of the philosopher's disciples complains that Strepsiades, by knocking on the door of the Think-Shop, caused "Socrates" to miscarry an idea.[69]

Socrates/Plato carried the midwife metaphor into metaphysics in the *Symposium* where it plays a role in the development of a key element in Platonic philosophy.[70] It dominates the speech in which Socrates presents his philosophy but which he attributes to Diotima, a wise woman of Mantinea.[71] Plato's identification of Diotima as a woman of Mantinea involves a pun on the word *mantis*, whether invented or exploited, for in several other passages in the dialogue he alludes to her mantic powers.[72] Was she actually from Mantinea? Was she a real woman at all? Prophetesses played a large role in the religious life of Mantinea,[73] and a stele found in that city and dated to the late fifth century depicts a priestess of Apollo who, according to Möbius, could only be Diotima.[74] Whether Möbius's identification is correct is a question that is probably unanswerable; for our purposes, however, it is less important than the question why Plato chose to use a woman—and, in particular, this woman—as the spokesperson of Socratic philosophy.

Plato specifically tells us that Diotima applied her mantic powers to medical problems, staying the attack of the plague at Athens for ten years by her sacrifices. This report of assistance given to the Athenians shows that Plato intended to portray Diotima as a person of renown beyond her homeland, and as one skilled in mantic healing methods (like those *manteis* condemned by the author of *Parthenoi?*). He adds that she was skilled (σοφή) in other, unspecified ways—a "wise woman." Most important, he identifies her as Socrates' teacher, both in matters of *eros* (which in Plato's view is metaphysical rather than physical) and in the Socratic method of question and answer, the means by which Socrates the midwife delivered his companions of their ideas.

Diotima herself thus functioned as a midwife of ideas for Socrates. One could, perhaps, take the further step of suggesting that Plato saw Diotima as an (actual) midwife. Although he does not specifically attribute this skill to her, the σοφια that Socrates does attribute to her may well have encompassed this skill, as do the words "wise" and "*sage*" when applied to women in contemporary English and French. Support for this view is also offered by the strong focus on medicine in the *Symposium*: the key role played by the doctor Eryximachus throughout the dialogue;[75] the speech of Aristophanes, which amounts to a parody of theories of sex determination as presented in the gynecological treatises; and the reference to Diotima's own powers over the plague. All these help to create a medical setting appropriate for the theme of male pregnancy in Diotima's speech. One might, in fact, reasonably ask whether anyone other than a super midwife would have been able to initiate Socrates into his own role of midwife of ideas. But this really misses the point. If Diotima was a (actual) midwife, it was of little significance to Socrates; what really mattered was her ability as spiritual or metaphorical midwife, which she was able to pass on to him.

Why did Plato choose to portray a woman as Socrates' teacher in the most basic aspects of his philosophy? David Halperin's insightful reading of Plato's *Symposium* provides the most convincing clue to this question. He argues that Diotima's identity as a woman (or rather, as a "woman," as constructed by a male), rather than being a puzzle, is actually essential to the message of the dialogue:

> Diotima's . . . presence endows the pedagogic processes by which men reproduce themselves culturally—by which they communicate the secrets of their wisdom and social identity, the "mysteries" of male authority, to one another across the generations—with the prestige of female procreativity [76]

Socrates, however, does not simply appropriate female procreativity; he devalues it by endowing male pedagogic processes with the prestige that rightly belongs to it. In the *Symposium* the philosopher explains that "those whose procreancy is of the body turn to women . . . those whose procreancy is of the spirit rather than the flesh . . . conceive and bear the things of the spirit . . . wisdom and her sister virtues."[77] Those who create things of the spirit have created something lovelier and less mortal than human children, such as the poems of Homer and Hesiod, and the laws of Lycurgus and Solon. Socrates/Plato asks, "Who would not prefer such fatherhood to merely human propagation."[78] Similar value judgments attend male pregnancy and Socratic midwifery as Plato describes them in the passage in the *Theatetus* quoted earlier, where even the pain of childbirth is something in which men excel women.

Of course, even in the Athens of the fifth century, philosophy remained a rather esoteric enterprise. The important point is not that philosophers entertained the idea of male pregnancy, or even that Plato elevated it to the pinnacle of his philosophical system, but that in doing this they reflected the views of the society at large. The Socratic notion of a midwifery of ideas, in which an older man literally educates (leads ideas out of) a boy through a close homoerotic relationship was of course not an invention of Socrates/Plato, even though the refinement of a spiritual rather than a physical relationship and the specific ideas that Socrates' companions gave birth to surely were. Greek pederasty had a long and respected history. Traditionally it played a central role in the introduction of young males into the value system of the dominant male culture. Whether it arose from military practices, as a means of inculcating courage in warriors, or from initiatory practices,[79] by the classical period pederasty had developed into an institution that acculturated young upper-class males to their social roles. In essence, it was the means by which the society's dominant (i.e., male) values were passed on from one generation to the next.[80]

Anthropologists have found that the practice of male homosexual initiation is often associated with male mimicry of female reproductive processes; the pattern has been studied extensively in a number of cultures.[81] In all of these societies the status of women is low, marriages are arranged, the sexes are segregated, and gender differences are polarized, often to the point of overt hostility.[82] Pederasty is seen as a necessary means of creating masculinity, often in a very direct and physical way through the ingestion of semen.[83] It is believed that boys, deprived of nurturing homosexual relationships with older males and allowed continuing association with the weakening effects of females, will fail to grow and develop into strong men. Gilbert Herdt provides an especially helpful account for comparative purposes in his study of the Samia.[84] Among the Samia, "drinking semen" is believed to be essential in the creation of a man from a boy, and the practice regularly extends beyond the purely ritual moment to become a "way of life" followed until the young male himself becomes a father.[85] As Halperin has so impressively pointed out to classicists, such rites graphically appropriate to males the female role of parturition: "after boys have been born, physically, and reared by women, they must be born a second time, culturally, and introduced into the symbolic order of 'masculinity' by men."[86]

Although Greek pederastic homosexuality in the classical period did not develop into elaborate and explicit initiation rites like those practiced in New Guinea, it nonetheless became formalized in terms appropriate to Greek interests and culture. As Pausanias says in the *Symposium*, some Greek cities (he notes especially those in Elis and Boeotia) had straightforward customs that simply allowed the man to have his way with a boy, but in Athens a complex courting ritual defined an etiquette of behavior.[87] As we saw, a more sophisticated version of this Athenian ritual appeared in the philosophical adaptation, "Platonic love." But whatever its form, Greek homosexuality played a similar role in inculcating male cultural values in the boy: it assured that Greek boys would be "born again" as "real men."[88]

By abrogating "true" or "higher" birthing to themselves, men devalued female birthing: women were considered capable only of giving birth to other females and to incomplete males whose masculinization men must complete through a rebirthing process. Thus the institution of male homosexuality impinged upon the status of Greek women especially in their primary role as childbearers. In the area of high culture, this devaluation was ratified by the appropriation of the *eros* of heterosexual reproductivity to the homosexual *eros* that led men to knowledge of the Platonic Good-in-Itself.

To return to the question at issue: did Greek men consider the death of women in childbirth as heroic and the equivalent of the death of men in battle? Neither the literary evidence nor the evidence of the funerary monuments supports this conclusion, and the vitality of the metaphor of male pregnancy and birthing in Greek culture confirms this negative finding. For the Greeks, giving birth to actual infants, very likely ephemeral creatures, although indeed something that only women could do, did not compare in importance with giving birth to "real men" (or to poems, laws, or philosophical truths, all accomplishments of men). How could dying as a result of such a relatively unimportant production be anything more than pitiable?

Eight

Women and Children: Issues of Control

Male concern with control of female reproductivity has appeared again and again in the preceding chapters.[1] Control even took precedence over the apparent goal of this reproductivity—the production of heirs for the *oikos*—as doctors advocated practices, such as early marriage and frequent pregnancies, that were known to be detrimental to successful childbearing. This focus on control of the female is demonstrated in a particularly striking way by the comparative lack of professional interest in the newborn and the young child that we see in the Hippocratic Corpus.[2] We see gynecology in the making, but not a Hippocratic pediatrics.

Doctors did sometimes treat children, and they recognized them as a distinct category of patient, even subdividing childhood into a number of stages, such as infancy, teething, those older than teething, and those approaching puberty, each with its own typical illnesses.[3] The treatises discuss particular problems that occur in children, such as sore throats, bladder stones, and convulsions (including epilepsy). Moreover, in the treatise *Epidemics* doctors report the reactions of children in a number of general outbreaks of illness, recording their observations in the constitutions.[4] Nevertheless, in the Hippocratic treatises women, and especially their reproductive problems, are accorded far more attention than infants and children, even though mortality was high in both groups. Eleven books of the Corpus are devoted to gynecology and prenatal development, and these occupy a total of 360 Littré pages, with additional material scattered in other treatises. In contrast, pediatric texts occupy only a few pages: only the brief treatise *Dentition* (2 Littré pages) is devoted to problems of infants. *Aphorisms* III 24–28, which adds approximately 2 more pages, deals briefly with illnesses characteristic of the different stages of childhood; a few other scattered references to children's illnesses are balanced, if not outweighed, by similar scattered passages about women's reproductive problems.

It is thus indisputable that Hippocratic doctors wrote far less about the care and treatment of children than about women's reproductive lives. A similar bias exists in the patients whose cases they reported. Of the patients in the *Epidemics*, 131, or 32 percent, are women, and approximately one-third of these patients (40) had problems associated in some way with pregnancy and childbirth. In contrast, the newborn is referred to only briefly, if at all. The condition of the infant is seldom reported: one infant (the first in a superfetation) is noted as live-born, one as dead, and two as grossly malformed. In most cases, only the sex is noted and, in 9 of the 40 pregnancy-related cases, we are not told anything at all about the infant or aborted fetus. No information is given about the postpartum condition of any normal, live-born infant. No doctor follows the fate of the newborn after birth, either in connection with its mother's case or independently. In general (nonchildbirth) cases, one newborn is mentioned in a discussion of swelling in wounds as having developed a swelling of the ear on the third day after birth;[5] only two other patients can be definitively identified as infants, one a two-month old and the other a four-month old, both in the late Book VII.[6] These infants are called *paidia*; the more specific term for an infant, *brephos*, appears only three times in the treatises, in *De alimento, Diseases of Women* I (in one manuscript only, and not in Littré), and the apocryphal *Epistles*.[7]

It is not possible to determine how many older children were treated by doctors since few patients can be unequivocally identified as children.[8] For example, the Greek word *pais*, which we translate as "child," was also used for slaves (of any age), just as black slaves in our own culture were regularly called "boy," despite their age.[9] In one case of a *pais* in the *Epidemics*, the age given, that of an eleven-year-old horse groom, puts the patient into the category of child as well as slave.[10] Four other cases of *paides* mention work, and thus must refer to slaves, although we cannot tell if these were also children.[11] Thirteen other patients labeled *pais* may, or may not, have been children.

Of the derivatives of the term *pais*, the feminine diminutive *paidiske* is almost always used to refer to a female slave.[12] In the *Epidemics* in one case the age given for a *paidiske* (twelve years old) identifies her as a child,[13] but in another case the *paidiske* is herself a mother (of a *meirakion*, probably himself past puberty).[14] Thus the term cannot reliably be used to identify children serving as slaves. However, we are probably on somewhat surer ground with the diminutive *paidion*, which is used in the *Epidemics* for the three cases whose infant status is assured by an age specification.[15] The word *paidion* appears seven times without an age specification,[16] but since it is the term most often used to refer to children in general passages, as well as to the newborn,[17] and even to the child within the womb, it seems reasonable to classify those identified by the term *paidion* as children, either slave or free.

The use of the genitive case to identify an individual's *kyrios* can, but need not, indicate childhood, even when used to identify a son or daughter. The possessive genitive was also regularly employed to denote ownership of a slave and to refer to wives. In the *Epidemics*, the expression is used to identify twenty-two patients, who may or may not have been children and/or slaves. The specific terms "son" (υἱός) and "daughter" (θυγάτηρ) appear infrequently; there is only one occurrence of "son" (v 40), which gives no information about age; "daughter" is applied to patients seven times; of these, two were themselves pregnant and hence not children,[18] one died as a result of impeded menarche, and two others were designated as *parthenoi*.[19]

The term *parthenos* is in four cases associated with menarche, and hence indicates a child, albeit one who passed over the boundary of childhood while under the doctor's care.[20] Three other patients are also called *parthenos*, but since one is noted to be twenty years old,[21] we cannot safely accept the other two as children. The term *kore*, which is also used for girls on the border of puberty, is similarly ambiguous since it is sometimes applied to married women. Nevertheless, since the connotation of bride is strong, and Greek girls were married at puberty, we might include the two cases of *korai* as children.[22]

An informal count based on these considerations of terminology yields a total of 21 patients who are reasonably certain to have been children by a strict definition, in comparison with the 40 patients with pregnancy-related problems, and the total of 131 female patients. If we count all possible cases of children, including *paides* and those identified with their *kyrios* by the genitive case, we reach a maximum total of 53, but some of these are slaves and wives, and the true count of children is surely less. On any count, however, the disparity is great between female patients and patients who are children, especially infants and young children.

Another way of estimating the employment of doctors for the treatment of children's illnesses is to consider the infrequency with which diseases such as measles, chicken pox, diphtheria, and scarlet fever are mentioned as typical childhood illnesses. Where these diseases are identifiable, they usually appear as illnesses of adults. Thus Potter has identified the description in *Diseases* III 7 as chicken pox complicated with a bronchopneumonia; the generic patient is described as an adult.[23] Mumps appeared as a local epidemic on the island of Thasos in 410, affecting mostly adolescent males, a fact that Grmek takes as evidence that mumps was not a new disease there.[24] Diphtheria does appear in the context of childhood illnesses in *Dentition* 24 and 31,[25] and in adults in *Diseases* II 26 and III 10, and the appendix to *Regimen in Acute Diseases* 10.[26] Grmek calls whooping cough an "inapparent disease" because it usually killed infants and young children and was thus "confused with other, undifferentiated causes of infant mortality."[27] Measles and rubella have perhaps similarly left no trace in the Corpus, although we cannot be sure that they affected Mediterranean populations in the classical period.[28]

The lack of reference in the Hippocratic treatises to these diseases as typical childhood illnesses thus rests in most cases not on their absence, and probably not on their absence in children. An explanation is suggested by modern Greek village attitudes to these illnesses in the 1960s, when Blum and Blum reported that out of a total of thirty-six children ten years of age or younger in three communities, only three children were said to have had measles, mumps, chicken pox, or whooping cough. The explanation was not the absence of these illnesses, but the fact that the villagers considered them as "compulsory diseases" of childhood and made no effort to take temperatures, put the children to bed, or keep them home from school, let alone consult a doctor.[29] Grmek's explanation of whooping cough as an "inapparent disease" of infancy and early childhood suggests that a similar attitude toward other childhood illnesses prevailed in antiquity.

What *did* move heads of households to call in a doctor for a child? In the *Epidemics* accidents and trauma account for eight cases, including a *paidion* gored by a boar (v 39), a *pais* struck on the head with an ostrakon by another *pais* (iv 11), a *pais*/horse groom kicked by a horse (v 16), a *kore* who fell from a cliff (v 55), two *paides* also injured in falls (iv 4, v 65), a *kore* who ate a poisonous mushroom (vii 102), and a twelve-year-old *paidiske* whom someone struck on the head with a door (v 28). The four-month-old *paidion* of Hegesipolis suffered a fatal inflammation of the umbilicus, and the doctor notes that the *paidion* of Hegetorides suffered similarly (vii 52). The two-month-old *paidion* of Timonax had a rash, with spasms and epileptic seizures, which proved fatal (vii 106). Five *paides* had illnesses associated with work or overwork. Five patients were females in the dangerous liminal stage of premenarche, a time at which they were susceptible to the illness of maidens.

These cases suggest that doctors were more often involved in the care of older, pubescent children than of infants, and that the problems they were called upon to treat were often literally traumatic.

145

Frequently the patients were slaves, valuable property filling a vital role as workers in the adult world. Moreover, a comparatively large number were menarchal girls, who by that very status were already of concern to fathers for their reproductive future. The focus of the Hippocratic doctor is clearly on those with, or approaching, adult status: working children and *parthenoi*.

The disparity between texts devoted to women's reproductive lives and those devoted to the care of infants and young children, and the disparity between the reports of treatment by doctors of parturient women and of their offspring are revealing in a culture in which a wife's primary role was defined as childbearing. Since newborns cannot survive without care, it must have been the case that the fathers (who made such decisions) were content to leave them to the traditional care of women. In fact, *Diseases* IV specifically refers to such care.[30] It is probable that the illnesses of older children were also treated by women within the household, as suggested by the paucity of reports by doctors of typical childhood diseases.[31] Moreover, the frequent reporting of the fate of children as a class of patients in general outbreaks of illness suggests that under such conditions the usual care givers in childhood illnesses, the mother and other women of the household, were themselves incapacitated. The social network of care of children by women within the home was disrupted, making the doctor's involvement more likely.

In contrast, it is clear that husbands were not content to leave pregnant women to the traditional care of women and midwives. Is this because they had less emotional investment in probably short-lived children than in wives?[32] That people who lived in preindustrial societies with high infant mortality did not love their children in the same way as do people in our own society is an idea that has, I believe, been effectively put to rest.[33] A more convincing explanation for the disparity in Hippocratic medical care for women and for children in classical Greece is to be found rather in the concern of Greek men for the legitimacy of their heirs. As we saw in chapter 3, male doctors treating or supervising the treatment of pregnant women were in a position to counter women's imagined or real propensity to resort to abortion or the introduction of supposititious children. In contrast, men apparently felt no need to increase control over their prepubescent children. This does not imply that they did not care about them, but that they felt comfortably in charge of them, as they did not in the case of their wives. Doctors thus had less incentive to replace the traditional care of children with a professional pediatrics.

The Cultural Context of Control

What lay behind this anxiety on the part of Greek men to control female reproductivity? In general, concern with control and self-control was a pervasive characteristic of the Greek system of moral values, and it was gender specific. Thus both Plato and Aristotle attribute moral excellence to the control of reason over the passions, view women as less able to exercise such control, and affirm the need for men to exercise it for them.[34] The male fear of letting a woman assume control found clear expression in the legal grounds for invalidating a will: a will could be declared invalid if it could be shown that the testator was insane—or under the influence of a woman.[35] In the medical sphere, Helen King has suggested that it was concern with preventing women from exercising control over men that influenced the Hippocratic doctors to provide much of the routine care for male patients that our culture assigns to (traditionally female) nurses.[36] We saw the potential dangers in female nursing in the case of Phrastor who, helpless in his illness, accepted the care offered by his former wife and her mother, women whose primary aim was to insinuate an illegal heir into his *oikos*.[37]

Belief in lack of female self-control underlay another deeply embedded characteristic of Greek culture, its honor/shame orientation.[38] A woman was viewed as a constant threat to the honor of the *oikos* through her inability to control her rampant sexuality. She could bring shame and dishonor by even the slightest hint of impropriety, even by innocently putting herself in the way of temptation. Hence the male members of the *oikos* felt obliged to watch her constantly, and this watching could easily turn into an obsession.

But these general Greek cultural values—some found consistently in cultures throughout the Mediterranean area, and in vari-

ous historical periods, wherever and whenever face-to-face societies occur[39]—do not explain why this anxiety and its restrictive
effects upon women varied both regionally and over time, and, in
particular, why in the late fifth century, at least in Athens, the situation of women seems to have reached its lowest point.[40] We need to
ask why the Greek stress on rational control and an honor/shame
culture proved to be especially detrimental to women's interests at
this particular time and place.

In looking for factors that may have worked to increase male
insecurity during the Hippocratic period, we might first postulate
the social and political instability resulting from the Peloponnesian
War and the years of warfare and shifting alliances that followed.
Evidence that gender roles came to be seen as problematic in the
stressful conditions of extended war and economic difficulty appears in both Attic tragedy and comedy, most clearly in such plays
as Aristophanes' *Lysistrata* and *Ecclesiazusae*, and in Plato's utopian
Republic. In fact, Plato's schemes so closely resemble the situation
in Aristophanes' *Ecclesiazusae* that we can assume the existence of
widespread debate and discussion about women's roles in Athens
at the turn of the century.[41]

One element in the troubled scene in postwar Athens that may
be particularly relevant to men's concern with control over their
women is the reimposition of Pericles' Citizenship Law in 403/402.
This law, which was originally passed in 451/450, decreed that
only those born of a citizen father and a citizen mother were eligi-
ble for citizenship.[42] When it was reenacted in 403/402, the law
was augmented by regulations prohibiting the marriage of citizens
with noncitizen women.[43] The evidence of Aristotle attests that
such restrictive laws were by no means unique to Athens but were
adopted by many *poleis* as they grew and developed:

> When a state becomes well off for numbers it gradually divests itself
> first of the sons of a slave father or mother, then of those whose mothers
> only were citizens, and finally only allows citizenship to the children of
> citizens on both sides.[44]

Complicating the picture as *poleis* grew in size and complexity
was a blurring of status boundaries. It became impossible to know

everyone. In Athens and other *poleis* with commercial interests, metics (resident aliens) often conducted profitable businesses and were well integrated into the community. By the late fifth century some metic families had lived in Athens for generations, as had that of the orator Lysias. Skilled metics, slaves, and free citizens worked side by side for the same wages.[45] As the author of an oligarchic pamphlet complained, slaves were indistinguishable from citizens by their dress and behavior.[46] Such a situation provided many opportunities for noncitizens to slip unnoticed into the citizenship rolls, and it must have become particularly acute in the late fifth century, when the crises of war caused a breakdown in earlier legal and customary restrictions on the citizenship.

In Athens, attacks on prominent figures via the citizen status of their mothers were frequent in Old Comedy during the final years of the Peloponnesian War (Euripides' mother is perhaps the best-known example), at a time when the Periclean law was apparently widely disregarded. Such attacks—and the reenactment of the law itself—provide evidence for the prevalence of disputes over citizen status. It is clear, however, that the reenactment of the law did not solve the problem. In 346 many were disenfranchised as a result of a scrutiny of deme membership,[47] and individual attacks on men based on the status of female family members appear frequently in the speeches of the orators.[48] When the restrictions on citizen status reached their most stringent point, female status thus immediately and directly affected the continuity of the male line.[49]

The threat posed by such attacks on status is vividly illustrated in the Demosthenic speech *Against Neaera*. In this speech, the speakers frankly admit that they are using an attack against the behavior and reputation of Neaera in order to get revenge against her live-in mate Stephanus.[50] The charge was that Stephanus lived with Neaera as his wife contrary to the law since she was a noncitizen (his defense was apparently that he kept her only as a concubine). The speaker also relates in detail earlier attacks against Stephanus on the grounds that he had twice given Neaera's daughter Phano in marriage fraudulently, representing her as his own child by an earlier, Athenian, wife. In the first of these cases, that involving the marriage of Phano to Phrastor, the charge had been brought by

Phrastor when Stephanus sought the return of Phano's dowry after Phrastor divorced her. The men reached a settlement out of court and Phrastor, influenced by the care Phano and Neaera gave him during an illness, subsequently even adopted the son whom Phano had born after the divorce. (When he tried to introduce the boy to his phratry as his son, however, he was rejected.) Phano was next married to a man, Theogenes, who held the office of archon basileus; however, when the Areopagus Council questioned her status and threatened Theogenes with a fine, he repudiated her.

The penalties involved in the charges against Neaera and Stephanus were severe: the penalty for a noncitizen who lived as the wife of an Athenian citizen was to be sold as a slave, while the man was fined one thousand drachmae;[51] the penalty for marrying off an alien woman fraudulently represented as an Athenian, an offense allegedly committed twice by Stephanus, was loss of citizen rights and confiscation of all one's property, one-third of which would go to the successful prosecutor.[52] The fact that Stephanus had twice been suspected of the latter offense but never actually prosecuted suggests that the charges were more a matter of rumor and reputation than of fact. And similarly much of the evidence brought forward in the present case involved slurs on Neaera's behavior and reputation meant to cast doubt on her status; for example, her presence at dinner parties with men was repeatedly put forward as evidence that she was a prostitute.[53]

The speech against Neaera makes it clear that any suggestion of impropriety on the part of a man's womenfolk could provide his enemies with a foothold for an attack in the courts that could have severe consequences for him and his entire *oikos*. The speech also demonstrates that the security of an *oikos* rested not only on the formal rules of citizen status but also on the actions and reputation of its women *as these might be interpreted* by a man's deme and phratry members, by the members of a jury, or even by the Areopagus Council. For a man to put the citizen status of his heirs beyond question, and to insure himself against disastrous penalties, meant maintaining the closest control over the reputation of the mother of those children—and also over other women in his household (if Phano were truly the daughter of Stephanus, she paid dearly for the reputation of Neaera). The increasingly restrictive definition of citizenship status that went with the development of the *polis* thus brought with it suspicions that haunted male lives and fed men's obsession with the control of their womenfolk.[54]

It was not, however, simply restrictive definitions of citizen status like those imposed by the Periclean Citizenship Law that resulted in such detrimental effects on women, as the case of Sparta shows. In Sparta citizenship was closely restricted, being available only to men who possessed an official allotment of land. How allotments were allocated is still a matter of dispute;[55] both parents must have been of citizen status, but, given the practice of wife-sharing, marriage between them could not have been a factor. This does not mean that families did not exist or were not important in the transmission of property in Sparta: ancient sources attest to significant variations in wealth among the citizens.[56] Nevertheless, citizenship rights were tied to the allotment, not to the possession of private land or wealth (except for the minumum requirement that a man be able to make his mess contribution), and this made the principle of communal identity far more significant than individual (patriarchal) family identity. In addition, citizenship status was not ambiguous. It was clearly marked out and enforced by living patterns: few citizen women would have had contact with helots, who lived on the land, or *perioikoi*, who lived in separate villages. Within this system, which offered few occasions for status disputes, women were granted considerable freedom and late marriage was acceptable. In contrast, most other *poleis* operated on a single system that linked the transmission of the private *oikos* and its wealth with the transmission of citizen status. In such patriarchally structured systems, control of women was essential. Plato confirms the connection between such patriarchal systems and the suppression of women when he ties an increased public role for women with the holding of women and children in common: he was simply taking the Spartan principle to its logical conclusion.

Conclusion: Women and the Polis

The contradictions that we have seen in the Greek system of handling childbirth were in large part created by one recurring motif, that of male concern to control the reproductivity of women. We have seen that this concern played a key role in fostering the practice of early female marriage and motherhood, a practice that endangered the lives and health of both mothers and infants. It was also a central factor in the replacement of traditional female care of women's reproductive health by that of the Hippocratic doctor, as well as in the creation of gynecological texts, developments that were ambivalent as far as women's health and the success of their reproductive activities were concerned.

Hippocratic medical care probably did little to improve women's chances of surviving the hazards of childbirth, which, as we have seen, presented serious risks to their health and life. Puerperal infections, malaria, and tuberculosis can all be traced in the Hippocratic literature as significant threats to parturient women, and they seem unlikely to have been alleviated by a shift from traditional to Hippocratic care. Such a shift could, in fact, have had detrimental effects on women's welfare as patients, for the replacement of female care givers by males added new stresses to the complications of childbirth for women accustomed to a sheltered existence. Moreover, the womb-centered approach that increasingly dominated the doctors' diagnosis and treatment of women encouraged frequent childbearing and must in many cases have prevented more accurate and helpful diagnosis and treatment. In fact, the clearest benefit for women resulting from the creation of the Hippocratic medical specialty of gynecology seems to have been to them as practitioners, rather than as patients: those women (midwives) who assisted doctors in the care of other women attained a degree of recognition in the larger community that is attested by the citing of midwifery as an occupational identity in epitaphs.

The male political community not only supported the extension of male care to women by employing Hippocratic doctors, but it also moved in the direction of the appropriation of the symbolic systems of female reproductivity by introducing a civic element into those rituals that served to acculturate girls and women to their childbearing role.[57] Thus "playing the bear" for Artemis was explained as a substitute sacrifice carried out for the salvation of the *polis*, and ancient sources report that participation in the festival was a prerequisite for marriage enforced by civic statute. A similar intrusion of civic (i.e., male) values into the symbolic systems of women's reproductive lives can be seen in the principal acculturating ritual for married women, the Thesmophoria. Although men were rigorously excluded from the festival itself, the ancient ceremonies of fertility had come to be structured in the political form of the male *polis*. Moreover, by its rehearsal of the trauma of the separation of mother and daughter, and by the paradigm of acceptance that it offered in the divine pair, Demeter and Persephone, the festival sent Greek women an annual message of compliance in the male-mandated early marriage of their daughters. Male control of female reproductivity was thus woven inextricably into the institutions of the *polis* itself.

After Gomme's optimistic assessment of women's "position" in classical Greece,[58] based upon the evidence of women's roles in tragedy, was countered by the use of a wider range of evidence, women's position in Greece for a time was judged much more pessimistically. Scholars emphasized women's isolation within the home and their lack of adult rights and powers to act on their own behalf or to share in the decisions of the *polis*. Recently, however, the pendulum has begun to swing back to a more optimistic view. Some scholars point out occasions when women did in fact leave their homes, and stress the informal power possible for them through the use of persuasion and household disruption. The subtlety of such analyses that discover new types of power and new ways in which women were able to connect with the outside community often make their conclusions seem attractive, and the debate continues. But while we may not be able to agree on how much isolation a system of separate spheres imposed upon women, or upon the extent and significance of the informal "power" they were able to exercise within such a system, the study of childbirth provides us with another, and less subjective, criterion by which we can judge the "position" of women. It has become clear in this study that many *poleis* fostered patriarchal methods of control over women's reproductivity that prejudiced their success in the primary role that the culture assigned to them, that of childbearing. The system was thus contradictory in terms of its own expressed aims. This self-contradiction provides a new and compelling argument for the conclusion that, at least in the extreme patriarchal form that it took in Athens and many other *poleis*, the Greek *polis* was detrimental to the interests of both women and *polis*.

PLATES

Pl. 1. Votive stele; New York, The Metropolitan Museum of Art, Fletcher Fund, 1924; MMA 24.97.92. All rights reserved, The Metropolitan Museum of Art

Pl. 2 Lekythos of Theophante; Athens, National Archaeological Museum; NM 1055.

Pl. 3. Lekythos of Pheidestrate and Mnesagora, Athens, National Archaeological Museum; NM 1077.

Pl. 4 Lekythos of Killaron; Paris,
Musée du Louvre, MND 726

Pl. 5. Stele; Cambridge, Mass., Courtesy of The Arthur M. Sackler Museum, Harvard University Art Museums, gift of Edward W. Forbes, in trust to the university; Sackler 1905.8.

Pl 6 Stele of Plangon and Tolmides, Athens, National Archaeological Museum; NM
749

Pl. 7. Stele of Nιkomeneia, Athens, Kerameικos Museum; P290.

Pl 8 Lekythos, Copenhagen, Ny Carlsberg Glyptotek, 226a

Plates

Pl. 9 Stele of Malthake; Athens, Piraeus Museum; Piraeus Museum 21

Pl. 10. Stele; Alexandria, Alexandria Museum

Pl. 11. Stele, Rhodes, Rhodes Archaeological Museum; 1470-3

Pl. 12 Stele of Phanostrate, Athens, National Archaeological Museum, NM 993.

Appendix A

Cases in the *Epidemics*

Book	Total Cases	Female Cases	Pregnancy-related cases	% Female	% Pregnancy-related
I	38	11	5	29[1]	13
III	28	12	5	43	18
II	29	16	11	55	38
IV	103	37	9	35 7	8.7
VI	19	6	1	32	5
V	105	27	6	25.7	5.7
VII[2]	87	22	3	25	3.4

1 These numbers include the patients used as examples in the third constitution, for the case histories alone, the numbers would be 28 percent gynecological cases (birth and abortion) and 36 percent female patients, agreeing substantially with Lloyd 1983, 67, n. 33 (27.3 and 35 7 percent—he seems to have counted each mention of a patient in the constitution, but some are duplicates). Corvisier (1985) counted considerably fewer cases: 315 in total, 76 women.

2. Excluding duplicates that also appear in V.

Appendix B

Cases Involving Pregnancy in the *Epidemics*

Note: The cases are presented in chronological order: Books I, III, II, IV, VI, V, VII. The translations of cases from I and III are reprinted by permission of the publishers and the Loeb Classical Library from W. H. S. Jones, *Hippocrates* Vol. 2, Cambridge, Mass.: Harvard University Press, 1962; the translations of the other cases are my own.

Book I XVI (2.646.9–13 Li.)

Though many women fell ill, they were fewer than the men and less frequently died. But the great majority had difficult childbirth, and after giving birth they would fall ill, and these especially died, as did the daughter of Telebulus on the sixth day after delivery.

Book I case 4 (2.684.10–688.8 Li.)

In Thasos the wife of Philinus gave birth to a daughter. The lochial discharge was normal, and the mother was doing well when on the fourteenth day after delivery she was seized with fever attended with rigor. At first she suffered in the stomach and the right hypochondrium. Pains in the genital organs. The discharge ceased. By a pessary these troubles were eased, but pains persisted in the head, neck and loins No sleep; extremities cold; thirst; bowels burnt; scanty stools; urine thin, and at first colourless.

Sixth day. Much delirium at night, followed by recovery of reason.

Seventh day. Thirst; stools scanty, bilious, highly coloured.

Eighth day. Rigor; acute fever; many painful convulsions; much delirium. The application of a suppository made her keep going to stool, and there were copious motions with a bilious flux. No sleep.

Ninth day. Convulsions.

Tenth day. Lucid intervals.

Eleventh day. Slept; complete recovery of her memory, followed quickly by renewed delirium.

A copious passing of urine with convulsions—her attendants seldom reminding her—which was white and thick, like urine with a sediment and then shaken; it stood for a long time without forming a sediment; colour and consistency like that of the urine of cattle. Such was the nature of the urine that I myself saw.

About the fourteenth day there were twitchings over all the body; much wandering, with lucid intervals followed quickly by renewed delirium. About the seventeenth day she became speechless.

Twentieth day. Death.

Book 1 case 5 (2.694.3–698.5 Li.)

The wife of Epicrates, who lay sick near the founder, when near her delivery was seized with severe rigor without, it was said, becoming warm, and the same symptoms occurred on the following day. On the third day she gave birth to a daughter, and the delivery was in every respect normal. On the second day after the delivery she was seized with acute fever, pain at the stomach and in the genitals. A pessary relieved these symptoms, but there was pain in the head, neck and loins. No sleep. From the bowels passed scanty stools, bilious, thin and unmixed.

Urine thin and blackish. Delirium on the night of the sixth day from the day the fever began.

Seventh day. All symptoms exacerbated; sleeplessness; delirium; thirst; bilious, highly-coloured stools.

Eighth day. Rigor; more sleep.

Ninth day. The same symptoms.

Tenth day. Severe pains in the legs; pain again at the stomach; heaviness in the head; no delirious; more sleep; constipation.

Eleventh day Urine of better colour, with a thick deposit; was easier.

Fourteenth day. Rigor; acute fever.

Fifteenth day. Vomited fairly frequently bilious, yellow vomit; sweated without fever; at night, however, acute fever; urine thick, with a white sediment.

Sixteenth day. Exacerbation; an uncomfortable night; no sleep; delirium.

Eighteenth day. Thirst; tongue parched; no sleep; much delirium; pain in the legs.

About the twentieth day. Slight rigors in the early morning; coma; quiet sleep; scanty, bilious, black vomits; deafness at night.

About the twenty-first day. Heaviness all over the left side, with pain; slight coughing; urine thick, turbid, reddish, no sediment on standing. In other respects easier, no fever. From the beginning she had pain in the throat; redness; uvula drawn back; throughout there persisted an acrid flux, smarting, and salt.

About the twenty-seventh day. No fever; sediment in urine; some pain in the side.

About the thirty-first day. Attacked by fever; bowels disordered and bilious.

Fortieth day. Scanty, bilious vomits.

Eightieth day. Complete crisis with cessation of fever

Book 1 case 11 (2.708.6–710.11 Li.)

The wife of Dromeades, after giving birth to a daughter, when everything had gone normally, on the second day was seized with rigor; acute fever. On the first day she began to feel pain in the region of the hypochondrium; nausea; shivering; restless; and on the following days did not sleep. Respiration rare, large, interrupted at once as by an inspiration.

Second day from rigor. Healthy action of the bowels. Urine thick, white, turbid, like urine which has settled, stood a long time, and then been stirred up. It did not settle. No sleep at night.

Third day. At about mid-day rigor; acute fever; urine similar; pain in the hypochondrium; nausea; an uncomfortable night without sleep; a cold sweat all over the body, but the patient quickly recovered heat.

Fourth day. Slight relief of the pains about the hypochondrium; painful heaviness of the head; somewhat comatose; slight epistaxis; tongue dry; thirst; scanty urine, thin and oily; snatches of sleep.

Fifth day. Thirst; nausea; urine similar; no movement of the bowels; about mid-day much delirium, followed quickly by lucid intervals; rose, but grew somewhat comatose; slight chilliness; slept at night; was delirious.

Sixth day. In the morning had a rigor; quickly recovered heat; sweated all over; extremities cold; was delirious; respiration large and rare. After a while convulsions began from the head, quickly followed by death.

Book I case 13 (2.742.12–746.3 Li.)

A woman lying sick by the shore, who was three months gone with child, was seized with fever, and immediately began to feel pains in the loins.

Third day. Pain in the neck and in the head, and in the region of the right collar-bone. Quickly she lost her power of speech, the right arm was paralyzed, with a convulsion, after the manner of a stroke; completely delirious. An uncomfortable night, without sleep; bowels disordered with bilious, unmixed, scanty stools.

Fourth day. Her speech was recovered, but was indistinct;

convulsions; pains of the same parts remained; painful swelling in the hypochondrium; no sleep; utter delirium; bowels disordered; urine thin, and not of good colour.

Fifth day. Acute fever; pain in the hypochondrium; utter delirium; bilious stools. At night sweated; was without fever.

Sixth day. Rational; general relief, but pain remained about the left collar-bone; thirst; urine thin; no sleep.

Seventh day. Trembling; some coma; slight delirium; pains in the region of the collar-bone and left upper arm remained; other symptoms relieved; quite rational. For three days there was an intermission of fever.

Eleventh day. Relapse; rigor; attack of fever. But about the fourteenth day the patient vomited bilious, yellow matter fairly frequently; sweated; a crisis took off the fever.

Book III case 10 (first series) (3.60.1–8 Li.)

A woman who was one of the house of Pantimides after a miscarriage was seized with fever on the first day. Tongue dry; thirst; nausea; sleeplessness. Bowels disordered, with thin, copious and crude stools.

Second day. Rigor; acute fever; copious stools; no sleep.

Third day. The pains greater.

Fourth day. Delirium.

Seventh day. Death.

The bowels were throughout loose, with copious, thin, crude stools. Urine scanty and thin.

Book III case 11 (first series) (3.60.9–62.10 Li.)

Another woman, after a miscarriage about the fifth month, the wife of Hicetas, was seized with fever. At the beginning she had alternations of coma and sleeplessness; pain in the loins; heaviness in the head.

Second day. Bowels disordered with scanty, thin stools, which at first were uncompounded.

Third day. Stools more copious and worse; no sleep at night.

Fourth day. Delirium; fears; depression. Squinting of the right eye; slight cold sweat about the head; extremities cold.

Fifth day. General exacerbation; much wandering, with rapid recovery of reason; no thirst; no sleep; stools copious and unfavourable throughout; urine scanty, thin and blackish; extremities cold and rather livid.

Sixth day. Same symptoms.

Seventh day. Death.

Book III case 12 (first series) (3.62.11–66.11 Li.)

A woman who lay sick by the Liars' Market, after giving birth in a first and painful delivery to a male child, was seized with fever. From the very first there was thirst, nausea, slight pain at the stomach, dry tongue, bowels disordered with thin and scanty discharges, no sleep.

Second day. Slight rigor; acute fever; slight, cold sweating around the head.

Third day. In pain; crude, thin, copious discharges from the bowels.

Fourth day. Rigor; general exacerbation; sleepless.

Fifth day. In pain.

Sixth day. The same symptoms; copious, fluid discharges from the bowels.

Seventh day. Rigor; acute fever; thirst; much tossing; towards evening cold sweat all over, chill; extremities cold, and would not be warmed. At night she again had a rigor; the extremities would not be warmed; no sleep; slight delirium, but quickly was rational again.

Eighth day. About mid-day recovered her heat; thirst; coma; nausea; vomited bilious, scanty, yellowish matters. An uncomfortable night; no sleep; unconsciously passed a copious discharge of urine.

Ninth day. General abatement of the symptoms; coma. Towards evening slight rigor; vomited scanty, bilious matters.

Tenth day. Rigor; exacerbation of the fever; no sleep whatsoever. In the early morning a copious discharge of urine without sediment; extremities were warmed.

Eleventh day. Vomited bilious matters, of the colour of verdigris. A rigor shortly afterwards, and the extremities became cold again; in the evening sweat, rigor and copious vomiting; a painful night.

Twelfth day. Vomited copious, black, fetid matters; much hic-coughing; painful thirst.

Thirteenth day. Vomited black, fetid, copious matters; rigor. About mid-day lost her speech.

Fourteenth day. Epistaxis; death.

The bowels of this patient were throughout loose, and there were shivering fits. Age about seventeen.

Book III case 2 (second series) (3.108.5–112.12 Li.)

In Thasos the woman who lay sick by the Cold Water, on the third day after giving birth to a daughter without lochial dis-charge, was seized with acute fever accompanied by shivering. For a long time before her delivery she had suffered from fever, being confined to bed and averse to food. After the rigor that took place, the fevers were continuous, acute, and attended with shivering.

Eighth and following days. Much delirium, quickly followed by recovery of reason; bowels disturbed with copious, thin, wa-tery and bilious stools; no thirst.

Eleventh day. Was rational, but comatose. Urine copious, thin and black; no sleep.

Twentieth day. Slight chills, but heat quickly recovered; slight wandering; no sleep; bowels the same; urine watery and co-pious.

Twenty-seventh day. No fever; bowels constipated; not long afterwards severe pain in the right hip for a long time. Fevers again attended; urine watery.

Fortieth day. Pain in the hip relieved; continuous coughing, with watery, copious sputa; bowels constipated; aversion to food; urine the same. The fevers, without entirely intermitting, were exacerbated irregularly, sometimes increasing and some-times not doing so.

Sixtieth day. The coughing ceased without any critical sign;

there was no coction of the sputa, nor any of the usual abscession; jaw on the right side convulsed; comatose; wandering, but reason quickly recovered; desperately averse to food; jaw relaxed; passed small, bilious stools; fever grew more acute, with shivering. On the succeeding days she lost power of speech, but would afterwards converse.

Eightieth day. Death.

The urine of this patient was throughout black, thin and watery. Coma was present, aversion to food, despondency, sleeplessness, irritability, restlessness, the mind being affected by melancholy.

Book III case 14 (second series) (3.140.14–142.4 Li.)

In Cyzicus a woman gave birth with difficult labour to twin daughters, and the lochial discharge was far from good.

First day. Acute fever with shivering; painful heaviness of head and neck. Sleepless from the first, but silent, sulky and refractory. Urine thin and of no colour; thirsty; nausea generally; bowels irregularly disturbed with constipation following.

Sixth day Much wandering at night; no sleep. About the eleventh day she went out of her mind and then was rational again; urine black, thin, and then, after an interval, oily; copious, thin, disordered stools.

Fourteenth day. Many convulsions; extremities cold; no further recovery of reason; urine suppressed.

Sixteenth day. Speechless.

Seventeenth day. Death.

Book II 2.4 (5.84.10–86.2 Li.)

The wife of Stumarges, after stopping much diarrhea from an intestinal disturbance of a few days, aborted a female child. She was well for four months, then became swollen.

Book II 2.13 (5.90.1–2 Li.)

The sixty-day male aborted in stopping [ἐπίσχεσιν] of birth was salutary [ὑγιηρόν].

[The text is obscure. Littré translates ὑγιηρόν as an adverb and interprets the case as an illness that was cured by an abortion. Wesley Smith (Loeb edition of Book II, forthcoming), however, takes ὑγιηρόν as an adjective applied to the fetus and translates, "The sixty day old male fetus, aborted after the delay of childbirth, was healthy."]

Book II 2.16 (5.90.5–6 Li.)

A nursing woman had pustules all over her body, then she stopped nursing, [the pustules] came to an end during the summer.

Book II 2.17 (5.90.7–12 Li.)

The wife of the shoemaker, who made leather things, gave birth and seemed to be delivered completely, but she retained some membranous part of the chorion; it came out on the fourth day with difficulty, for she was suffering from strangury. Conceiving again almost immediately, she gave birth to a male. She had strangury for many years; at last the menses did not flow. But when she bore a child, the strangury stopped for a time.

[The text is obscure. I interpret it as two births by the same woman, whom the doctor apparently cared for over a long period of time.]

Book II 2.18a (5.90.13–15 Li.)

A woman had pains in the hip joint before she became pregnant, but when she became pregnant, she did not suffer any more. But on the twentieth day after the birth she had pains again. She bore a male.

[II 2.18b follows immediately in the text, and Galen suggested that this chapter combined two histories.]

Book II 2.18b (5.90.15–92.2 Li.)

A woman pregnant either in the third or the fourth month had an eruption on the right lower leg, of the sort for which we use frankincense powder; also on the right hand beside the thumb. I don't know what she bore, for I left at six months. She lived, as I think, at Archelaos's, near the cliff.

Book II 2.19 (5.92.3–7 Li.)

The wife of Antigenos, who was of the house of Nikomachos, gave birth to a child, fleshy, with the parts mostly articulated, four fingers long, without bones; the afterbirth was thick and round. She was asthmatic before the birth, then at the time of the birth she vomited up a little pus like that from a boil.

[Galen says this is a singular birth, if it is not an abortion.]

Book II 2.20 (5.92.8–12 Li.)

A woman giving birth to twin daughters in a difficult labor and not completely purged, swelled up generally; then the belly became big, and the rest of the swelling went down. There was a red flow up to the sixth month, then very white all the time. The discharge kept her from intercourse, and excessive red flowed at the regular times.

[There is disagreement over whether the text for this last sentence reads in this way or indicates her address: she lived in a house looking on the gates.]

Book II 2.23 (5.94.7–9 Li.)

Prior to giving birth the [inflammation] in the area of the pharanx starting up and inclining to one side did not ulcerate. It went to the left side, then the pain went into the spleen without a crisis.

Book II 4.5 (5.126.10–14 Li.)

The servant of Stymargeos, in whom there was swelling since she bore a daughter. The mouth of the womb was turned, pain in hip and leg. Cut beside the ankle [venesection], she found relief, although trembling encompassed her whole body. But it is necessary to go to the cause [*prophasis*] and the beginning [*arche*] of the cause.

177

Book IV 6 (5.146.9–12 Li.)

With the summer solstice the wife of Achelous aborted on the 6th day; she was nauseated with chills and sweating; crisis on the fourteenth day. I don't know how many months old the fetus was. She said she had aborted another fetus that was male at twenty days; if that was true, I don't know.

Book IV 10 (5.148.24–150.4 Li.)

The woman of Thersander, slightly leucophlegmatic, while nursing had an acute fever. Her tongue was burning hot and all the rest (of her body) at that time. Her tongue was hardened like thick hailstones, and there were worms in her mouth. About the twentieth day she had an incomplete crisis.

Book IV 20 (5.160.6–8 Li.)

[In a katastasis] . . . the Tenedian woman aborted, as she said, a thirty-day male; belly liquid, thin; tongue parched; crisis on fourth day.

Book IV 22A (5.162.4–6 Li.)

The wife of the brother of Apemantos aborted a female of sixty days, as she said, on the seventh day. Around the ninth day she was disturbed; after the crisis she had pains on the right, as from a relapse. She conceived quickly and aborted.

Book IV 22B and C (5.162.7–8 Li.)

Another woman bore a daughter with white discharges; another with red, as is normal.

Book IV 24 (5.164.6–10 Li.)

The daughter of the Agoranomos at Tekomaios's [house], beginning a pregnancy without a sign, at two months had phlegmatic vomits, then bilious; she was relieved. She had difficult labor; completely purged. Similar vomiting up until the thirtieth day, then the belly was disturbed and the vomiting ceased. Passed food undigested. She did not have menses for two years. In the winter she had hemorrhoids.

Book IV 25 (5.166.8–12 Li.)

[This case appears in a series of many cases that Littré suggests were collected at Perinthus during the epidemic of cough described in VI 7.1.] The wife [of the man whose own illness has just been described] aborted on the seventh day a female infant of seven months. The problem became evident on the fourth day, for in the beginning she had pain in the feet. When the fever ceased, her breathing was loosened, but was hindered; pain in hands and arms. Relapse at the end of a long time; shivering; urine suppressed before the crisis.

Book IV 36 (5.178.20–21 Li.)

The woman with the twisted jaw; in the fifth month of pregnancy it was drawn to the left.

Book VI 4.4 (5.306.12–308.6 Li.)

The wife of Agasios, when she was a girl, had rapid breathing. After a slightly difficult delivery she experienced a great distress: suddenly a creaking noise seemed to be coming from her chest, and on the next day she had asthma [gasping for breath] and suffered pain in the right hip. Whenever she suffered this pain, she also had asthma; whenever the asthma ceased, so did the pain. She vomited foamy matter that started out bright colored and settled down to vomits like thin bile. She suffered pains especially when she worked with her hands. She should abstain from garlic, pork, sheep, beef, and, among activities, from crying and anger.

Book V 11 (5.210.12–212.4 Li.)

At Larissa, in the wife of Gorgias, the menses stopped for four years, except for a very little; on whichever side she lay, it produced throbbing and pressure in her womb. This woman became pregnant, and then she became doubly pregnant (superfetation). The child was delivered in the ninth month, living, female, with an ulcer on the hip; the afterbirth followed. A very abundant flow of blood followed on the next day and on the third and fourth days, with congealed clots; fever continued for the first ten days; red blood passed off below from her the rest of the time. Her face swelled up very much, as well as her lower legs and feet, and one thigh. She would not eat, but a strong thirst continued; the coldest water was helpful, but wine not at all. Her belly after the first child was delivered was a little reduced, but not completely; otherwise it was harder, but no pain was in it. On the fortieth day from the first the superfetation came out, fleshy. Her belly collapsed; all the swelling, the slight flow, and the odorous blood [ceased], and she was healthy.

Book v 13 (5.212.11–19 Li.)

A woman in Larissa, pregnant in the tenth month. Blood flowed out of her for fourteen days, the most on the three days before the delivery of the child. On the fourteenth day the child came out of the womb dead, with the right arm grown to its side. The afterbirth came on the third day, at the same hour of the night as the child. While discharge flowed moderately after that for three days and nights. After that a fever seized her for two days and two nights, and her whole belly hurt, and her hips, but mostly her lower belly.

Book v 18 (5.215.20–218.13 Li.)

The wife of Antimachos in Larissa was pregnant about fifty days. She had no appetite the whole time. The last seven days she had pain in the heart and was seized with fever. She did not pass anything below during this time; a cathartic potion was given to her that was stronger than needed, and she vomited bile inflamed by the lack of food and the fever (for she had not even taken anything to drink), but only a little. She also vomited clotted matter in a violent way; then she was nauseated, and it left off. She seemed to be weak and was not willing to drink water and vomit. After this a pain gripped her lower belly, for it was ulcerated by the drug, and bloody bits of flesh flowed out of her after the feces. The weakness and the nausea were continually greater. There were five kotyles [about two and a half pints] of the evacuated matter. The belly stopped when a lot of water was poured over it, but she was not able to accept anything else. It seemed that she would have lived if she had been able to drink the water and vomit it immediately before it went down.

Book v 53 (5.238.4–9 Li.)

In the wife of Simon, abortion on the thirtieth day. This happened to her when she had drunk something [an abortifacient], or it was spontaneous. Pain; vomiting of much bile, pale, leek-green, when she drank; she bit her tongue. Her tongue was big and black; the white in her eyes was red. Sleepless. On the fourth day in the night she died.

Book v 90 (5.254.5–6 Li.)

In the wife of Epicharmos, before giving birth, dysentery; the pain was intense; excreta filled with blood, phlegm. When she gave birth, she immediately was healed.

Book v 103 (5.258.9–12 Li.) = vii 49 (5.418.1–4 Li.)

In the wife of Simon [compare 5.533], shaken in childbirth, a pain in the chest and side, expectoration like pus; wasting [*pthisis*] set in; fevers for six months. Diarrhea again; cessation of the fever; the belly stopped; she died in about seven days.

Book vii 6 (5.376.14–378.3 Li.)

In the sister of Harpalides, pregnant about four or five months, an aqueous swelling in the feet, and the eyeballs swelled up, and all the skin puffed up, as in those suffering from dropsy. Dry cough; she could breathe only in an upright position; asthma of such a kind [as in such cases], and choking sometimes from breathing, so that she stayed seated on the bed and could not lie down; if there were any hope of sleep, it was when she was seated. Fairly much without fever. The fetus for the most part was motionless, as if it were dead, and it fell differently [Littré: following the movements of the woman]. The asthma lasted nearly two months. Using honey-sweetened beans and thickened honey, and drinking Aethiopian cumin in wine, she was relieved. After that, coughing, she brought up much [sputum], ripe, phlegmatic, white, and her breathing abated. She bore a female child.

Book VII 41 (5.408.11–19 Li.)

Around the setting of the Pleiades, an acute fever seized the wife of Olympiades, who was in her eighth month, after a fall. Tongue parched, dry, rough, sallow, eyes sallow, and skin corpselike. She aborted on the fifth day, easily free of it. Sleep, as it seemed, like a coma; in the evening she did not perceive those arousing her; she yielded to a sneezing powder. She took a drink of juice, coughed a little drinking it down. The voice was not lost, nor did she bring up anything. Eyes struck dumb; breathing elevated, drawn through the nose. Color bad; sweat on her feet and legs when she was near death; she died.

Book VII 49 (5.418.1–4 Li.) = v 103 (5.258.9–12 Li.)

Book VII 97 (5.450.24–452.3 Li.)

In the mother of Terpides, from Doriscus, an abortion of twins occurring in the fifth month as a result of a fall. She delivered one immediately, as in a sort of chiton; the other she delivered four days after, more or less. Later she conceived in the belly again. In the 9th year terrible pains in the belly for a long time. They began sometimes from the neck and spine and settled down in the lower belly and groin; sometimes [they began] from the right knee and settled down there. And when the pains were in the belly, the bowels were flatulent; when they ceased, heart pain occurred. There was no choking [suffocation]. Cooling of the body as of one lying in water, at the time when the pain came. The pains kept returning the whole time, milder than in the beginning. Garlic, silphium, bitter things in general, did not help, nor sweet things, nor pungent things, nor white wine; red wine and baths seldom. In the beginning terrible vomits came upon her and a refusal of foods, and during the pains the menses did not appear.

Notes

Historiographical Introduction

1. An exception to this was Fasbender 1897.
2. Other significant research on Greek gynecology includes the works of Leslie Dean-Jones, Guilia Sissa, and Jody Pinault. A number of scholars, including Valerie French, Danielle Gourevitch, and Rousselle in her book *Porneia*, focus on later Roman gynecology, although they often include some discussion of the earlier Greek background. The work of Foucault on sexuality has both a Roman and a male orientation.
3. Grensemann 1975, 80–115; 1987; 1989, also Lonie 1981, 71.
4. Lonie 1981.
5. Lloyd 1979, 1983.
6. King 1983, 1985, 1986, 1987, 1989.
7. Rousselle 1980.
8. Manuli 1980, 1983.
9. Hanson 1989; see also King 1989.
10. Important recent studies of the case histories in general include Deichgräber's (1982) analysis of the patients in Thasos; Langholf's (1977) syntactical study, including text and commentary of the individual cases in II, IV, and VI; and Grmek's (1989) retrospective diagnoses of a number of the cases.
11. Gourevitch 1988, French 1987.
12. Keuls 1985.
13. Wells 1975.

14. Weinberg 1984, 1987.
15. Borza 1979.
16. In particular, the very influential trio of books on ancient sexuality, Winkler 1990; Halperin 1990; and Halperin, Winkler, and Zeitlin 1990, which were explicitly written as developments of Foucault's work.
17. Richlin 1991, 160; on a more general plane, see Newton 1988, esp. nn. 22 and 23, with references.
18. See Lerner 1986.
19 See Foucault 1979 [1975]; interpretations of Foucault are ever multiplying, but analyses that I have found particularly useful are Sawicki 1991, and Goldstein 1984.
20. A good example is the doctor/author's prescription for the illness of maidens, *Parth.* (8.468 21–23 Li.).
21. Walcot 1970, Humphreys 1978, 1981; and, more recently, Versnel 1987; D. Cohen 1989; Foxhall 1989, and Halperin 1990. For a theoretical discussion of the use of anthropology in classical feminist studies, see Culham 1987.
22. See Friedl 1962; Campbell 1963, 1964; Blum and Blum 1965, on medical care; Alexiou 1974 and Danforth 1982 on funerary traditions.
23. Levy 1963.
24. For criticism of the use of such parallels, see Danforth 1984; Herzfeld 1987.
25. Kleinman, referred to in most of his works, but see esp. 1980.
26. Zeitlin 1981, 1982; Winkler 1990.
27. See Lerner 1986, esp. Chap. 3, which provides references to the vast bibliography on this question.

Chapter One. The Lives of Greek Women

1. A good statement of this appears in Browner and Sargent 1990.
2. Delaney 1987; Martin 1987, Jacobsen 1984; Gélis 1991.
3. Pl. *Laws* 680d–681d; Arist. *Pol.* 1252a24–1252b30.
4 In the sketch that follows, much of the ancient evidence comes from upper-class sources, such as Xenophon's *Oeconomicus* and the speeches of the Attic orators, but the basic form of the *oikos* and the role it played in the community, can be extended to all citizen landowners. This approach is supported by parallels with modern Greek village studies in which quite modest households function similarly to the *oikos*.
5. Dem. 46.22; Plut. *Solon* 20; Schaps 1979.
6. Du Boulay 1974, 19; see also Du Boulay 1986, 145–46; Dubisch 1986.
7. See, e.g., Hirschon 1989.

8. E g., Friedl 1962, 1963; Campbell 1963, 1964, esp. chap. 10; Dubisch 1986; Alexiou 1974; Blum and Blum 1965; and Danforth 1982; see Levy 1963 for a discussion of the possible explanations of similarities, and Danforth 1984 and Herzfeld 1987 for criticism of such comparative studies, answered by D. Cohen 1991, 38–41.

9. Walcot 1970; Versnel 1987; D. Cohen 1989, 1991.

10. Du Boulay 1974, 137; Sanders 1962, 129.

11. Hipp. *Nat.Child* 15.3 (7.494.11–17 Li), 18.8 (7.505.28–31 Li.), 20 5 (7.509.29–510.9 Li.), 21.1 (7.511.21–29 Li.), *Dis. Wom.* 1 1 (8.12. 6–14.7; 21–22 Li.); Parm. *ap.* Arist. *PA* 648a29–32. Some sources consider women to be cold rather than warm: Empedocles *ap.* Arist. *PA* 648a29–32; Hipp. *Vict.* 1 34 (6.512.13–19 Li.); Arist. *GA* 775a4–23 (weaker, colder, moves less, ages more rapidly); Aristotle discusses the dispute on hot and cold in *PA* 648a20–650a3; see also Lloyd 1983, 172–73; Brulé 1987, 335–59.

12. On the pollution following childbirth, see Parker 1983, 49–52.

13. Hipp. *Nat.Child* 30.1–2 (7 531 23–532.19 Li.); see further discussion.

14 Hanson 1989, 48.

15 Harris 1982; Pomeroy 1983; Patterson 1985, in Sparta the decision was made by a group of elders representing the interests of the *polis* (Plut. *Lyc.* 16). In the legal code of Gortyn, a divorced mother whose husband did not take the child when she offered it to him in the presence of three witnesses was herself given the right to decide whether to raise or expose the child (Willetts, 1967, col. III 47–49, col. IV 8–17).

16. Harrison 1968, 71; in drama, where the motif is common, especially in the fourth century, tokens to allow later identification were often left with the child.

17. Men. *Perik.*, an old woman who finds twins, a boy and a girl, gives the boy to a rich woman who "needed" a child, and kept the girl for herself

18. See, e.g , Harrison 1968, 71; Pomeroy 1983, 208; Golden 1981; 1990, 87.

19. Golden 1990, 87.

20. See Germain 1969 for a discussion and collection of the sources; Pomeroy 1983; Patterson 1985. Many discussions fail to distinguish between exposure and infanticide; in particular, this is a weakness of recent arguments that seek to determine on the basis of demographic probability whether, and in what proportions, females were selected for exposure; see Boswell 1988, 41–45. Such failure vitiates several recent arguments from demographic probability: Engels 1980, arguing that systematic female *infanticide* was impossible because it would lead to the extinction of the group (*contra* W.V. Harris 1982;

Golden 1981); Golden 1981, arguing that female *infanticide* was necessary to avoid an oversupply of widows (*contra* Sallares 1991, 157–158); and Brulé 1987, 370–73, arguing that exposure/infanticide was necessary to make up for an inbalance in the sex ratio of marriage partners when men married fifteen to twenty years later than women.

21. Sanders 1962, 129.
22. Campbell 1963, 92; see also Du Boulay 1974, 123
23. Du Boulay 1983, 244–46.
24. Blum and Blum 1965, 73–75.
25. Du Boulay 1983.
26. McKee (1984) suggests that the higher mortality of males from conception through childhood provides a biological reason for the prevalence of "benign neglect" of females and perhaps even for the higher status accorded to males in general.
27. McKee 1984; on the other hand, Agathonos et al. (1982) report that twice as many boys as girls were involved in fifty-four cases of traumatic child abuse that they studied in modern Greece; they suggest that this is a consequence of the greater expectations of boys in a culture that puts a high value on being male.
28. On one sort of evidence, the so-called "feeding-bottles" of the fourth century, which may have been used as lamp fillers rather than for the feeding of children or the sick, see Kein 1957. It should, however, be possible to determine age at weaning from skeletal evidence for the introduction of cereal in a child's diet; see Sillen and Smith 1984.
29. The miniature wine jugs, or *choes*, that portray scenes from that celebration almost all picture boys. The children are usually assumed to be three years of age; the evidence includes a passage in Philostr. *Heroicus* 12.2, which speaks of a festival for three-year-olds in the month Anthesterion, but does not name Choes; a second-century tombstone (Conze no. 1977) portraying a boy and inscribed, "when he was of the age for *choic* things, death came before the Choes"; and the second-century Iobacchoi inscription that lists crucial events in the life of a man and places participation in Choes between birth and *ephebeia* (*IG* II^2 1368.127–31). On the other hand, many of the *choes* depict crawlers who appear to be considerably younger than three. If Choes celebrated weaning, variation in age would be expected, ideally, in a society lacking modern facilities for the handling of food, nursing would continue until three, but in reality it probably ended sooner for many children, boys as well as girls. On Choes, see Parke 1977, 107; Deubner 1932, 13, 16, 28–31, Rumpf 1961; Green 1971; Bazant 1975 R. Hamilton (1992) argues that the Choes vases do not celebrate an occasion for children because the children, despite

being the most frequently portrayed element in the scenes, are not invariably portrayed with items that are unique to the scenes (grapes, tables, cakes, and the *choes* themselves) But a twenty-second-century archaeologist coming upon a collection of twentieth-century Christmas cards might as easily decide that they were not about a festival celebrating an infant because infants were not invariably present with other elements that were unique to these cards (snow and ivy).

30. Makler 1980.
31. Xen. *Lac.* 1.3; *Oec.* 7.6; Arist. *HA* 9.608b15. *Contra* Pomeroy 1975, 85, the ration lists for Ionian women working at Persepolis indicating extra rations for women who bore sons (Hallock 1969, 37–38, 344–53), provide evidence only for Persian practices.
32. Xen. *Oec.* 7.6.
33. Campbell 1964, 151.
34. Doumanis 1983, 37. Doumanis studied the mother-child interaction in two groups of twenty children fourteen to sixteen months old in Epirus and in Athens; although she notes that the groups were evenly divided between girls and boys, she consistently refers to the children as "he" and provides no information about differences in their treatment according to sex.
35. Wells 1975; see, too, Gélis 1991, 229, which cites pelvic malformations due to malnutrition as the principal cause of difficult labor in early modern Europe.
36. Loudon 1991, 44–45.
37. At the *amphidromia*, these helpers were purified, and the mother probably moved from being polluting to others to a state of being "impure, but not polluting others"; Parker 1983, 51.
38. Golden 1990, 23–24
39. Gould (1980, 40–42) argues that only girls who were heiresses (i.e., had no living brothers) were introduced; they served in lieu of a male heir, providing a conduit across a gap in the male line; such introductions would have taken place only after the girl's probable future status as an *epikleros* was recognized Golden (1985a) also argues for the introduction of some girls.
40. See Golden 1986.
41. Schaps 1977.
42 Campbell 1964, 186.
43. Plut. *Lyc.* 14–15
44. Xen. *Oec.* 7.5.
45. Hirschon 1989, 108; whether the ideal is carried out in practice is, of course, another matter.
46. See Golden 1990, 33, 125, 128.

47. See Pavlides and Hesser 1986, 73–94; many of these items are now purchased as villagers seek to become more "modern."
48. Xenophon's Ischomenus assumed that his young wife could read lists of household goods, Xen. *Oec.* 9.10, and in Lys. 32.11–18 a widow argues against her father's misuse of her children's inheritance in a family council, bringing in as evidence family records, both of course were members of the upper class; see too Dem. 41.8–21, and discussion of literacy in chapter 3. Child care and other activities: Golden 1990, 33, 72–79, 125, 128.
49. Ar. *Lys.* 638–47; Turner 1983, 181–205, 310–82.
50. Solon, frag. 27 (West); Hipp. *Coac.* 30, 502 (2.700, 5–6, Li.); see Dowden 1989, 29 and 210 n. 37; Brulé 1987, 360–61.
51. *Anth.Pal.* 6.280; cf. Daux 1973a, 1973b. Gallant (1991, 18–19) speculates an age span of sixteen to nineteen for the marriage of Greek girls, on the grounds that all the ancient evidence *could* refer to upper-class girls, and that parallels with Roman and early modern Europe suggest it.
52. It is interesting that in modern Greece girls who anticipate an increase in status with marriage (especially a move from village to town) are believed able to control themselves until marriage at twenty-five to thirty as their families build up the necessary dowries, while girls without such prospects are considered to lack a motive for self-control and hence to require an early marriage. A degree of rationality and self-control is thus allowed to exist in females. Friedl 1962, 66.
53. Xen. *Oec.* 3.13.
54. Dem. 27.4, 28.15; 29.43.
55. Hipp. *Epid.* III Case 12 (first set) (3.62.14–66.11 Li.)
56. Guarducci 1950, 4:72, sect. xii, lines 17–19.
57. Pouilloux 1954, no. 141, *Inv.* 1032, lines 21–22 and pp. 371–78.
58. Xen. *Lac.* 1.6; Plut. *Lyc.* 15.3.
59. Campbell 1964, 82–83.
60. See chapter 6.
61. Hipp. *Dis.Wom.* 1 2 (8.14.8–22.4 Li.); *Superfet.* 34 (8.504.4–506.7 Li.); Manuli 1980, 402–5; 1983, 160–62, Sissa 1990, 44–55, 121–22; Loraux 1987, 216–17.
62. Xenophon's reference to the parents in the plural suggests that the girl's mother might have had some influence on the decision, Xen. *Oec.* 7.10; while [Arist.] *Oec.* 3.1 (frag 184 [Rose]), says that a proper wife does not interfere in the arrangement of her children's marriages, such an injunction may in itself indicate that such involvement was common.
63. Solon frag. 27, lines 9–10 (West); Hes. *WD* 695–97; and Pl. *Laws*

721b, 785b. Arist. *Pol.* 1335a6–35 gives as a reason for the age gap the desirability of having both partners reach the end of fertility at the same time: at age fifty for women and seventy for men.

64. Hunter (1989a, 294 and n. 3) found no examples of land as dowry, but also no rule against it

65 On dowry, see Goody 1990, 13–16, 79–86 (general), 389–90 (classical Greece).

66. Schaps 1977, 78.

67. Lys. 19.14–16.

68. Lys. 19.59; Schaps 1979, 78–81.

69. Friedl 1963, 113–135; 1962, 53–56; compared with classical Greece by Levy 1963. Although the 1983 revision of the Greek Civil Code no longer specifies a parental obligation to provide dowry, dowry remains a central issue even for urban families, where it is likely to take the form of a house or apartment; Hirschon 1989, 118–28, 260.

70. Men. *Dys.* 842, Dem. 44.49, 46 18; Patterson 1991.

71. See Redfield 1982.

72. W. Thompson 1967.

73. See, e.g., Campbell 1964, 60–61.

74. Alexiou and Dronke 1971; Alexiou 1974; Barringer 1991.

75. Burkert 1985, 161; for references, see Bennett and Tyrrell 1991.

76 Danforth 1982, 86–87.

77 Eur. *Med.* 238–40, trans. Way.

78 Campbell 1964, 61–63, 73–74, 78, 83–84 (observations in 1954–55); Friedl 1962, 60–64 (observations in 1955–56); Du Boulay 1974, 137, 155 (observations in 1966; she reports that at the time of her observations extended families no longer consisted of more than parents and one married son) These were rural communities with an economic base of farming or herding, and hence most likely to be comparable with conditions in classical Greece. A quite different pattern of family organization exists among modern urban Greeks, who are dependent upon wage earning, lack capital and credit, and confront a housing shortage. In this situation, dowry takes the form of living accommodations, often a self-contained apartment carved out of the maternal parents' living quarters; the couple lives an autonomous existence from the beginning of the marriage, with the husband, not the mother-in-law, having complete control over the wife (Hirschon 1989, 123–28, 153–54; observations in 1971–72). On the association of virilocal marriage patterns with the suppression of women, see Loizos and Papataxiarchis 1991, 8–10.

79. Gallant (1991, 21–26) assumes a model household that includes the husband's widowed mother in the early years of marraige, citing the subdivision of houses in Olynthus as classical evidence of patrilocal

marriage. But the single instance of a subdivided house at Olythus, House A12, also had an entryway broken through to the house next door (A13), and the excavators suggested that half of A12 was taken over by the occupant of A13. There is no evidence that the division was done to accommodate newlyweds, and certainly no evidence that the marriage pattern would have been patrilocal as opposed to matrilocal (both forms coexist in modern Greece: Du Boulay 1974; Hirshon 1989).

80. Lys. 1.6–7, trans. Freeman 1946.
81. Hunter 1989a.
82. Isager 1981–82, 85–86.
83. Pl. *Laws* 776ab. Meyers (1989) suggests that archaeology may reveal evidence for such joint family residence in housing clusters.
84. Schaps 1977.
85. This correction of Angel's figure of thirty-five (Angel 1969, 430–31) is discussed later.
86. Golden 1990, 136; consider the grave relief of Ampharete in the Kerameikos Museum, which portrays her playing with her infant grandchild in death as she did in life; *IG* II^2 10650, about 410 B.C.
87. For example, Lys. 1.6–7; Vernant 1980–81, 404, Cole 1984, 243 and n. 62.
88. Corvisier 1985, 121, 161–65.
89. Postpubertal subfertility: Petersen 1961, 440; Gray 1979, 221–27; fertile period: Hipp. *Dis.Wom.* 1 17 (8.56.16–17 Li.).
90. Hipp. *Ster.* 214 (8.414.18–22 Li.)
91. Hipp. *Epid.* II 6.29 (5.138.6–9 Li.).
92. Hipp. *Epid.* v 42 (5.232.9–16 Li.).
93. Arist. *Pol.* 1335a 13–23.
94. See Weinberg 1984, 1987, and my chapter 4; among the diseases whose effects are enhanced are malaria, tuberculosus, influenza, and polio.
95. Lloyd 1983, 70–76; Nickel 1979; Manuli 1983, 154 and 186–87 (app. 1); Herfst 1979 [1922], 52–63, discusses the ancient sources.
96. Hipp. *Dis.* 1.5 (6.146.19 Li.).
97. Hipp. *Dis.* 1.8 (6.154.19–21, 24–156.1 Li.).
98. Hipp. *Nat.Child* 30.1–9 (7.531.20–532.13 Li.); Lonie (1981, 244–45) expresses "considerable doubt" that the author had ever observed a delivery; we cannot of course know what this particular author may have observed, but since elsewhere in the treatise he lays considerable stress upon observation, and there is no evidence that male doctors were prohibited from participation in childbirth cases, it seems unlikely that he would have missed the opportunity at some time to observe a delivery.

99. Hipp. *Dis.Wom.* 1 1 (8.10.10–11 Li), trans. Lonie 1981; see Hanson 1987, 1991.
100. Hipp. *Dis.Wom.* 1 34 (8.80.4–5 Li.); *Artic.* 57 (4.246.9 Li.).
101. Pl. *Theat.* 149d.
102. Hipp. *Superfet.* 4.2 (8 478.14–15 Li.).
103. Plin *Nat.Hist.* 25.94.150; King 1988, 54–55; Walton, Beeson, and Scott 1986, s.v. "herbal remedies", on the dangers of henbane, Majno 1975, 387.
104. King 1988.
105. Angel 1969, 430–31, but see Golden 1981, 327.
106. Noted by Patterson 1981, 78, n. 71.
107. See, for instance, Buikstra and Konigsberg 1985; Bocquet-Appel and Masset 1982; M. Cohen 1989, 110–11; 206, n 29; and 218, n. 106
108. Sallares 1991, 111–13; Gallant (1991, 19–20) opts for forty and thirty-eight as ages of death for men and women, but it is unclear why he chose those particular numbers, aside from his claim to be more optimistic than most critics in his assessment of Angel's figures.
109. See Herrmann and Bergfelder 1978; Holt 1978; Suchey et al. 1979; Gejvall 1983, 86–87.
110. Patterson (1981, 45) calculated that on the average women would have to bear five children to ensure population replacement, on the basis of U.N. Model Life Table no. 35 (United Nations 1955).
111. Sallares 1991, 135–36; the passages cited are Is 2.3, 5.5, 6.10, 8.40, 11.37; Lys. 16.10; Dem. 40.6–7, 43.74, 44.9, and 57.28, 37.
112. Based on figures for the population of Rouen during the seventeenth and eighteenth centuries in similar conditions of birth control, Brulé (1987, 368) estimated the number of children born to women who married between ages fifteen and nineteen as nine. However, a fertility rate of seven live births per woman is considered almost impossible to sustain over an extended period; see United Nations 1955, 14.
113. Loudon 1991, 56–63; Weinberg 1984, 1987; the number of children born does not necessarily increase in direct proportion to the lowering of the age of marriage, see Brulé 1987, 369.
114. Hipp. *Epid.* v 53 (5.238.4–9 Li.); *Dis.Wom.* 1 67 (8.140 Li.).
115. Hipp. *Dis.Wom.* 1 67 (8.140–42 Li.); on postabortion sterility, see Gray 1979, 242.
116. Ar. *Thesm.* 502–16; Powell (1988, 354–57) is skeptical about the reality behind these male suspicions, but has no doubt about the suspicions themselves.
117. This figure is based on the evidence of the classical cemetery at Olynthus, where 49.7 percent of the burials are infant or juvenile; however, these remains included no infants below six months of age,

when mortality would have been at its highest (Robinson 1942, 146–71, esp. 170–71) On the basis of the most applicable U.N. Model Life Table (no. 35: life expectancy ca. twenty-five years), 60 percent of the children will die before age thirty (United Nations 1955). Golden (1990, 83) estimates 30–40 percent mortality in the first year of life; see Frier 1982, 245; 1983.

118. See chapter 8, for a discussion of Hippocratic treatment of infants and children.
119. [Dem.] 59.55–56, trans. Murray (Loeb); for a different view, see King 1991
120. Blum and Blum 1965, 51, 167; see also Sanders 1962, 129, 149–54.
121. See D. Cohen 1989; 1991, chap 6.
122. See chapter 6.
123. See chapter 6.
124. Hirschon 1983; Campbell 1964; Du Boulay 1986.
125. Turner 1983, 215–28, 232–382; Henderson 1987b, 114–17; 1987a.
126. Turner 1983, 400–412.
127. Plut. *Alc.* 22.5.
128. Ar. *Peace* 991–92; *Lys.* 554, see Henderson 1987b, 116, n. 81; 1987a, xxxix; Turner 1983, 248–51.
129. See chapter 5.
130. See esp. Hirschon 1983.
131. Dem. 57, esp. 30–31, 35.
132. Pl. *Laws* 781c.
133. W Thompson 1972, 218–19; in her study of widows, Hunter (1989a) found eighteen who remarried (six of these were of uncertain status and may have been divorcées) Gallant (1991, 26–27) found that 65 percent of his count of widows in the forensic speeches remained unmarried.
134. Dem. 30.33; 27.5, 36.8; such an arrangement usually occurred in cases in which the wives had no living fathers or brothers who would be able to make the arrangements.
135. Plut. *Per.* 24.
136. Hunter (1989a) refutes the common claim that they might elect to stay in the husband's home (e.g , MacDowell 1978, 88–89); no such cases are known, although the widow in Lys. 32 remained in her husband's house with her three children for a year before she ran out of supplies; at that time her father arranged for her marriage and took the children into his own home to raise.
137. Hunter 1989a, 298.
138. Thuc 2.45
139. Hipp. *Epid.* vi 8.32 (5.356.4–15 Li.).

140. Hirschon 1989, 108; see also Du Boulay 1974, 122; Caraveli 1986, 181, for a lament about widowhood.
141. W. Thompson 1972, 221, n. 52, from the *Demographic Yearbook 1968*.
142. [Dem.] 59.22; Golden 1990, 100; Brulé 1987, 351–55.
143 See Turner 1983, 198–99, 206–14; Brulé 1987, 351–55.
144. Schaps 1979, 14–16; Foxhall 1989; Hunter 1989a; 1989b.
145. Hipp. *Nat.Child* 13 (7.489.25–492.7 Li.): the doctor, however, does not say that the woman asked him directly; he merely says that "the story came to" him, thus sidestepping the issue of who it was that invited or authorized his action
146. Henderson 1987b
147. Hyperides frag. 205 (Blass); Bremmer 1987, 191–94.
148. Lys. 1.
149. Bremmer 1987, 195.
150. E.g., Ar. *Plut.* and *Eccles.*; Bremmer 1987, 202–6.
151. See esp. Friedl 1967.
152. Nelson 1975.
153. Lamphere 1975.
154. Morsy 1978; Hunter (1989b, 47), in discussing cases in which women were active in family affairs and considered *kyria* of their own property as widows, points out that they had "an authority that no law gives, and no law protects."
155. See Hunter 1989b; widows were legally dependent upon their grown sons, even though they may at times have exercised de facto control over their own property. It is not the case that women were guaranteed support from the state throughout their lives if they gave birth to a son, as Garland maintains (1990, 257).
156. For example, the treatment of metic heiresses paralleled that of citizen women, although the metics fell under the jurisdiction of the polemarch and the citizen women under that of the archon; Dem. 46.22.
157. Is. 3.39.
158. Harrison 1968, 164
159. See Harrison 1968, 13–15.
160. Is. 3.39.
161. Plut. *Per.* 36–37.
162. [Dem.] 59 59–61.
163 In [Dem.] 59.122 the speaker says that men have *hetairai* for pleasure, concubines for the daily care of their bodies, and wives for the procreation of legitimate children and to be faithful guardians of the household.
164. Starr (1978) argues against the prostitute role, however.

165. Hipp. *Fleshes* 19 (8.610.3–5 Li.).
166. Hipp. *Nat.Child* 13 (7.489.25–492.7 Li.), trans Lonie 1981.
167. Lonie 1981, 164.
168. Faster to age in lifetime: Hipp. *Seven Months' Child* 9.

Chapter Two. Hippocratic Medicine and the Epidemics

1. Hipp. *Art, Nat.Man, Reg.Health.*
2. On Thucydides' knowledge of medicine, see Cochrane 1929; Weidauer 1953; a different view is offered by Parry 1969; see also Hornblower 1987, 110–35
3. Ar. *Wasps* 71–87; *Plut.*; on medical terms in tragedy, see Collinge 1962; Miller 1944.
4. Pl. *Protag.* 311bc; see too *Phaedr.* 270cd.
5. See L. Edelstein 1945.
6. Pl. *Rep.* 405c–407d, trans. Cornford 1945.
7. Pl. *Phaedr* 270c–e; *Protag.* 311bc; Meno in the *Papyrus Anonymous Londinensis* (see W. G. S. Jones 1947).
8. This is called the Hippocratic Question; useful reviews are provided by Lloyd 1975; Kudlien 1977; Smith 1979; and King 1989, 16–20.
9. See, e.g., Laín Entralgo 1970, 141.
10. On Presocratic philosophy, see Kirk, Raven, and Schofield 1983.
11. On humoral theory, see W. H. S. Jones 1922–, 1·xlvi–li; Lloyd 1978, 24–28; Foster and Anderson (1978, 56–60) trace its subsequent history down to the present day.
12. *Nat.Wom.* 15 (7.332.9 Li.), 33 (7.370.8–9 Li.); *Dis.Wom* II 118 (8.256.4 Li.).
13. Hipp. *Epid.* II 1.7 (5.76.17–78.18).
14. See Langholf 1990, esp. chap. 3 on crises.
15. This is one possible meaning of the title *Epidemics*—the travels of doctors in the demes; see Langholf 1990, 78–79. Deichgräber (1982) traced the travels of the doctors who wrote the *Epidemics* by the addresses that they give for many of their patients; see also Robert 1975.
16. One of the best known of the Hippocratic treatises is the environmental work *Airs, Waters, Places.*
17. On the training of doctors, see Lloyd 1978, 12–21.
18. For example, Hippocrates' *Art* is highly rhetorical and sophistic; *Nat.Man* 1 refers to lectures on philosophical medicine, and the style of the book is sophistic; *Reg.Health* is directed to laymen.
19. Blum and Blum 1965, 142.
20. Hipp. *Reg.AcuteDis.* (appendix) 28, trans. Potter (Loeb) (2.448.12–450.2 Li.).
21. Hipp *Epid.* I 26 (2.678.5–680 4 Li).

22. See Langholf 1990, 78–79.
23. The non-Athenian context raises the question whether we are justified in integrating this evidence with material from Athenian sources A positive answer is provided by the evidence demonstrating that the Athenians from the late fifth century knew Hippocrates as a famous doctor and were very interested in the latest in medical theories; see nn. 1–4.
24. One such patient is Philiscus, who is mentioned by name in the third constitution of Book i (i 8 [2.646.9–13 Li]) and discussed in detail in the first case history.
25. Thuc. 2.47–54; Thucydides spent his long exile in the north where he would have had ample opportunity to come into contact with Hippocratic doctors; on Thucydides' knowledge of medicine, see n. 1.
26. Hipp. *Epid.* i 8 (2.646.9–648.6 Li.), trans. Jones (Loeb).
27. Smith attributes these distinctions to Dioscurides and Capiton in the first century A.D. and does not agree to their ranking of the books in terms of time and excellence (1979, 235–39; 1989).
28. Galen 7.854 K.
29. This figure differs from that of Lloyd (1983, 67, n. 33) who gives 44.7 percent. As Lloyd notes, such statistics can be difficult to compile because of textual problems and decisions about what constitutes a case (there are, however, no infants of indeterminate sex to complicate matters in this book). In Book ii, in addition to the clearly defined individual cases, I have also counted patients referred to by name as examples in cases that essentially belong to another patient. The following are the male cases that I have counted: in the second section, chapters 5, 6, 7, 9 (2 cases), 14, 23 (2 cases); and in the third section, chapters 3, 4 (2 cases), and 11 (2 cases), for a total of 13 male patients The female cases are: in the second section, 1, 2, 3, 8, 13, 16, 17 (one patient, two births), 18 (2 cases), 19, 20, 22 (this name could be either male or female; the birth mentioned is assigned to ii 2 23 by Smith and Langholf, whom I follow), 23 (2 patients, one childbirth); in the third section, 13; in the fourth section, 5 and 6 The total of female patients is 16.
30. On the Cough of Perinthus, see Grmek 1989, 305–39.
31. E.g , vi 4.18 (5.312.1–4 Li.); vi 2.12 (5.284.1–2 Li.); see Deichgräber 1971, 72–75; Di Benedetto 1977, 258–59.
32. *Epid.* vi 3.12 (5.298.4–9 Li.); Pl. *Soph.* 253b ff ; *Pol* 260e ff ; *Phaedr.* 263b ff. According to Frenkian 1941, Plato recognized a resemblance between Hippocrates and his own method of collection and division in *Phaedr.* 265a–270e, but he does not explicitly attribute a method of collection and division to Hippocrates in this passage.
33. Nikitas 1968, 118–20

34. Smith 1989, 151–52.
35. Nikitas 1968; Smith 1989; Robert 1975, on the other hand, maintains that the three books had a single author, and explains the differences between them as a result of the less finished state of iv.
36. Nikitas 1968; his conclusions are rejected by Di Benedetto (1977), who, on the basis of a brief analysis of these books, dates ii, iv, and vi earlier than i and iii; his argument is not compelling, however.
37. Nikitas 1968, 83–85.
38. See Langholf 1977.
39. Galen 7.854 (Kühn).
40. Langholf 1977.
41. Langholf (1977) points out that vii could not be derived from v C because in many instances its cases are longer and more complete, but neither could v C be an excerpt of vii because it also contains independent passages, as, for example, v 86 and v 71, the first part of which is missing in the parallel passage, vii 82.
42. Deichgräber 1971, 144–45; Grensemann 1969; Robert (1973) suggests an even more exact date, 357 or 356; on the other hand, Papanikolaou (1965 [not seen]) dates vii in the third or second centuries and v to the same dates as Deichgräber. Since dating is based on references to datable events in the cases, these dates hold for the original authorship of the cases, not for the editing that put them into the form that we have as Books v and vii.
43. Heraclitus, DK 22 B48.
44. Hes. WD 757, 759.
45. Hipp. *Sac.Dis.* (6.354.20 Li.).
46. Heraclitus, DK 22 B36, B77, B117, B118. .
47 W. H. S. Jones 1909, 49, 50, 52
48. *Epid.* v 25 (5.224.6–13 Li.); on shamanistic cures by object removal, see Rogers 1942, 1217–18.
49. On iatrogenic disorders in the Hippocratic treatises, see Von Staden 1990, 85–88; Lloyd 1987, 124–35.
50. v B: Hipp. *Epid.* v 33 (5.230.4–5 Li.); v C· v 76 (5.248.4–8 Li.) = vii 38 (5.406.5–7 Li.).
51. Robert, 1989; Robert also identified three passages in Book vii that do not appear in Book v in which the form of expression (but not explicit criticism of mistakes) suggests a group practice. On Hippocratic admission of mistakes, see Von Staden 1990, 85–88; Lloyd 1987, 124–35.
52. Hipp. *Epid.* vi 2.15 (5.284.12 Li.); Smith 1989, 152.
53. This does not exclude the possibility that the woman (at least the free-born wife) exercised some initiative in the matter, see Gould 1980, 49–50.

54. Hipp. *Precepts* 6 (9.258.5–15 Li.); Pl. *Rep.* 341c; Lloyd 1978, 15; Cohn-Haft 1956, 19–20, 32–45.
55. Deichgräber 1982: a number of these patients also appear on a Thasian inscription that lists officeholders (*theoroi*, or state ambassadors), demonstrating that this doctor was treating members of old, well-established families and their households (including slaves).
56. Friedl 1958.
57. Hipp. *Fract.* 36 (3.540.9–12 Li.).
58. On sore throat with fever, see *Progn.* 23 (2.174.14–180.5 Li.).
59. Goody 1986, 83–84.
60. See Lonie 1983; Vitrac 1989; and generally on the development of literacy, Goody 1977, 1986; Havelock 1982; Lang 1984

Chapter Three. The Treatment of Female Patients in the Epidemics

1. These numbers for Book I include the patients used as examples in the third constitution; for the case histories alone, the numbers would be 28 percent gynecological cases (birth and abortion) and 36 percent female patients. These latter figures agree roughly with those cited by Lloyd (1983) 67, n. 33, who gives 27.3 percent female of all mentioned patients, 35.7 percent of patients in the cases (he seems to have counted each mention of a patient in the constitution, but some are duplicates).
2. Hanson 1989, 48; Hanson finds this imbalance extending to the *Epidemics* as a whole; in her calculations she discounts the male birth in II 2.18, (apparently because it is noted in the context of pregnancy alleviating a pain rather than as a case of postpartum complications), and omits the male fetuses of II 2.13, IV 6, and IV 20, and the female abortion of II 2 4, as well as the male infant of II 2.17. In all, there are twenty cases in which sex is specified and fourteen cases in which it is not. Of the twenty cases in which sex is specified, six are male (a ratio of three in ten, not one in eleven). The preponderance of females is still noteworthy.
3. M. Harris and Ross 1987, 168
4. See King 1989.
5. Hipp. *Epid.* I 8 (2.642.4–648.4 Li.).
6. *Epid.* I 9 (2.656.6–658.12 Li.); III 14 (3.98.1 Li.).
7. I 1 (2.602.4–5 Li)
8. I 6 (2.638.4 Li.).
9. I 9 (2.658.6–12 Li.).
10. I 8 (2.646.9–648 6 Li.), quoted in chapter 2.
11 II 2.18a (a pregnancy case, but these problems occurred before conception); IV 30 (5.172.19–174.10 Li.).
12. IV 32 (5.176.9–12 Li.)

13. Theoretically this was early for her to identify the sex, since males were thought to develop fully in thirty days, but *Nature of the Child* mentions earlier fetuses that were not fully articulated and yet were identified as male; *Nat.Child* 18.7 (7.504.18–506.2 Li.).

14. *Epid.* III case 6 (first set) (3.52.7–8 Li.): silent, depressed, despairing of herself; III case 2 (second set) (3.112.10–11 Li.): despondent, irritable, melancholic; III case 11 (second set) (3.134.2 Li.)· an ill-tempered woman; III case 15 (second set) (3.142.5–146.6 Li.): grieving, silent; *Epid.* v 18 (5.216.20–218.13 Li.): uncooperative (from weakness only?). In other treatises similar attitudes on the part of doctors are revealed: *Parth.* (8.466.9–10 Li.), woman's nature is prone to despondency; *Dis.Wom.* I 62 (8.126.12–14 Li.): difficulties in questioning female patients because of their modesty and ignorance; *Dis.Wom.* I 67 (8.140.15–16 Li.): general suspicion that women will resort to abortion. Problems with patients were, however, not limited to women: doctors complain that patients in general (probably the generic male) often failed to call for medical assistance in time or refused to follow the doctor's instructions (*Prorrhet.* II 6 (9.24.2–4 Li.); *Progn.* 1 (2.112.11–12 Li.)); *Art* 7 (6.10–12), men do not seem to have done this from despondency, however.

15. Pl. *Symp.* 189b–193.

16. Grensemann 1975, 9, at least his part C.

17. VI 32 (5.356.4–15 Li.).

18. Hipp. *Dis.Wom.* II 153 (8.328.1–14 Li.): "Whenever a woman after childbirth takes up a burden greater than [her] nature, either winnowing, or splitting wood, or running, or any other such thing, the next day she will suffer problems with regard to this especially. . . . It is necessary to abstain from drinks as much as possible, and to protect the womb so as not to agitate it. . . . Such things are necessary afterward: if they don't keep quiet but move about, treat with hellebore, and if it doesn't help, also make them vomit, remain unwashed, and be quiet and rest."

19. VI 8.6 (5.344.8–16 Li.).

20. VII 96 (5.450.20–23 Li.).

21. v 91 (5.254.7–10 Li.); VII 123 (5.468.3–5 Li)

22. v 12 (5.212.5–10 Li.), VII 64 (5.430.1–2 Li.).

23. Hipp. *Dis.* I 8 (6.154.19–21, 24–156.1 Li.) includes the giving of an upward-working cathartic to a pregnant woman as an instance of a mistake by a doctor, and the giving of a pain-killer to a woman in labor who gets worse or dies as an instance in which the doctor is liable to be blamed.

24. Hipp. *Epid.* v 2 (5.232.9–16 Li.).

25. *Dis.Wom.* 1 2 (8.14.8–22.4 Li.) trans. in Hanson 1975, 572–75; 7 (8.32.1–34.5 Li.); 32 (8.76.1–22 Li.); 11 127 (8.272.9–274.9 Li.); 151 (8.326.14–20 Li.); 201 (8.384.1–386.16 Li.); 203 (8.386.21–392.11 Li.); *Nat.Wom.* 3 (7 314.14–316.8 Li.), 26 (7.342.18–20 Li.), 73–75 (7.404 10–19 Li.), 87 (7.408.6–9 Li.); *Places in Man* 47 (6.344 3–348.15 Li.); numerous cases in the *Epidemics:* 111 case 12 (second series) (3.136 1–12 Li.), diagnosed by Hanson 1989, 1v 30 (5.172.19–174.10 Li); v 12 (5 212.5–10 Li.); v1 1 1 (5.266 1–4 Li.); v1 8.32 (5.4–15 Li.), v11 64 (5.428.14–430.2 Li.) (cf. v 67), v11 96 (5.450.30–33 Li.); v11 123 (5.468 4–6 Li.).
26. Pl. *Tim.* 91c–d, trans. Jowett, in E. Hamilton and Cairns, 1961.
27. Hipp. *Parth.* (8.466–470 Li.).
28. Griffith 1898, prescriptions 1, 6, 8, 11; on the other hand, Merskey and Potter (1989) argue that passages in which the womb is said to move are not associated with symptoms at a distance, and that when such symptoms are attributed to the womb, it is not specifically said to move; therefore they diagnose every case of movement of the womb as prolapse.
29. Kudlien (1967, 10, 88) identified it as primitive, a "relic of ur-mythical knowledge."
30. Blum and Blum 1965, 53, 116, 132 (caused by the Evil Eye), 189–92. The wandering womb lived on in the Hippocratic tradition in early modern Europe; see Gélis 1991, 59–61.
31 Keuls 1985, 76–78.
32. Pl. *Tim.* 91b–c, trans Jowett, in E. Hamilton and Cairns, 1961.
33 See esp. King 1988; Loraux 1987.
34. Hipp. *Epid.* v1 5, 11 (5.318.14–15 Li.); *Dis.Wom* 1 33 (8.78.4–7 Li.); *Genit* 9.3 (7 316.20–318.23 Li.); see Hanson 1989.
35. Succussion: *Artic.* 42–44 (4.182ff. Li.); *Dis.Wom.* 1 68 (8.142.20–144.16); 11 144 (8.318.5–7 Li.) = *Ster.* 248 (8.462.3–5 Li.) = *Nat.Wom.* 5 (7.316.20–318.23 Li.); *De exc.foet.* 4 (8.514.14–516.7 Li.); *Epid.* v 103 (5.258.9–12 Li.) = v11 49 (5.418.1–4 Li.); it was also used on male patients: v1 8.28 (5.354.4–5 Li.), a successful succussion of a man whose liver had a folded lobe. The author of *On Joints* 42 (4.182.13–184.4 Li.), on the treatment of humpback, says that, while he admires the inventor of succussion, he will not use the method himself because it is mostly used by charlatans (but consider chs. 43 and 44 [4.184.5–188.16 Li.], where he gives directions for its use in other conditions); see too Lloyd 1987, 69 n. 78.
36. Hipp. *Epid.* v 53 (5.238.4–9 Li.)
37 Hipp. *Dis.Wom.* 1 67 (8.140.15–16 Li.); the cases cited by Preus 1975, 1 78 (8.188 Li.) and 1 74 (8.160), do not seem to support this point.

Fleshes 19 (8.610.3–5 Li.): the doctor reports having seen many fetuses aborted by public prostitutes who routinely aborted themselves.

38. On the real risks of the products prescribed as emmenagogues, expulsives, and uterine purgatives that could have been used for abortions, see Fontanille 1977, 146–48; Riddle 1992.

39. *Dis.Wom.* 1 78 (8.184.19–186 2 Li.), (8 186.4–6 Li.), (8.186.6–7 Li.), (8.186.22–24 Li.), (8.188.13–14 Li.), (8.188.14–17 Li.), (8.188.18–20 Li.); 1 91 (8.218.13–15 Li.), (8.220 16 Li.).

40. *Nat.Wom.* 32 (7.350.6 Li.).

41. Hipp. *Dis.Wom.* 1 21 (8.60.4–62.3 Li.), 25 (8.64.12–68.17 Li.); *Epid.* vii 73 (5.432.18–19 Li.); *Aph.* v 31 (4.542.12–13 Li.), 34 (4.544.3–4 Li.); vii 27 (4.584.1 Li.).

42. E.g., Hipp. *Dis.Wom.* 1 74 (8.154 9–160.20 Li.).

43. *Dis.Wom.* 1 78: (8.178.12–14 Li.), (8.180.14–18 Li.), (8 182.20–21 Li.), (8.184.4 Li.), (8.188.8 Li.), (8.188.17 Li.).

44. *Nat.Wom* 32 (7.350.20 and 21 Li.), 95 (7.312.15–18 Li.).

45. *Dis. Wom.* 1 78 (8.188.8 Li.) after a discussion of the expulsion of dead fetuses, and (8.188.17 Li.) before a similar discussion.

46. *Dis.Wom.* 1 78 (8.182.14 Li.).

47. *Dis.Wom.* 1 78 (8.178.1–12 Li.).

48. Riddle 1992, 76.

49. Riddle 1992, 81.

50. Ibid.

51. That they were so used was the interpretation of Hähnel 1936, accepted by Edelstein 1943; Preus 1975, 251–56; Fontanille 1977, lists over one hundred recipes for "abortifacients," although many of these are emmenagogues or contraceptives; for a discussion distinguishing these and considering evidence for their use and effectiveness, see Riddle 1992. Questioning doctors' involvement. see Lonie 1981, 165, n. 301; R. Bernier 1990; Nardi 1971.

52 Preus 1975, is especially interesting in this regard For example, he interprets the genitive absolute, τρωσμῶν γινομένων, of *Dis.Wom.* 1 68 (8.142.13 Li.) as implying assistance in delivery in an induced abortion, and identifies the recipient of expellant sneezing powder, whose nose and mouth are to be held shut, as the fetus rather than the woman (p. 253) Preus routinely refers to the French rather than the Greek text of the Littré edition, which may account for some misreadings.

53. *Nat.Child.* 13 (7.488.22–492.6 Li), quoted in chapter 1; see Lonie 1981, 165.

54. Hipp. *Oath* (4.630.9–10 Li.); the most influential solution to the problem was that offered by L. Edelstein 1943, who claimed that

Oath was not part of the mainstream of Hippocratic medicine but an esoteric document that was the product of a Pythagorean group. Edelstein, however, following Hähnel 1936, misread the material about expulsive remedies as evidence for the widespread acceptance and practice of elective abortion; he also focused too narrowly on Pythagoreanism. See Kudlien 1970 and Burkert 1992, 179, n. 26.

55. Nardi 1971, 66–71; Fontanille 1977, 58–60, 67–68.
56. Nickel 1972.
57. It can, however, be found in the Cyrene Cathartic Law (Sokolowski 1962, 115, B 24–27, trans. and interpreted by Parker 1983, 346): "If a woman throws out (i.e. miscarries), if it is distinguishable (i.e. if the fetus has recognizable form), they are polluted as from one who has died, but if it isn't distinguishable, the house itself if polluted as from a woman in childbed." Aristotle also made the distinction, allowing abortion to limit family size before sense and life have begun, *Pol.* 1335b24–26.
58. Since the extent of the pregnancy is very underestimated (it must be of at least a month's duration, not six days), and the possible effectiveness of this maneuver is very overestimated, it may be that we are dealing here with an imaginary scenario constructed as a frame for the author's theories on the development of the fetus. If so, he has carefully constructed the "abortion" to involve minimal input on his part and minimal risk to the woman.
59. Crahay 1941; the oration *For Antigenes, on the Abortion*, attributed to Lysias (frag. x [Gernet]), as interpreted by Sopater, would support this, but its authenticity was questioned even in antiquity; it appears to be a schoolroom exercise, and the issues raised by later sources may reflect concerns of their own time (although Gernet accepts it as genuine in his commentary; see Gernet and Bizos 1967); Nardi 1971, 82–93, collects all the relevant texts with discussion.
60. The author of *Fleshes* 19 (8.610.3–5 Li.) refers to the many aborted fetuses of prostitutes that he has seen.
61. Riddle (1992, chap. 2) argues that the distinction between contraception and abortion was recognized in antiquity· texts (albeit late) differentiate between remedies with hormonal (contraceptive) effects (ἀτόκιον), and those which aborted the conceptus or fetus (φθόριον), and both Plato and Aristotle assume that fertility can be controlled (although without specifying the means, for abortion or exposure would achieve the same results)
62. Blum and Blum 1965, 73–74.
63. Eur. *Hipp.* 293–96; Sor. *Gyn* 1.2.4
64. *Nat.Wom.* 6 (7 320 7–8 Li), 40 (7.384.10–12 Li.); *Dis Wom.* 1 21 (8.60.16–17 Li), 68 (8.144.22–24 Li.).

65. See chapter 1, nn. 95–96. Another possible exception is IV 22, in which two births are briefly noted as having occurred, one with a white (abnormal) and one with a red (normal) discharge. Aside from recording his involvement, it is difficult to see any reason why the doctor would have reported these undistinguished cases, but the text of the manuscript is too corrupt to place weight upon it.

66. On the gynecological treatises in general, see Lloyd 1983, 62–86; on the embryological treatises, see Lonie 1981. Hanson (1989) deals specifically with women in the *Epidemics* with reference to the gynecological treatise *Diseases of Women* I, for which she is preparing a critical edition and translation; see Hanson 1975.

67. Rousselle 1980, 1090–92.

68. Manuli 1980, 396 and n. 2.

69. Lloyd 1983, 63, 84.

70. Hanson 1991, 78–79.

71. Implicit in the *engye*, or contract of marriage, *Men. Mis.* 444–45; *Perik.* 1013–4; *Sam.* 726–27; also see [Dem.] 59.122.

72. Theogn. 582, Soph. *Oed.Tyr.* 1485, 1497; DuBois 1988.

73. Implicit in the many remedies for female sterility in the gynecological treatises, according to Hanson 1990, 327.

74. The nurse's advice in Euripides' *Hippolytus*.

75. See Hanson and Armstrong 1986.

76. Hipp. *Seven Months' Child* 4 (7.440.13– 444.22 Li.); *Dis.Wom.* I 62 (8.126.4–10 Li.).

77. Hipp. *Dis.Wom.* I 62 (8.126.4–19 Li.), 67 (8.140.14–19 Li.), Eur. *Hipp.* 293–96.

78. Hipp. *Nat.Child* 13 (7.490.5–7 Li.).

79. Hipp. *Nat.Child* 30 (7.532.14ff.; 534.8–10 Li.).

80. Riddle 1992, esp. 81, 91; see earlier comments, in the discussion of abortion.

81. Hipp. *Dis.Wom.* I 62 (8.126.5–15 Li.).

82. Blum and Blum 1965, 50, 150–51.

83. *Fleshes* 19 (8.614.8–11 Li.).

84. *Dis.Wom.* I 68 (8.144.22–24 Li).

85. *Dis.Wom.* I 34 (8.80.20–21 Li.), I 46 (8.160 7 Li.), instructions to doctor to employ a woman: I 21 (8.60.15ff , Li.); *Nat.Wom* 6 (7.320.7–8 Li.), 40 (7.384.10–12 Li.); the assistant or the patient: *Nat.Wom.* 2 (7.312.18 Li.), probably the patient herself: *Nat.Wom.* 107 (7.422.14–15 Li), *Dis.Wom.* I 40 (8.98.1–2 Li.), II 141 (8.314.15–16 Li.), 146 (8 322 15–16 Li.), 157 (8.332.16 Li.); *Ster.* 213 (8.408.17; 410.3 Li.); see Lloyd 1983, 70–72.

86. See Grensemann 1975, 9.

87. Cf. Sor. *Gyn.* 1.3: ἵνα καὶ διὰ θεωρίας τὴν τέχνην ἰσχύσῃ παραλαβεῖν.
88. W. V. Harris 1989, 22–24. 67, 96; figures on women, 106; figures on classical Attica as a whole, 114; female literacy restricted to upper-class women and *hetairai*, 96, 107; see also Cole 1981; Powell 1988, 342–43.
89. Xen. *Oec.* 7.5 and 9.10.
90 Manuli 1983, 187.
91. Sor. *Gyn.* 1.3; Harris 1989, 203, Thomas 1989 does not mention midwives.
92. Havelock 1982, 189; W. V. Harris 1989, 22; Stoddart and Whitley (1988), in studying regional variations in literacy in Greece and Etruria from the eighth to the fourth centuries, found that writing was used from the seventh century by craftsmen in Athens (pp. 765–766) and in Etruria from the sixth century (p. 770); in contrast, in Crete its use seems to have been limited to the inscribing of laws by scribal experts; I know of no similar study of the regions in which Hippocratic doctors were most active, but the medical texts themselves, especially the *Epidemics*, assure us that writing was not the prerogative of the upper class or official scribes.
93. Ar. *Kn.* 188ff.
94. It seems reasonable to consider the Hippocratic doctors as professionals, even though they were not certified by any official body. *Webster's Ninth New Collegiate Dictionary* defines a profession as, "a calling requiring specialized knowledge and often long and intensive academic preparation."
95. Pl. *Rep.* 454d2; this is argued by Pomeroy 1978. Herfst (1979 [1922]) put the case for midwives acting in a professional sense (although he claimed female doctors only later and on the evidence of Pliny). Manuli (1980, 396 n. 1) reviewed the argument against this "radical hypothesis"; however, she omitted the explicit reference to female physicians in the *Republic*. Tarrant (1988) expressed doubt that midwives did anything more technical than comfort the mother, cut the cord, and attend to cleanliness, arguing that women, who had "comparatively little financial means," would not be able to support a profession of midwifery. In this he overlooked the considerable attention devoted to obstetrics and gynecology in the Hippocratic Corpus: *someone* was supporting these clearly professional activities, whether they were carried out by males or by females. As with all significant expenditure, it would have been the male guardians of the women who paid the bill. A full discussion of the later evidence for women as physicians is provided in Firatli and Robert 1964, 175–78,

no. 39 (stele of Mousa, a female physician of the second–first centuries A.D.).

96. Although the Hippocratic doctor did not stand at the pinnacle of social status, being essentially a craftsman who worked with his hands, he nonetheless participated in the upper-class pursuits of rhetoric and philosophy and, if Plato's portrayal in the *Symposium* is true to life, may even have hobnobbed with the upper levels of society.

97. Such women would have been marginal members of the society, freed slaves, metics, poor citizens.

98. See Kudlien 1979, 88–89; Krug 1985, 195–97; Firatli and Robert 1969, 175–78.

99. *IG* II², 6873; Peek 1955, 342. Consider, too, Hyginus's tale of Hagnodike, who disguised herself as a man in order to study medicine with Herophilus and to treat women. When charged by the Athenians with seducing her female patients, she defended herself before the Areopagus by revealing her true sex, and, when her female patients supported her work, the Athenians amended their law to allow free women to study medicine (Hyg *Fab.* 254); see Von Staden 1989, 40–41.

100. Foucault 1979 [1975].

101. And over the lives of male patients as well, but that is another story

102. On the issue of control, see Padel 1983, Bouvrie 1990, 50–59.

103. Poisons: Ar. *Thesm.* 561–62, 428–31; supposititious children: 338–39, 407–9, 502–16, 564–65.

104. Ar. *Thesm.* 502–16. Henderson 1975, s.v. "κύτταρον," translates the last phrase: "limp and withered like a little shot pine-cone."

Chapter Four. The Risks of Childbirth

1. Schofield 1986, 235.

2. Loudon 1991, 34.

3. Wells 1975.

4. See, e.g , Russell 1983, and Gélis 1991, 229. The evaluation of risk and the way in which statistics are presented lends itself to a degree of subjectivity. Hopkins (1987, 118, n. 10), in discussing deaths in the Roman Empire, says that maternal deaths in childbirth in preindustrial societies "may have been grossly exaggerated," citing the evidence of Gutierrez and Houdaille 1983 and Schofield 1986 for eighteenth-century England and France. It is true that these studies revealed a lower death rate than their authors had expected, averaging about 100–110 per 10,000 births, but the figures for England are 100 times the death rate in 1980 and for France 70 times the rate in 1975–77,

and the authors consider these rates to be very high. Whether we can apply the eighteenth-century figures to antiquity is also a question In both England and France, the average age of marriage hovered around 25, and in England 12 percent of the women never married, while in classical Greece virtually all women married and most marriages occurred before the age of 20, most frequently around 15. Since early marriage exposes women to higher-risk early childbirth and to more occasions of childbirth in their childbearing career, it involves an overall higher risk (Gutierrez and Houdaille attribute the decline in death rate over the 130 years of their study to a rise in the average age of marriage from 24 to 26 [pp. 986–87]). Moreover, these figures were for rural areas, and there were large regional differences in death rates in the French study, reaching a high of 291 per 10,000 in Mogneneins; if the average figure of 100–110 did not apply to Mogneneins in the eighteenth century, one cannot assume that it would apply to Greece in the fifth century B.C.

5. See chapter 1.
6. Wells 1975, 1237; Owsley and Bradtmiller 1983; I have been unable to find the source of the photograph published by Angeletti 1990, of an apparent eight-month fetus in breech position; she suggests that the situation was compatible with preeclampsia, which she believes to have been the cause of the unfavorable Hippocratic prognosis for eight-month infants; however, there is no information in the references she gives about the site where these remains were found (Greece?), or their date.
7. Hopkins 1966, 1987.
8. See, e.g., Grmek 1975.
9. See esp. Grmek 1989
10. Eisenberg 1977; Kleinman 1980, 72–80, Helman 1984, 65–73.
11. Quotation from Kleinman 1973a, 208–9; see also Freidson 1975, part 2.
12. Merck Manual, s.v. "puerperal infection."
13. On childbed fever, see Semmelweis 1983 [1860]; Penniston 1986; Gélis 1991, 249–52.
14. See Seligman 1991; an illustration of non–hospital-associated puerperal fever is provided by the case of Mary Wollstonecraft, who died of puerperal fever after a delivery that took place at home under the attendance of a midwife; the placenta was retained and extracted— apparently only partially and with contamination resulting—by a physician called to the home. See Godwin 1990 [1798].
15. This will not involve aspects of the epidemiology of childbed fever, which are not relevant to the disease in classical Greece.
16. Brief histories of puerperal fever before the introduction of antibiotics

are provided by Peckham 1935, and Gélis 1991, 249–52.

17. Denman 1768.

18. W. Harris 1845; Semmelweis's discoveries were announced in England in a lecture by C. H. F. Routh in 1848 (Semmelweis 1983 [1860], 174–75); Alexander Gordon in 1795 had preceded him by about half a century with his statement that puerperal fever is contagious and carried by the hands of doctors and medical attendants, but Harris was not entirely convinced. On the distinction that Semmelweis saw between his views and those held in Britain, see Semmelweis 1983 [1860], 133, 136–50, 176 and 176 n. 12.

19. Grmek 1989, 391, n. 72.

20. Grmek 1989, 132; he omits three cases included by Fasbender 1897, 189–93: iii 10, 11, and 12 (first series), and includes iii 2 (second series), labeled as doubtful by Fasbender.

21. Fasbender (1897, 189, n. 2) comments that this was remarkably late— if the earliest stage was not overlooked; however, in England and Wales in 1976, a rise in temperature to 38° C within fourteen days after birth was notifiable as puerperal infection; in Scotland the time period was twenty-one days, Walker, MacGillivray, and Macnaughton 1976, 404.

22. Tonsillitis as a common complication of the postpartum period is noted by Reynolds and Newell 1902, 516.

23. Fasbender 1897, 189–93; the cases are iii 10, 11, and 12 (first series; pain is noted without site specified in iii 10, in the hip in iii 11, and in the *kardia* in iii 12.

24. On interference in live delivery, *Superfet.* 4 (8.478.4–16 Li.) and 15 (8.484.10 Li.); following the death of the fetus, *Superfet.* 5, 6, 7 (8.478.17–480.12 Li.); *Dis.Wom.* i 70 (8.146 21–148.2 Li.), *Excision of the Fetus* 1 (8.512.1–514.3 Li.); on the use of pessaries: *Superfet.* 36 (8.506.11–13 Li.) and 42 (8.508 7–8 Li.); *Dis.Wom.* i 78 (8 172.14–198.2 Li.), with many recipes. Rousselle (1980, 1097–98) argues that the use of garlic, a known antiseptic, in preparations, as in the fumigations of *Dis.Wom.* ii 133 (8.286.9 Li.) and *Ster.* 230 (8.440.2 Li.), effectively negated risk; even if this were so, it takes care of only a small proportion of the cases of internal application (forty-four instances in the gynecological books), which often featured *dreck* as a primary ingredient. Loudon (1991, 72) identifies the main determinant of maternal mortality as the care given by the birth attendant, including dangerous and unwarranted interference.

25. Loudon 1991, 34.

26. Ibid

27. Merck Manual, s.v. "preeclampsia."

28. Malinas and Gourevitch 1982, discussing *Dis.Wom.* i 32 (8.76.1–22

Li.) suffocation in pregnancy; see also Gourevitch 1984, 160–62, Angeletti argues that the difficulties attributed to an eighth-month delivery are to be attributed to "a mild toxemic disease" (Angeletti 1990, 89).

29. *Epid.* II 2.20 (but of the belly), and V 11
30. *Epid.* VII 6.
31. *Epid.* I cases 4, 11, 13, III 14 (second set).
32 Loudon 1991, 34.
33. See Gélis 1991, 226–36, for the situation in early modern Europe.
34. See Weinberg 1984, 1987; among the diseases whose effects are enhanced are malaria, tuberculosis, influenza, polio; Sallares (1991, 131–32) is probably right to attribute the excess female mortality between the ages of fifteen and forty-five in modern preindustrial populations, as well as in ancient Greece, to this weakening of immunity in pregnancy.
35. Arist. *HA* 582a21–24; 583b26–28; *GA* 775a13–16; *Peri makrobiotos* 466b15–16; 467a31–32.
36. *Epid.* I 8 (2.646.9–13 Li.).
37. Littré suggested that this case belonged to the Cough of Perinthus (VI 7.1 [5.330.11–336.11 Li.]), which, according to Grmek 1980, 1989, 305–28, involved diphtheria and probably influenza, whooping cough, night blindness, and bronchopneumonia.
38. Weinberg 1984, 814, 818; see also Weinberg 1987; Diro 1982; Watkinson and Rushton 1983. Rutman and Rutman (1976) employ the hypothesis of malaria to explain the high death rate for women in the childbearing years in the seventeenth century in the Chesapeake and in Salem, Massachusetts.
39. Although W. H. S. Jones (1907 and 1909) argued that malaria was a new disease in Greece in the fifth century, most scholars today agree that it was present earlier, although it underwent a resurgence at this time, possibly as a result of the entry of large numbers of infected individuals into Greece with the Persian army; see Grmek 1989, 275–83; Borza 1979, and *contra*, Hammond 1984, answered by Borza, 1987; Borza's discussions are especially relevant because they deal with the situation in northern Greece, the area in which the doctors of *Epidemics* were practicing
40 E.g., *Epid.* I 10–11 (2.670.16–672.3 Li.), *Aph.* II 25 (4.478.1–3 Li.), *Dis* II 40 (7 56.3–4 Li.), 42 (7.58.22–23 Li.), 43 (7.60.6 Li.); *Progn* 20 (2.168.6–14 Li.); *Affect.* 18 (6.226.5 Li.); for a full discussion of all the relevant passages, see W. H. S. Jones 1909, 61–73.
41. Another empirical source for the number lore, especially as it appears in the gynecological treatises, might have been experience with pregnancy even today we distinguish between the first, second, and third

trimesters. Numbers such as this serve as handy general mnemonic devices for recalling the stages of pregnancy or calculating delivery date, as in *Epid.* II 3.17 (5.116.12–13 Li.): "That which moves in seventy days is finished in thrice that." Nevertheless, in some cases the concern with numbers seems to have its source in number magic. For example, the number seven had a special significance, as in the treatise *Sevens* and the widely held belief that the seven-months' child survives while the eight-months' child does not; see Hipp. *Seven Months' Child, Eight Months' Child*, and Hanson 1987.

42. Timken-Zinkann 1968, for an alternative theory, see Langholf 1990, 47–50.
43. Hipp. *Epid.* I 8 (2.646.12 Li.).
44. On the meaning of *kausos*, see Grmek 1989, 289–92.
45. *Epid.* I case 1 (2.682.4–684.9 Li); Grmek 1989, 295–304
46. The modern medical literature on malaria is abundant; useful brief discussions may be found in the Merck Manual and in Havard 1990, s.v. "malaria"; for a more extensive discussion, with bibliography, see Manson-Bahr and Apted 1982.
47. Zulueta (1973) has argued against the presence of falciparum malaria in classical Greece on the grounds that the species of mosquito most important for its transmission in modern times resists infection with some types of the parasite and that time was required for selection to overcome this; see too Bruce-Chwatt and Zulueta 1980, 14–19. But see Grmek 1989, 278–81, which reviews the evidence for the presence of falciparum.
48. On blackwater fever, see Manson-Bahr and Apted, 1982, on blackwater fever in the Hippocratic writings, see Grmek 1989, 284–304; *kausos* with black urine, *Epid.* I 9 (2.652.8–9 Li.).
49. Edmonds 1900, 260 (emphasis added).
50. *Progn.* 20 (2.172.3–4 Li.); *Aph.* v 55 (4 552.6–8 Li.); Soph. *Oed.Tyr.* 25, trans. in W. H. S. Jones 1909, 33.
51. Foy and Kondi (1935) and Grmek (1989) discussed possible cases of blackwater fever in the *Epidemics*, but confined themselves to males; the apparent assumption was that women in the postpartum period could only suffer from puerperal infections.
52. Hipp. *Nat.Man* 15 (6.68.8–9 Li.), on melancholia, see W. H. S. Jones 1907, 45–47; 1909, 98–101.
53. Other possibilities include typhoid; Grmek so diagnosed the wife of Hemoptolemos in VII 11 (5.382 13–386.22 Li.) from the characteristic color of the stools (ὑπόκιρρα), explaining the absence of reference to a rash by suggesting that the light rash of typhoid would not have been seen as significant by the doctor (Grmek 1989, 346–50). Scurlock

identifies the *kausos* in which the daughter of Telebulus died (ı 8 [2.646.12 Li.]) as typhoid, apparently because of the emphasıs on nosebleeds, but this was the epidemic in which Philiscus dıed of blackwater fever according to Grmek (Scurlock 1991, 57, n. 223).

54. Corvisier (1985, 110, n. 23) diagnoses it as puerperal fever.
55. W. H. S. Jones 1909, 43 and 43, n. 1; he refers to Edmonds 1900; most of the footnotes are devoted to animals.
56. W. H. S. Jones 1909, 123–26.
57. E.g., *Dis.* ıı 48–49 (7 72.6–76.13 Li.); *Int.Aff.* 10–12 (7.188.26–192.19 Li.); *Epid.* ıv 24 (5.172.1–5 Li.); v 103 (5.258.9–12 Li.) = vıı 49 (5.418.1–4 Li.), the wife of Simus after childbirth; vıı 50 (5.418.5–17 Li), 51 (5.418.18–420.10 Li.); for a collection of the references, see Meinecke 1927.
58. According to the modern definition, tuberculosis is "a chronic granulomatous infectious disease caused by bacteria of the genus *Mycobacterium*"; Manchester 1984, 162. The Greeks, of course, were not aware of the bacterial agent responsible and therefore dıd not recognıze the various forms of tuberculosıs as the "same" disease, as, for example, tuberculosis of the spine, or Pott's disease, characterized by a sharply angular curvature of the spıne that can sometımes be ıdentıfied ın ancient representations.
59. Hipp. *AWP* 4 (2.22 Li.); on modern recognition of this, see Youmans 1979, 203–5.
60. See chapter 3, n. 35.
61. Grmek 1989, 191.

Chapter Five. Appeal to the Gods

1. Blum and Blum 1965, 125–32.
2. Ibıd., chaps. 12 and 13.
3. Megas 1958, 144–45, 148, 151–52; Dubisch 1991.
4. New York, Metropolitan Museum of Art MMA 24.97.92; see Rıchter (1954, no. 67), who dates the relief to 425–400; and Mitropoulou (1977, 45, no. 66), who dates ıt more closely to 410; see also Stoop 1960, 30, 32; and Van Straten 1981, 100 and fig. 43. Pıngiatoglou (1981, 140, n 7) questions its authentıcıty, but apparently without having seen it; she is followed by Vedder 1988, 178, n. 81.
5. Hom. *Il.* 19.187; 21.103.
6. Eur. *Iph.Taur* 1464–69, Iphigeneia. Hes. frags. 23a, 26; Wernicke 1895b, 1382; Kondis 1967, 222–23.
7. *Anth.Pal.* 6.201–2, 270–74, 276 to Artemis (200 to Eileıthyıa); Pıngiatoglou (1981) offers a collection of the archaeologıcal, epıgraphıcal,

and literary evidence for Eileithyia (especially useful for unpublished material from Paros), she also briefly discusses other childbirth deities, including Artemis, who bear the epithet "Eileithyia."

8. Callim. *Anth.Pal.* 6.146.

9. See Rouse 1902, 251–58; Baur 1901; Cole 1984, 243, n. 62; Mitropoulou 1977, 101–2; Van Straten 1981, with catalogue of offerings in the form of bodily parts; compare with dedications to Eileithyia, Pingiatoglou 1981.

10. See esp. Bruneau 1970, 191–95.

11. Demangel 1922, 78–79 and figs. 11 and 12; 84–85 and fig. 17; compare a similar representation in a dedication to Hera Eileithyia in the Argive Heraeum, Waldstein 1892, 20 and pl. viii.19; also a seventh-century figure from Crete, Ducrey and Picard 1969.

12. Dikaios 1961; Heuzey 1882; Myres 1914; Pingiatoglou (1981, 91, n. 243) lists five such groups; see also Vedder 1988, 178 and pl. 25 2.

13. Paus. 1.29.2; Sybel 1881, nos. 4542h and 4542k; Philadelpheus 1927, 159–60, nos. 3, 5–6, figs. 3 and 4; and Baur 1901, 492.

14. Kondis 1967, 190, 203; Price 1978, 121–22; Themelis 1971, 20–24; excavation reports in *Praktika* (1950) figs. 5 and 7; *Ergon* (1960) 29, fig. 38.

15. Salviat 1959.

16. "Chronique des fouilles," *BCH* 82 (1958) 808–14; 85 (1961) 920–27; 100 (1976) 781–83; 101 (1977) 692; Pingiatoglou 1981, 118–19; Weill 1985.

17. Hipp. *Epid.* iii, first case, second set.

18. Linders 1972. These are duplicates of those at Brauron, see Papademetriou 1963, 112 and *Praktika* 1949, 84–85; 1950, 187; 1956, 75–76. He explains the duplication by a removal of the offerings to Athens, but Linders has shown that the lists in Athens were arranged according to the storage places of the dedications in *Brauron*, and suggests that they were simply copies of records in Brauron that were set up in Athens, as we know was done with Delian inscriptions and some Eleusinian decrees (Linders 1972, 73).

19. Linders 1972, 9, 14.

20. Mommsen 1899, 343ff.

21. Linders 1972, 58–59.

22. Osborne 1985, 154–72.

23. *IG* ii² 1517.214; son of Dieukhes (a physician: Galen 11.163, 795 [Kühn]; Ath. 1.5a); together with his brother Diakritos, who was a doctor (*IG* ii² 1744, prytanis in mid-fourth century), and three other men, one also known to have been a doctor, Epeukhes joined in a dedication at the Athenian Asklepieion (*IG* ii² 4359; see Aleshire 1989, 94–95).

24. See the evidence of the epigrams in the *Anthology*; also the scholiast on Callim. *Hymn* 1.77.
25. Kondis 1967, 223.
26. See Baur 1901.
27. On Asclepius and his cult, see E. Edelstein and Edelstein 1945.
28. At the Asclepieion in Athens 51.39 percent of the dedications were by women according to Aleshire 1989, 45–46.
29. Roebuck 1951; Lang 1977.
30. Roebuck 1951, 121–23; Lang 1977; on the possible uterus, see Van Straten 1981, 124, no. 15.118.
31. *IG* II² 1532–37 and 1539; Van Straten 1981, nos. 1.8, 1.25–311; Aleshire 1989.
32. Herzog 1931, 148 n. 15; Van Straten 1981, 129–30, no. 30.2.
33. Van Straten 1981, no. 30.10.
34. Van Straten 1981, no. 30.7, with bibliography.
35. Herzog 1931; E. Edelstein and Edelstein 1945, 1:221–37, T423
36. *IG* IV², 1, nos. 121–22; Herzog 1931; E. Edelstein and Edelstein 1945, 1:221–37, T423, nos 1, 2, 25 (but pregnant with worms), 31, 34, 39, 42; also a request for offspring at Lebena, T426, no. 2.
37. These parallel appeals made to Apollo at Delphi for offspring. Fontenrose (1978) lists one historical, four quasi-historical, and seven legendary responses on this subject, all to men. Requests by individuals for cures (for wounds, madness, speechlessness, and unspecified illness) number eight quasi-historical and nine legendary; one petitioner (Q135) is a woman, Telesilla of Argos, for an unspecified sickness
38. E. Edelstein and Edelstein 1945, 1:239–40, T426.
39. Hipp. *Aph.* v 50 (4.550.5–6 Li.) = *Epid.* II 6.16 (5.136 7–8 Li.); see too *Dis.Wom.* I 71 (8 150.19–20 Li.) in a mole pregnancy, and II 110 (8.236.20–21 Li) in treating a red flux.
40. Bernhard 1926, 31–32, nos. 100, 101, 108.
41. E. Edelstein and Edelstein 1945, 2:158–73.
42. Case no. 25, Herzog 1931, 80; Hiller read ζωϊυφιων, *IG* IV, ed. Minor, p. 74, line 32; Ploss (1891, 299) considered it a cesarean.
43. *Epid.* v 18 (5.218.10 Li.), 42 (5.232.14 Li.), 50 (5.236 16 Li.); VII 10 (5 380.21 Li.).
44. E. Edelstein and Edelstein (1945, 2·170 n. 35) consider them to be simply miracle stories, rejecting Herzog's medical interpretation (see further in text).
45. Hipp. *Nat.Child* 30, trans. Lonie 1981; see also *Prorrhet* 26 (9.58 Li).
46. It was only in the fourth century that doctors opened the profession to paying students without claim to Asclepiad descent; see Sherwin-White 1978, 262–63.
47. See Sherwin-White 1978, 275–76; Jouanna 1988.

48. Herzog 1931, 145 and 145, n. 15; Aleshire (1989, 65–66) identified nine dedicants to Asclepius at Athens as doctors, often by the medical nature of their offerings; Cohn-Haft 1956, 117ff.
49. In the British Museum, see Phillips 1973, pl. 10.
50. E. Edelstein and Edelstein 1945, 1:263, T458.
51. Bousquet 1956 (SEG 16.326); Langholf 1990, 25–27; Jouanna (1988) points out that since the Delphic privileges were extended only to descendants of Asclepius in the male line, this inscription need not refer to a guild of physicians but may refer to a gentilic organization; not all Asclepiadai were doctors, and not all doctors were Asclepiadai in the male line.
52. Herzog 1928, 52ff., no. 1.
53. Herzog 1928, 18ff., no. 8A.
54. Linders 1972, II^2 1517.214.
55. See Lloyd 1979, 37–49; Lanata 1967; Burkert 1983.
56. Hipp. Sac.Dis 1 (6.354.13–14; 358.19 Li.).
57. Text: 8.466–70 Li.; in my translation I have retained the confusion between singular and plural found in the Greek text; for discussion, see Lefkowitz 1981, 12–25; King 1983; 1985, 175–82.
58. Hipp. Regimen 1 2–10 (6.468.6–486.11 Li.); Nat.Man 1–3 (6.32.1–34.7 Li.); Breaths 1–5 (6.90.1–96.19 Li.); Pl. Phaedr. 270a–d.
59. On the relationship between philosophy and medicine, see L. Edelstein 1967, Longrigg 1963; W. G. S. Jones 1946; Laín Entralgo 1970, 142–51. The question of philosophy in Magna Graecia offers more problems, especially in the case of Empedocles, who functioned as an iatromantis and claimed to be an immortal god (DK 31 B112), but who also analyzed the mechanics of human physiology (DK 31 B84, 100).
60. Hipp. Superfet. 34 (8.504.20–506.7 Li.).
61. Ar. Wasps 1037–43, trans. Rogers.
62. This strangling illness of men was not taken into consideration by King in her interpretation of the strangling illness of parthenoi (King 1983; 1985, 175–82). Since the problem afflicts men as well as women (and, in fact, the author of Parthenoi explicitly says this about the ailment he is discussing), the explanation cannot be framed exclusively in terms of references to female anatomy.
63. The term ἠπίαλος occurs in Superfet. 34 (8.506.2 Li.).
64. Aristophanes' linking of ἦγχον and ἀπέπνιγον is not noticed by King; it seems to vitiate her argument that the use of ἄγχω in Illness of Maidens is not equivalent to πνίγω but provides a specific reference to "the role of Artemis at transitions in a woman's life which involve bloodshed" (King 1985, 117).
65. E.g., in the Oresteia of Aeschylus.
66. Hdt. 6.84.

67. Hipp. *Sac.Dis.* 1 (6.354.12–15 Li.), see Lloyd 1979, 12–13, and 12, nn. 18 and 20.
68. Hipp. *Sac.Dis.* 1 (6.358.19–360.9 Li.).
69. Empedocles DK 31 B111.
70. Ar. *Clouds* 749–52; Pl. *Gorg.* 573a; belief in the ability of magicians to influence the moon continues in modern Greece, Blum and Blum 1965, 175 (a woman healer); 196 (Dionysius the Sorcerer).
71. Eur. *Med.*, passim.
72. Pl. *Symp.* 201cd; other references to mantic powers, 202e–203a, 206b
73. Pl. *Theat.* 149c.
74. Plut. *De superst.* 116A; see also Pollux 7.188.
75. Eur. *Hipp.* 293–96.
76. On magical healing in Greece, see Lanata 1967; Lloyd 1979, 10–58; Halliday 1936, 280–84.

Chapter Six. Acculturation to Early Childbearing

1 United Nations 1954, 6–8; Lancaster 1990, 281; Loudon 1991, 56.
2. Hes. *WD* 698.
3. Pl. *Laws* 785b; *Rep.* 460e.
4. Arist. *Pol* 1335a13–23.
5. Plut. *Lyc.* 15.3.
6. Xen. *Oec.* 3.13.
7. Plut. *Mor.* 271D; vases portraying brides' fear Keuls 1985, figs. 101 and 102, and p. 130; references to the unwed maiden as untamed, wild creature are collected by Carson 1990, p. 144 and n. 22.
8. Trillat 1986, 14; King 1985, 103–18, esp. 106–9.
9. Rousselle (1980, 1090; 1988, 67–68) interprets the symptoms as a sign of a serious infection, in particular, of the abortion of an extra-uterine pregnancy. King 1983; King 1985, 103–18.
10. Veith 1965; Simon 1978; accepted by Laín Entralgo 1970, 167–68, Gourevitch 1984, 27, 112–28; Manuli 1983, 153. King (1985, 105–6, 110–13) is critical of both Veith and Simon. A useful review and critique of the intellectual history of hysteria appears in Micale 1989 and 1990.
11. As both King (1985, 106–9) and Trillat (1986, 14) have pointed out, the word does not appear in the Greek but is found only in Littré's captions.
12. Walton, Beeson, and Scott 1986, s.v. "hysteria."
13. Veith 1965, 273.
14. Veith 1965, 273; see more recently Shorter 1986, who documents the

rise and fall of paralysis as the "symptom of choice" in the nineteenth century.

15. B. Simon 1978, 239.
16. B. Simon 1978, 243, 258; consider also his more cautious statement about the Hippocratic syndrome. "Are these conditions the same ones we call hysterical conversion? It seems likely" (243).
17. See Foster and Anderson 1978, 96–99; Helman 1984, 73–74, 146–60, 184–85; Yap 1977; Rubel, O'Nell, and Collado-Ardón 1984; and Foulkes 1972.
18. Rubel 1964.
19. Foulkes 1972.
20. Good 1977.
21. Morsy 1978.
22. See Rubel 1964; Rubel, O'Nell, and Collado-Ardón 1984.
23 Bauman (1939) identified the illness as a "Volkskrankheit," in the form of a "suggestionsepidemie," which he traced to a religious source: a holy legend or the self-sacrifice of a maiden inspired by a divinity. Shorter (1986) demonstrates that even an approach that accepts hysteria as an "actual disease entity" does not preclude a focus on the shaping of the symptoms by the cultural context; a similar approach is suggested by Micale 1990, 42–47
24. B. Simon 1978, 251.
25. Manuli 1980, 402; King 1985 is also skeptical
26. Perlman 1989; quotation from p. 126.
27. The literary and evidence is collected in Wernicke 1895a; see Perlman 1983 and 1989; E. Simon 1983, Calame 1977, 63–70; Cole 1984, Kahil 1977; Osborne 1985; R. Hamilton 1989.
28. Schol. Ar. *Lys.* 645; Suda, s v ἄρκτος ἢ Βραυρωνίοις. A somewhat similar etiological myth for the bear festival at Mounychia tells of the demand for a human sacrifice of a girl that was averted by the substitution of an animal; Paus. *ap.* Eustathius *Il.* 2.732; *Anecd.Bekk.* 1.144. On the development of the temple legends, see Sale 1975.
29. Ar. *Lys.* 638–47.
30. Harpocr. *ap.* Suda, s v. ῍Αρκτος ἢ Βραυρωνίοις, Burkert 1966, 3–5
31. Eur. *Heracl.* 777; Men. *Epitrep.* 438; Thuc. 6.54ff ; Arist. *Ath.Pol.* 18 2; this is the accepted identification of these offices, but Walbank (1981), in support of the reading of the text by Stinton 1976 (καὶ χέουσα τὸν κρόκωτον, an emendation of Sourvinou-Inwood's reading), has argued that all of the cult titles belonged to Artemis at Brauron.
32. Kahil 1963, 1965, 1976, 1977, 1981, 1983; R. Hamilton 1989.
33. A third vase seems to portray the metamorphosis of a figure into a bear, and E. Simon (1983, 88) suggests persuasively that it is a representation of a dramatic performance involving the story of Kallisto and

her son Arkas and not a part of the evidence about the Arkteia; see R. Hamilton 1989.

34. Brelich 1969, 248–49.
35. Ar. *Peace* 873, Arist. *Ath.Pol.* 54.7 and Pollux 7 107; accepted by Henderson 1987a, 156 on line 645; Perlman 1983, 117, Cole 1984 ("probably"); *contra*, Delmousou 1988a, 1988b.
36. Schol. Ar. *Lys.* 645, Suda, s.v. Ἄρκτος ἢ Βραυρωνίοις
37. Chirassi 1964, 26; Coulton 1976; Sourvinou-Inwood 1971, 1988, Osborne 1985, 165; Henderson 1987a, Dowden 1989, 28–30.
38. Sourvinou-Inwood 1988.
39. See review, Keuls 1990.
40. Sourvinou-Inwood 1988, 56
41. Sourvinou-Inwood 1988, 57.
42. Kahil 1977.
43. Brelich 1969, 273.
44. Kondis 1967, 190, 203; Price, 1978, 121–22; archaeological reports in *Ergon* (1958) 36, fig. 38; 37, fig. 39; (1959) 16, fig. 15; 17, figs 16–17; (1960) 23, fig. 32; 24, fig. 33; 29, fig. 38; *BCH* 83 (1959) 595, fig. 25; 596, fig. 27; 84 (1960) 665, figs. a and b; 666, fig. 7; 85 (1960) 640, figs. 4–5
45. Papademetriou 1963; Pomponius Mela II 3, 46.
46. Wernicke 1895a, 1171, following Mommsen.
47. Kahil 1977.
48. Perlman 1983.
49. Harpocr. *ap.* Suda, s.v. Ἄρκτος ἢ Βραυρωνίοις, *Anecd.Bekk.* s.v. Ἀρκτεῦσαι; Schol. Ar. *Lys.* 645
50 E. Simon 1983, 86; on the contrary, Parke (1977, 140) would confine the rites to a few.
51. Another suggestion of exclusivity is the use of the term δεκατεύειν for "playing the bear," attested by Harpocration and Hesychius, its significance was unknown even in antiquity, for Harpocration suggested that it means a tithe (one in ten girls would participate), and Hesychius that it could refer to the ten-year-olds who served. Perlman (1983) suggested that the latter explanation derived from *Lys.* 645, but it was accepted by Mommsen 1898, 453, and Montepaone 1979, 356; Perlman reconciled the notion of a tithe with participation by all by suggesting that the tithe denoted selection not in the strict sense of one in ten, but in the more general sense that the participants had to meet requirements of age and citizenship and were regarded as sacred to the goddess.
52. Dowden (1989, 27–28) categorically rejects this but still postulates "some sort of universal involvement," with the elite undergoing a fuller version of initiation than ordinary girls

53. R. Hamilton (1989, 459–60 and n. 18) postulated two Brauronia, a penteteric public festival in which grown women and men participated, and an annual private ritual of the bears that involved only girls, influenced perhaps by the parallels he so rightly stresses between the Artemis cult at Brauron and Alkman's *partheneia*. In this he does not imply, however, that playing the bear was a private rite in the sense of being carried out alone by single individuals, or that the *krateriskoi* were dedicated "privately" by girls who went to the shrine alone and individually dedicated their vases (personal communication).

54. R. Hamilton 1989, 471 and table 4.

55. Dohan 1934, 524, 525; Jucker 1963; Amyx 1988, 2:652–57. In a few scenes on the Corinthian vases women appear in the company of padded dancers (komasts); Payne (1931, 118–24, esp. 121) held that the presence of komasts implies a Dionysia, while Amyx, on the basis of vases unknown to Payne, assigned both komasts and women to a festival of Artemis. Nevertheless, it is interesting that Suda, s.v. Βραυρών, says that there was a Dionysia in Brauron (and also many *pornai*, an allegation that has been strongly denied—see Lloyd-Jones 1983, 92, n. 31; however, Brelich [1969, 276–79] points out that prostitutes would have come to Brauron for the Dionysia).

56. Sokolowski 1962, no. 115, B9–23.

57. Hipp. *Hebd.* 5 (8.636.19–26 Li.), Solon 27.7 = 19 (Campbell); Heraclitus DK A18; Arist. *HA* 581a.

58. See esp. Rubel in Landy 1977, quotation from p. 128 (= Rubel 1964).

59. Osborne 1985, 165, has suggested that, like an illness, the experience of participation may have triggered menarche; his acceptance of the age range as five to ten makes this highly unlikely, but it is certainly a possibility for those ten to fifteen.

60. On separation from the mother, see Jenkins (1983) who refers to a fifth-century red-figure skyphos portraying Persephone reaching out for Demeter as she is carried away by Hades; and Foley 1982, 169–70; Sourvinou-Inwood (1987a, 140) and Redfield (1982, 187–88) stress the trauma of separation from the father, but the ancient evidence does not suggest that fathers resisted their daughters' early marriage, and they were, after all, the ones in control.

61. [Homer] *Hymn to Demeter* 470–82; for text and commentary, see Richardson 1974, esp. 74–86, for variants on the myth; because the hymn links the story with the institution of the Eleusinian mysteries, it may contain details relevant to that celebration that do not pertain to the Thesmophoria. For that reason, I have given only the basic story outline.

62. Detienne (1989) demonstrates the importance of the evidence provided by Aristophanes; the main witness, however, is a late scholion to

Lucian 275.23–276.28 (Rabe); for references to other sources, including archaeological remains, see Burkert 1985, 242–46. Detienne (1989) relied especially upon Ael. frag. 44 (Hercher) and Paus. 4.17.1, both, as he admits, "marginal, dubious stories." Arguments for the participation of unmarried women, slaves, and prostitutes rest upon Luc. *Dial.Meretricii* 2.1, where a mistress/prostitute says she has seen the girl her lover is planning to marry at the Thesmophoria; and Men *Epitrep*. 522, where a father-in-law complains that his son-in-law is paying double for the Thesmophoria (for a wife and for a slave-mistress). These contradict Is. 6.49–50 and Ar. *Thesm* 294, which attest that slaves were not permitted, and Call. frag. 63, which says that unmarried women were excluded While it is possible to reconcile the sources by new hypotheses (an alternative festival for women excluded from the regular festival, Deubner 1932, 53–54; the exclusion of unmarried women applied only to those charged with carrying out the rites, Farnell 1977 [1896–1909], 3:84), the comic purposes of both Lucian and Menander make reliance upon them dubious when other sources contradict them.

63. See Nilsson, 1957 (1906), 313
64. For Athens, next to the Pynx, see H. Thompson 1936 For Thebes, on the Kadmeia, see Xen. *Hell*. 5.2.29. For celebrations outside the city at Paros, Thasos, Smyrna, Miletus, Troizene, Gela, see Richardson 1974, 250.
65. Is. 3.80, 8.19.
66. Their only opportunity for such an extended stay away from the home. Burkert 1985, 242.
67. Detienne (1989) stressed the occurrence of blood sacrifice during the Thesmophoria itself; since the remains were decayed, the sacrifice must have taken place at the festival of the previous year. Their survival for a year seems unlikely, however. Deubner (1932, 52–53) suggested that the remains were thrown down during the festival Skira, four month earlier; Parke (1977, 159) agreed, but E. Simon (1983, 19–20) was still doubtful about the survival of the remains and suggested instead the Stenia, two days before the Thesmophoria.
68. Detienne 1989.
69. Riddle 1992, 25–26; so too the branches upon which the women slept (chaste tree, ἀγνός, see Detienne 1977). Perhaps both reflect the chastity required *during* the rites
70. E.g., E Simon 1983, Burkert 1985, 242–46; Brumfield 1981, 70–103.
71. See Lewis 1980 For woman-centered interpretations, see next note; Detienne (1989) read the festival as an expression of male fear of the androcidal tendencies of women
72. Winkler 1990, chap. 7, Zeitlin 1981, 1982; other interpretations that

center upon women· Jeanmaire 1939 (a female initiation ceremony),
so too Lincoln 1979; Kerényi 1975 and Abram 1985 focused on menstruation.

73 Winkler 1990, chap. 7.
74. Winkler 1990, 199.
75. Arist. *GA* 729a10–12, 28–33; 729b14–22; *Met.* 1044a34.
76. Ar. *Thesm.* 832–47, see also Ar. *Lys.* 651.
77. Zeitlin 1981, 1982.
78. Zeitlin 1982; quotation from p. 142.
79. Megas 1958, 53–54.
80. B. Simon 1978, 251–57; quotation from p. 257. Kraemer 1979.
81. Zeitlin 1982; Abram 1985; Chirassi 1979.

Chapter Seven. The Attitudes of the Polis *to Childbirth: Putting Women
into the Grid*

1. Michon 1905, 198; Riemann 1940; Loraux 1981; Vernant 1980–81,
   404; Keuls 1985, 138; and Vedder 1988, 190, 182. Vedder expressed it
   in its most extreme form when she claimed that the group of tombstones portraying labor scenes discussed in this chapter provided a
   "direkt" analogy with memorials for men who had died in battle, and
   that both the warriors and the women were similarly portrayed as "in
   Aktion."
2. Plut. *Lyc.* 27.2–3 (as emended by Latte). The case for the emendation
   is made by Wallace 1970; one good manuscript reads των ιερων, and
   Wallace argued that this reading is confirmed by the text of Herodotus
   9.85 before the mistaken emendation of *that* text changed ιρέας to
   ιρένας. Despite the difficulty in attributing to scribal error the shift
   from τῶν ιερῶν to ἐν λέχῳ, MacDowell 1986, 120–22, accepts the
   emendation because it "gives precisely the sense required" by "the
   Spartan principle that a man's aim in life is to be a good soldier and a
   woman's to be the mother of good soldiers." But the argument is circu-
   lar: if the text depends upon the principle, it cannot be used in support of the principle.
3. *IG* v 1, 713–14, 1128, 1277, in childbirth; 701–10, 918, 1124, 1125, in
   battle.
4. Wolters in Wolters and Friederichs 1885, no. 1042, first identified the
   scene on the stele of Malthake (no. 8 in this chapter) as labor, citing
   the epigram of Neotima (*Anth.Pal.* 7.730, quoted and discussed later);
   Wolters 1892 discussed other members of the group and called attention to the loosened clothing as a sign of childbirth (see my n. 10); see
   also Michon 1905; Riemann 1940; Loraux 1981, with emphasis on private memorials; Vedder 1988, gives a full discussion and bibliography

of the group; see also Vedder 1989, a special study of the stele in the Sackler Museum, Harvard University.

5. Michon 1905, 198, first suggested the equation of death in childbirth with death in battle; see my n. 1.

6. Ar *Lys.*651; *Thesm.* 832–47.

7. Loraux 1986, 24.

8 Loraux 1981. Loraux also added as evidence an epitaph (Peek 1955, no. 548 [IG II/III² 11907], dated after 350) that applies the term *iphthime*, which she translates as "courageuse," to a woman named Kratista who died in childbirth. But the term *iphthime* is Homeric, and the Homeric evidence does not support the translation "courageous" when the epithet is applied to a woman. Homer applies the adjective to women in seven passages. Two of these use the epithet in contexts that offer no suggestion as to its exact meaning: *Od.* 12.452, of Queen Arete of the Phaeacians; *Od.* 15.364, of Ktimene, Penelope's youngest child. In three passages the context is one of traditional female behavior: *Il.* 5.415, of Aigialeia in mourning, *Od* 16.332, of Penelope when she must be informed of her son's safety lest she be frightened and cry; and Od. 23.92, of Penelope when she is admonished by her son *Od.* 10.106 applies the term to a giant Laestrygonian woman; a translation of "stalwart" or even "huge" is appropriate, but would not justify using the same translation for a normal-sized woman. Finally, the adjective is applied to the wife of Sthenelos in connection with her illustrious descent; it is true that she is also described as giving birth at seven months, but in this she is portrayed as the passive victim of Hera, and the epithet is not applied to her behavior during the delivery. The epithet is also applied to cattle at *Il.* 23.260 (and similarly four times in the Homeric *Hymn to Hermes·* 94, 302, 394, 402). It is justified in this epitaph only because the usage is a special case, a pun on Kratista's name (Loraux calls it a "nom prédestiné).

9. Although the iconography of white-ground lekythoi used as funerary offerings is often considered in conjunction with grave reliefs, no labor or childbirth scenes appear on them, see Kurtz and Boardman 1971, 102–5; Shapiro 1991, 653–55.

10. Wolters in Wolters and Frederichs 1895 and Wolters 1892, loosened clothing: the epithet λυσίζωνος was applied to childbirth divinities: Theoc. 17.60; Pind. *Ol.* 6.39; for references to later literature, see Aubert 1989, 444 and n. 48, 449 and n. 59. Vedder (1988) suggested that the major iconographical clue was an accentuation of the belly by the arrangement of the clothing.

11. An exception was Brückner 1888, see Michon 1905. Vedder (1988) briefly discusses the history of the debate, which now seems resolved in favor of the identification.

12. New York, Metropolitan Museum of Art MMA 24.97.92; see plate 1 and chapter 5, n. 4. Another portrayal of this posture in a clear context of childbirth is provided by an Eretrian pyxis that depicts Leto in labor; see Speier 1932, 83 and pl. 28; Pingiatoglou 1981, 20–22, pl. 8.
13. Vedder 1988, 1989.
14 Omitting Istanbul, Archaeological Museum 572 (Vedder 1988, pl. 24, no. 1), only the woman's head and upper torso are preserved; Thasos, Archaeological Museum 1172 (Vedder 1988, pl 24, no. 2), a three-quarter life-sized scene reconstructed from a number of fragments in accordance with the type scenes on intact pieces—Devambez (1955) questioned the funerary context, arguing that the scene was part of a choregic monument depicting Phaedra; and a badly damaged stele in Messembria, Mihailov 1970, 290, no. 330 bis, and pls. 167, 168. Pingiatoglou (1981, 87, n. 237) added two unpublished fragments of stelai in the Paros Museum, nos. 983 and 370; of the first, she says only that it is somewhat similar to the Rhodes stele and slightly different from the stele of Malthake, omitting to specify even the number of figures in the scene; she gives no description at all of the second and no illustration of either. Her principle of selection is also unclear: she includes two Roman pieces in the group, the relief from Ostia, Ostia Museum 5204, post-Flavian; and the Basil relief of the second century A.D., Phillips 1973, pl. 3.
15. Athens, National Archaeological Museum NM 1055: Vedder 1988, pl. 21, 2; Conze 1893–1922, no. 309, pl. 75.
16. Athens, National Archaeological Museum NM 1077: Conze 1893–1922, no. 308, pl. 74; Schmaltz 1970, 132, no. A140.
17. Paris, Louvre MND 726: Vedder 1988, pl. 21.1; Michon 1905, 190–99, pl. 13
18. Cambridge, Mass., Arthur M. Sackler Museum 1905.8: Chase 1924, 103; Vedder 1989.
19. Vedder 1989.
20. Athens, National Archaeological Museum NM 749: Johansen 1951, 51, n. 26.
21. Athens, Kerameikos Museum P290: Vedder 1988, pl. 22.2; Riemann 1940, 24–28, no. 25, pl. l.6.
22. Ny Carlsberg Glyptotek 226a: Vedder 1988, pl. 22.1; Schmaltz 1970, 137, no. A205.
23. Piraeus Museum 21. Conze 1893–1922, no. 155, pl. 46; Brückner 1888, 518, no. 5.
24. On the use of this epithet, never applied to citizens and rarely to metics, see Nielsen et al. 1989, 419, they suggest that its use is a strong indication that the inscription commemorates a slave.
25. First noted by Furtwangler, cited in Brückner 1888, 518

26. C. Clairmont, personal communication, August 1989.
27. Alexandria: Vedder 1988, pl. 23.2; Pfuhl 1901, 268–70, no. 7, pl. 18.1 (no. 6 similar but older, less well preserved); Breccia 1922, 134, no. 83b (no. 82b is the older stele), Noshy 1937, 106.
28. New York, Metropolitan Museum MMA 04.17.1: Merriam 1887; Brown 1957.
29. Rhodes, Archaeological Museum 1470–3: Vedder 1988, pl. 25.1.
30. E.g., Athens, National Archaeological Museum NM 819.
31. Volos Museum, corridor A, 1: Arbanitopoulos 1928, 147–49 and pl. 1; 1909, 215–19; Brown 1974; first half of the second century.
32. Peek 1955, 1606.
33. Stele of Ampharete, Athens, Kerameikos Museum. Clairmont 1970, no. 23; *IG* II² 10650; see Schmaltz 1983, 119.
34. Sourvinou-Inwood 1987a, 1987b, 1990.
35. Halperin 1990, 30–36; Mason 1984, 61; 1987.
36. Arist. *GA* 729a28–33, 729b13–15.
37. Henderson 1987b, 109.
38. See chapter 1.
39. On "quiet" warrior monuments, see Clairmont 1972, 52, 54.
40. One anomalous scene, Leiden, National Museum of Antiquities RO I A5 (see Schmaltz 1970, A34) shows the warrior seated on a rock. A second man is holding out his hand in farewell, while the warrior raises his right hand to his helmet (perhaps to remove it, signifying that he is finished with war?), and rests his left hand on his shield. There is no indication that he is wounded, suffering, or in less than full control of himself.
41. See Clairmont 1972, with list in n. 4. In general, also see Stupperich 1977; and Schweitzer 1941, 35–48.
42. Aristonautes, Athens, National Archaeological Museum NM 738. The motif is more often found in Boeotia on painted stelai, for example, Mnason in the Thebes Museum; see Schweitzer 1941, 38 n. 4.
43. Although wounded warriors are portrayed on Attic white-ground lekythoi, they are figures from myth, such as Sarpedon and Patroclus (see Schweitzer 1941, nn 10, 11). Moreover, the function of these ceramic lekythoi was quite different from that of the stone grave monuments, whether these were in the form of stelai or lekythoi: the ceramic lekythoi were offerings to the dead, whereas the stone stelai and lekythoi were display markers for the grave; see Stupperich 1977, 182–83.
44. The fate of the Amazons who fought against Athens provided a warning to women of the consequences of violating this dichotomy: their anonymous death "justly punishes them for usurping the name of warriors"; Loraux 1986, 148

45. Although by the fourth century, pity was becoming increasingly acceptable in memorials to the dead, this did not extend to monuments celebrating the civic contribution of the citizen soldier (Loraux 1986, 114–15), nor to the private monuments that made use of scenes from the public memorials (Clairmont 1970, 100–102; 1972, 55–58).

46. The disparity between Greek attitudes toward death in childbirth and death in battle that is expressed in these monuments is confirmed by the difference in the public treatment of these two forms of death, a point I owe to Christoph Clairmont. For men who died in battle, fifth-century Athens developed a system of public honor to celebrate death in warfare, which included the *epitaphios* and the common public monument, or *polyandrion* (see Loraux 1986). This must have been very clearly felt in antiquity, as it usurped the traditional family role (and especially the role of women) in the honoring of the dead (see Shapiro 1991, 646). In contrast, no similar public honors were offered for victims of childbirth, whose deaths remained a private, family matter, just as their lives had been.

47. Clairmont 1970, 62–63; Benson 1990.

48. See Schmaltz 1983, 112–14.

49. See n. 33.

50. *Anth.Pal.* 7, no. 730, trans. Paton (Loeb); Wolters in Wolters and Friederichs 1885, no. 1042; Michon 1905.

51. Standing figure the deceased: Athens, National Archaeological Museum NM 766, Clairmont 1970, no. 27; NM 4507, Kallipolites 1968, 85ff., figs. 2–3.

52. Pl. *Rep.* 454d2; Pomeroy 1978.

53. Athens, National Archaeological Museum NM 993; Clairmont 1970, no. 53; *IG* II² 6873; Peek 1955, 342. See Kudlien 1979, 88–89; Krug 1985, 195–97. Consider, too, Hyginus's tale of Hagnodike, who disguised herself as a man in order to study medicine with Herophilus and to treat women. When charged by the Athenians with seducing her female patients, she defended herself before the Areopagus by revealing her true sex, and, when her female patients supported her work, the Athenians amended their law to allow free women to study medicine, Hyg. *Fab.* 254; see Von Staden 1989, 40–41.

54. In addition to the label above the seated figure on the right, which reads "Phanostrate," the letters ΦΑΝΟΣ appear on the left, and M and traces of an A (?) below. Both Conze (1893–1922) and Clairmont (1970) read ΦΑΝΟΣΤΡΑΤΗ, and Clairmont suggested μα[ῖα as a further identification of the standing figure. Daux (1972, 552) says that he alone has seen the name ΑΝΤΙΦΙΛΗ and suggests that the lower line reads Μελιτέως; Vedder 1988, followed Daux. I have not seen the inscription, but I accept the authority of Conze and Clair-

mont; while Daux's reading would remove one example of a seated figure who is not the deceased, it does not affect the primary sense of the monument as the memorial of a midwife-physician

55. See Nielsen et al. 1989.

56. Vedder 1988, 189

57. Another example is provided by Clairmont 1970, no 25, a nurse, the other figure (dedicator) is portrayed as a child, recalling the nurse's profession

58. See French 1987, 69–84.

59. Eur. *Hipp.* 616–24, trans. Hadas and McLean.

60. Hom. *Il.* 5.875.

61. Hes. *Theog* 886–900, 924–26.

62. Eur. *Bacch.* 88–100, 519–36.

63. Aes. *Eum.* 658–61.

64. Eur. *Hipp* 618–23.

65. Eur. *Or* 552.

66. See chapter 1, n 70; DuBois 1988.

67. Arist. *GA* 729a10–12, 729b14–22.

68. Pl. *Theat.* 150b–151a, trans. Cornford, in E. Hamilton and Cairns, 1961 (emphasis added).

69. Ar. *Clouds* 135–37; see Halperin 1990, 138–39.

70. For discussion of the metaphor, see Edie 1963, 554–57; Morrison 1964, 51–55; more recently Tomin 1987, brings the bibliography on the question up to that date; see too Tarrant 1988. The *Phaedrus* continues the application of the metaphor in the metaphysical explication of reality: Pl. *Phaedr.* 244a, 250e, 256e, 261a. The determination of Socratic versus Platonic content in Plato's dialogues is one that goes beyond the scope of this investigation. Aristophanes' use of the metaphor in 423 proves that it was widely associated with the actual Socrates long before Plato entered the picture, but beyond that, as we consider the use that the Platonic Socrates made of it in the dialogues, we will have to content ourselves with a hybrid Socrates/Plato.

71. Pl. *Symp.* 201d–212a.

72. Other Platonic references to mantic powers, aside from the pun on "Mantinea": *Symp.* 202e–203a, 206b; see also *Phaedr.* 244a–245c, which associates *eros* with mantic powers.

73. Fougères 1898, 221ff.

74. Fougères 1888, 376–80 and pl. iv; Möbius 1934, 45–60, esp. 58.

75. L. Edelstein 1945.

76. Halperin 1990, 144.

77. Pl. *Symp.* 208e–209a, trans. Joyce, in E. Hamilton and Cairns 1961.

78. Pl. *Symp.* 209cd, trans. Joyce.

79. The Greeks associated it with the development of courage, as in the

Sacred Band at Thebes, but recent scholarship has seen its origins in initiatory practices, see Sergent 1987, esp. 49–54.

80. On Greek homosexuality, see the speeches of Phaedrus and Pausanias in Plato's *Symposium*, and Aeschines' *Against Timarchus*; see also Dover 1978; Halperin 1990; Winkler 1990.

81. See Herdt 1981; Godelier 1986, 52–55; and the collection of essays in Herdt 1984.

82. Herdt 1981, 65–72.

83. See Herdt 1981, esp. 227–42. Pseudomenstruation (induced bleeding from the nose or penis) is also employed to purge the body of all traces of the mother's blood acquired during gestation, birth, and nursing; see Herdt 1981, 223–27.

84. Herdt 1981, esp. 232–39, 255–94, 318–25.

85. Herdt 1981, 234.

86. Halperin 1990, 143.

87. Pl. *Symp.* 182a–e

88. Greek pederasty as initiatory· Bremmer 1980, 1989, 1990; Parker 1983; Sergent 1987.

Chapter Eight. Women and Children· Issues of Control

1. On the importance of control of women in Greek culture, see Bouvrie 1990, 50–59.

2. See J. Bernier 1990, 209–20.

3. *Epid.* 1 4 (2.630.4 Li.), see also VI 3.7 (5.296.3–4 Li.), VI 8.11 (5.348 6–10 Li.); Aph III 24–28 (4.449.12–500.28 Li); *Progn.* 19 (2.168.3–5 Li.).

4. *Epid.* 1 4 (2.622.6 Li.), 1 4 (2.630.4–5 Li.), 1 8 (2.650.8 Li.), 1 9 (2.668.3 Li.), III 8 (3.84.11 Li.), IV 36 (5.178 17 Li.), VI 1.12 (5.272.5–12 Li.), VI 3.7 (5.296.3–4 Li.), VII 105 (5.456.11).

5. *Epid.* II 3.18 (5.120.7–9 Li.).

6. *Epid.* VII 52 (5.420.11 Li.), 106 (5 456.14 Li.)

7. Hipp. *De Alim.* 37 (9.110.18 Li.); *Epis* 23 (9.396.16 Li.); *Dis.Wom.* 1 71 (8.150.9 Li.).

8 Children are defined here in purely physical terms, as those who have not yet reached puberty, traditionally set at fourteen for both sexes in Greece. It seems clear that socially the lines were drawn in quite different terms in classical Greece than in our own culture (e.g., capacity to work may have been a more important determining factor than physical puberty in the case of slaves, and males, in contrast to females, were not considered fully adult—capable of full political activity—until the age of thirty), but this is another issue.

9. On the term *pais*, see Golden 1985b; on slaves as patients, Kudlien 1968.
10. *Epid.* v 16 (5.214.20–216.10 Li.).
11. *Epid.* iv 20 (5.158.1–2 Li.), iv 27 (5.172.3 Li.); iv 31 (5.174.20 Li.); iv 50 (5.190.11–15 Li.). The concentration in Book iv may mean that this is an idiosyncrasy of this particular author's work or interests, however.
12. Kudlien 1968, 17.
13. *Epid.* v 28 (5.226.17 Li.).
14. *Epid.* vii 105 (5.456.4–5 Li.), indicated by the article with the genitive case.
15. *Epid.* vii 52 (5.420.11 Li.), 106 (5.456.14 Li.)
16. *Epid.* ii 3.18 (5.120.6 Li.); iv 19 (5.156.4 Li.), two cases; v 39 (5.230.21); vii 117 (5.462 21 Li.); vii 118 (5.464.3 Li); vii 52 (5.422.2 Li.).
17. *Epid.* ii 2 4 (5.84.10–86.2 Li.); ii 2.19 (5.92.3 Li.); v 11 (5.210.12–212.4 Li.); v 13 (5.212.11–19).
18. *Epid.* i 8 (2.646.12 Li); iv 24 (5.164.6 Li.).
19 Impeded menarche, *Epid.* vii 123 (5.468.4 Li.); *parthenoi*: i 8 (2.648.3 Li.); iii case 6, first set (3.50 2 Li.).
20. *Epid.* i 8 (2. 648.2 Li.); iii case 6 (first series) (3.50.1 Li.); iii case 12 (second series) (3. 136 10–11 Li.); vii 123 (5. 468.4–6 Li.); in ii 2.8 (5. 88.3–8 Li.) the doctor is not sure.
21. *Epid.* v 50 (5.236.11 Li.).
22. *Epid.* vii 77 (5.434.9 Li.), vii 102 (5.454.10 Li.).
23 *Dis.* iii 7 (7.124.18–126.16 Li.); Potter 1980, 74–77 and 108.
24. Grmek 1989, 136.
25. Hipp *Dent.* 24, 31 (8.548 1–2, 16–17 Li.).
26. *Dis.* ii (7.40.9–42.20 Li.); iii 10 (7 128 16–130.16 Li.); *Reg.AcuteDis.* App. 10 (2.442 7–456.6 Li.); Grmek 1989, 338, 436; Potter 1980, 76–79, 110–11.
27. Grmek 1989, 335.
28. Grmek 1989, 336.
29. Blum and Blum 1965, 53.
30. *Dis.* iv 54 (7 596.5–8 Li.).
31. In Xen. *Mem.* 2.2 Socrates includes care during childhood illnesses among the things for which his son should be grateful to his mother.
32. See, e.g , Finley 1981, 159.
33 For Greece, see Golden 1990, 82–94, which gives references to the debate in other cultures.
34. Arist. *NE* 1102b14–19, 1145b8–1152a37; Pl. *Tim* 42ab, and the charioteer Reason in the *Phaedrus*.
35. Is. 2.1,20,26; 6.21; Dem 46.14, 16, 48.54–56.

36. King 1991.
37. [Dem] 59.55–56; see chapter 1 and also subsequent discussion.
38. See, e.g., D. Cohen 1991, 54–69. Psychological explanations have been given as well, especially by Slater 1968; while I am concerned here to point out the ways in which political strategies adopted by the *polis* fostered male anxiety on this issue, we should not overlook traditional Greek family roles and relationships, which probably did much to nourish the seeds of neurosis.
39. On honor/shame as a characteristic of Mediterranean societies, see, briefly, D. Cohen 1991, 54–69, and, at greater length, the papers collected in Peristiany 1966. Recently the ubiquitous and nebulous nature of the model has led to a questioning of its value as an explanatory concept; see Herzfeld 1980, and the essays in Gilmore 1987, with review by Kertzer 1987.
40. Pomeroy 1975, 78, 120–31, 136–39, 149–50, 176–89.
41. This, rather than direct influence of one work on the other, seems to be the preferred explanation for the close parallels; see Ussher 1973, xv–xxv; Demand 1982.
42. See Patterson 1981.
43. According to Patterson, the Periclean law established necessary conditions of citizenship but did not regulate marriage per se, which may not have been considered necessary before the reenactment, see Patterson 1981, 137, n. 12.
44. Arist. *Pol.* 1278a25–34, trans. Rackham (Loeb).
45. Randall 1953, esp. 209.
46. [Xen.] *Ath. Pol.* 10–12.
47. Dem. 57.2.
48. Dem. 57, in which the citizenship of the speaker was challenged because his mother had worked as a nurse and sold ribbons in the agora; attacks in Aesch. 3.78–79, 171–72, and Dinarchus 1 15, on Demosthenes through his mother Kleobule's Scythian origin (Kleobule's mother was Scythian, but Kleobule was probably born in 405 during the period of amnesty before the reenactment of the Periclean law in 403/402), discussed in Davies 1971, 121–22, and Hunter 1989b; attacks on a man through his wife/concubine, Dem 59, discussed later.
49. See Davies 1977–78, although without specific reference to the effects upon women.
50. Dem. 59.
51. Dem. 59.16–17.
52. Dem. 59.52.
53. Dem. 59.25, 28, 34, 48.
54. See Davies 1977–78, on the atmosphere of "tensions, prejudices and

insecurities," "sense of siege," and "deep-status anxiety" occasioned by vulnerability to attack on citizenship status.

55. See Powell 1988, 80–81, for discussion and references; I agree with Powell's hypothesis that there were two types of land, one of which was linked with citizen status.

56. Hdt. 6.61; 7.134; Thuc. 1.6; Xen. *Lac.* 5.3, 6.4; *Hell.* 6.4.10–11; Arist. *Pol.* 1270a18.

57. See Strauss 1985, with bibliography on symbolic anthropology.

58. Gomme 1925.

Glossary

abortifacient: a substance that prevents implantation of a conceptus or expels it after implantation.

apostasis: the condition that occurs when the products of pepsis are isolated or excreted in the blood, pus, urine, or in skin eruptions, or joint ailments.

blackwater fever: a dangerous complication of falciparum malaria characterized by black urine.

cathartic: a purgative, either an emetic or a laxative.

chorion: the outer membrane of the fetal sac.

constitution: a description in the *Epidemics* of the weather conditions and illnesses experienced in a given locality over a period of time, often a year.

contraceptive: a substance that prevents conception.

crisis: decisive turning point in an illness, whether toward recovery or death; a favorable crisis could be followed by a relapse and further crises.

diaphragm: the muscle that divides the thorax from the abdomen.

eclampsia: severe toxemia of pregnancy, marked by convulsions.

emetic: a drug that causes vomiting.

emmenagogue: a drug given to bring on menstruation.

epistaxis: nosebleed, usually a favorable sign in Hippocratic theory.

erysipelas: streptococcus infection marked by skin inflammation and fever.

hellebore: a herb with depressive effects on respiration and the heart (similar to digitalis), frequently used as a purgative by Hippocratic doctors.

humors: basic fluid constituents of the body, whose balance assured health and whose inbalance caused illness; number and identification vary, but most treatises presuppose four humors: phlegm, blood, yellow bile, and black bile.

hypochondrium: the soft parts of the body below the cartilage of the breastbone and above the naval.

hypogastrium: the lower abdomen.

iatrogenic disorders: illness caused by medical treatment.

ilium: the largest pelvic bone.

kardia: heart or cardiac region.

kausos: a type of remittent fever, sometimes identifiable as malaria (see Grmek 1989, 289–92).

lochia: discharge following childbirth, lasting about six weeks.

menarche: the first menstrual period.

metastasis: change of location of symptoms, as when a cold "goes down" into the chest (also called coction).

mole: an abnormal mass in the uterus, especially one containing fetal tissue.

parity: number of offspring born to a woman.

pepsis: Hippocratic concept, in which offending humors are overcome by the body through a sort of cooking or ripening.

phrenes: midriff, heart, viewed as the seat of the mental faculties, hence mind (a plural form; the singular *phren*, which is not found in prose, is indistinguishable in meaning). There was disagreement over the location of the mental faculties, with some opting for the heart and others for the brain.

phrenitis: inflammation of the phrenes, marked by remittant fever with pain in hypochondrium and delirium.

preeclampsia: abnormal condition of pregnancy characterized by hypertension and edema; may develop into eclampsia.

phthisis: wasting illness, often identifiable as tuberculosis.

prognosis: foretelling the course of an illness, considered to be the mark of a good doctor.

purging/purgatives: purging was a method of ridding the body of excess humors through the use of purgatives (emetics or laxatives).

succussion: bodily suspension as a treatment; in cases of childbirth, the woman might be suspended on a frame and lifted and dropped in the hope of shaking the baby loose.

superfetation: a second conception supervening upon an existing pregnancy.

toxemia: the presence of toxins in the blood, resulting in convulsions (preeclampsia and eclampsia).

trepanning: boring a hole in the skull, an ancient operation perhaps first practiced for magical reasons; it was sometimes used as a treatment for headaches, and was a lifesaving measure when injury to the skull caused fluid buildup.

urinalysis: the Hippocratic doctor looked for color, consistency, sediment, results of shaking or letting stand.

uterine suffocation: suffocation believed to be caused by the womb's movement obstructing respiration (see wandering womb).

uvula: the pendent lobe at the back of the soft palate.

venesection: cutting a vein in order to rid the body of excess blood through therapeutic bleeding.

wandering womb: the theory that the womb was free to wander about the body, seeking out moisture either willfully or mechanistically; the cure recommended by doctors was intercourse and pregnancy.

Abbreviations

AAA	*Archaiologika Analekta ex Athenon; Athens Annals of Archaeology*
ABSA	British School at Athens. *Annual*
AC	*L'Antiquité Classique*
ACF	Collège de France. *Annuaire*
AD	*Archaiologikon Deltion*
AE	*Archaiologike Ephemeris*
AHB	*Ancient History Bulletin*
AJA	*American Journal of Archaeology*
AJAH	*American Journal of Ancient History*
AJP	*American Journal of Philology*
AK	*Antike Kunst*
Annales (ESC)	*Annales. Économies, Sociétés, Civilisations*
BCH	*Bulletin de Correspondance Hellenique*

BICS	London University Institute of Classical Studies. *Bulletin*
C&M	*Classica et Mediaevalia*
CJ	*Classical Journal*
CP	*Classical Philology*
CQ	*Classical Quarterly*
CRAI	Académie des Inscriptions et Belles-Lettres, Paris. *Comptes Rendus des Séances*
CSCA	*California Studies in Classical Antiquity*
CW	*Classical World*
EMC	*Echos de Monde Classique (Classical Views)*
GRBS	*Greek, Roman and Byzantine Studies*
HSCP	*Harvard Studies in Classical Philology*
JDAI	Deutsches Archaeologischen Institute. *Jahrbuch*
JHS	*Journal of Hellenic Studies*
MDAI (A)	Deutsches Archaeologischen Institute. Athenische Abteilungen. *Mitteilungen*
MDAI (R)	Deutsches Archaeologischen Institute. Römische Abteilungen. *Mitteilungen*
PP	*La Parola del Passato*
QUCC	*Quaderni Urbinati di Cultura Classica*
RE	*Real-Encyclopädie der klassischen Altertunswissenschaft*
RhM	*Rheinisches Museum für Philologie*
SAWW	Akademie der Wissenschaften, Vienna. Philosophische-historische Klasse. *Sitzungsberichte*

236

StudMed	*Studi Medievali*
TAPA	American Philological Association. *Transactions*
ZPE	*Zeitschrift für Papyrolgie und Epigraphik*

Bibliography

Abram, Dorothy P. 1985. Poisons and Powers in Myths of Demeter and Klytemnestra. *Temenos* 21:7–22.

Agathonos, L., N. Stathacoupoulou, H. Adam, and S. Nakou. 1982. Child Abuse and Neglect in Greece: Sociomedical Aspects. *Child Abuse and Neglect: The International Journal* 6:307–11.

Aleshire, Sara B. 1989. *The Athenian Asklepieion: The People, Their Dedications, and the Inventories* Amsterdam: J. C. Gieben.

Alexiou, M. 1974. *The Ritual Lament in Greek Tradition.* Cambridge: Cambridge University Press.

Alexiou, M., and P. Dronke. 1971. The Lament of Jephtha's Daughter: Themes, Traditions, Originality *StudMed* 3, no. 12.2:819–63

Amundsen, D. W., and C. J. Diers. 1969. The Age of Menarche in Classical Greece and Rome. *Human Biology* 41:125–32

Amundsen, D. W., and G. B. Ferngreen. 1977. The Physician as an Expert Witness in Athenian Law. *Bulletin of the History of Medicine* 51.202–13.

Amyx, D. A. 1988. *Corinthian Vase-painting of the Archaic Period.* 3 vols. Berkeley: University of California Press.

Angel, J. L. 1969 The Bases of Paleodemography. *American Journal of Physical Anthropology* 30:427–35.

Angel, J. L. 1977. Anemias of Antiquity. Eastern Mediterranean. In *Porotic Hyperostosis. An Enquiry,* ed. E. Cockburn, 1–5. Detroit Paleopathology Association.

Angel, J. L. 1978. Porotic Hyperostosis in the Eastern Mediterranean. *Medical College of Virginia Quarterly* 15:10–16.

Angeletti, Luciana Rita. 1990. *De Octimestri Partu* and Pathology of the Last Trimester of Pregnancy *Medicina nei Secoli Arte e Scienza* 2:75–92.

Arbanitopoulos, A. S. 1909. *Katalogos ton en toi Athanasakeioi Mouseioi, Bolou. Archaioteton.* Athens· K. Eleutheroglaki.

Arbanitopoulos, A. S. 1928. *Graptai stelai Demetriados-Pagason.* Athens: Hetaireias P. D Sakellarios.

Aristophanes. 1982 [1924]. Trans. B. B. Rogers. 3 vols. Loeb Classical Library. Cambridge, Mass.· Harvard University Press.

Aristotle. 1990 [1944]. *Politics.* Ed. and trans. H. Rackham. Loeb Classical Library. Cambridge, Mass.: Harvard University Press.

Arthur-Katz, M. 1989. Sexuality and the Body in Ancient Greece. *Metis* 4:155–79.

Aubert, Jean-Jacques. 1989. Threatened Wombs: Aspects of Ancient Uterine Magic. *GRBS* 30:412–49.

Barden, J. C. 1991. Failure to Meet Goals on Infant Health Is Masked by Drop in Mortality Rate. *New York Times* September 2, p. 9.

Barringer, J. 1991. Europa and the Nereids: Wedding or Funeral? *AJA* 95:657–67.

Baur, Paul. 1901. *Eileithyia.* Tübingen. H. Laupp, Jr.

Bauman, E. D. 1939. Die Krankheit der Jungfrau *Janus* 43:189–94.

Bazant, Jan. 1975. Iconography of Choes Reconsidered. *Listy Filologické* 98:72–78.

Bernardi, Bernardo. 1985. *Age Class Systems: Social Institutions and Politics Based on Age.* Cambridge: Cambridge University Press

Bennett, L. J., and W. B. Tyrrell 1991. What Is Antigone Wearing? *CW* 85:107–109.

Benson, Carol A. 1990. Recurring Figure-types in Grave Stelai: Evidence for Pattern-books? Conference paper, American Institute of Archaeology.

Bernhard, O. 1926. *Griechische und römische Münzbilder in ihren Beziehungen zur Geschichte der Medizin.* Zurich· Verlag Orell Füssli.

Bernier, J. 1990. Enfants malades et maladies des enfants dans le *Corpus Hippocratique.* In *La maladie et les maladies dans la collection hippocratique,* ed. P. Potter, G. Maloney, and J. Desautels, 209–20. Actes du VI Colloque international hippocratique. Sillery, Quebec: Editions Du Sphinx

Bernier, R. 1990. *Embryogenèse et avortement chez les auteurs hippocratiques.* In *La maladie et les maladies dans la collection hippocratique,* ed. P. Potter, G. Maloney, and J. Desautels, 363–80. Actes du VI Colloque international hippocratique. Sillery, Quebec: Editions Du Sphinx.

Blum, Richard, and Eva Blum. 1965. *Health and Healing in Rural Greece: A Study of Three Communities.* Stanford: Stanford University Press.

Blümel, C. 1966. *Die klassisch griechischen Skulpturen der Staatlichen Museen zu Berlin.* Berlin: Akademie-Verlag.

Blumenfeld-Kosinski, Renate. 1990. *Not of Woman Born. Representations of Caesarean Birth in Medieval and Renaissance Culture.* Ithaca: Cornell University Press.

Bocquet-Appel, J., and C. Masset. 1982. Farewell to Paleodemography. *Journal of Human Evolution* 11:321–33.

Borza, Eugene N. 1979. Some Observations on Malaria and the Ecology of Central Macedonia in Antiquity. *AJAH* 4:102–24.

Borza, Eugene N. 1987. Malaria in Alexander's Army. *AHB* 1:36–38.

Boswell, John. 1988. *The Kindness of Strangers.* London: Allen Lane. Penguin Press.

Bousquet, Jean. 1956. Inscriptions de Delphes. *BCH* 80:579–90, and pl. 10.

Bouvrie, Synnove des. 1990. *Women in Greek Tragedy.* Oslo: Norwegian University Press.

Breasted, James Henry. 1930. *The Edwin Smith Surgical Papyrus.* Oriental Institute Publications, vols. 3–4. Chicago: University of Chicago Press.

Breccia, E. 1922. *Alexandrea ad Aegyptum: A Guide to the Ancient and Modern Town and to Its Graeco-Roman Museum.* Bergamo: Istituto Italiano D'arti Grafiche.

Brelich, A. 1969. *Paides e parthenoi.* Rome: Edizioni Dell'Ateneo.

Bremmer, J. 1980. An Enigmatic Indo-European Rite: Paederasty. *Arethusa* 13:279–98.

Bremmer, J. 1987. The Old Women of Ancient Greece. In *Sexual Asymmetry: Studies in Ancient Society,* ed. J. Blok and P. Mason, 191–215. Amsterdam: J. C. Gieben.

Bremmer, J. 1989. Greek Pederasty and Modern Homosexuality. In *From Sappho to De Sade,* ed. J. Bremmer, 1–14. London: Routledge

Bremmer, J. 1990. Adolescents, *Symposion,* and Pederasty. In *Sympotica: A Symposium on the Symposion,* ed. Oswyn Murray, 135–48. Oxford: Clarendon Press.

Brown, Blanche R. 1957. *Ptolemaic Paintings and Mosaics and the Alexandrian Style* Cambridge, Mass.: American Institute of Archaeology.

Brown, Blanche R. 1974. The Painted Stelai of Demetrius. *AJA* 78:161.

Browner, C. H., and C. F. Sargent. 1990. Anthropology and Studies of Human Reproduction. In *Medical Anthropology: A Handbook of Theory and Method,* ed. T. M. Johnson and C. F. Sargent, 215–29. New York: Greenwood Press.

Bruce-Chwatt, Leonard J., and Julian de Zulueta. 1980. *The Rise and Fall of Malaria in Europe: A Historico-epidemiological Study.* Oxford. Oxford University Press.

Brückner, M. 1888. Von den griechischen Grabreliefs. *SAWW* 116.514–20.

Brulé, P. 1987. *La fille d'Athènes. La religion des filles à Athènes à l'époque classique. Mythes, cultes et société.* Annales Littéraires de l'Université de Besançon, no. 363. Paris: Les Belles Lettres.

241

Brumfield, Allaire Chandor. 1981. *The Attic Festivals of Demeter and Their Relation to the Agricultural Year.* Salem, N.H.: Ayer.

Bruneau, P. 1970. *Recherches sur les cultes de Delos.* Paris: E. Boccard.

Brunt, P. A. 1971. *Italian Manpower 225 B.C.–A.D. 14.* Oxford: Clarendon Press.

Buikstra, J. E., and L. K. Konigsberg. 1985. Paleodemography: Critiques and Controversies. *American Anthropologist* 87:316–33.

Burkert, W. 1966. Kekropidensage und Arrhephoria. *Hermes* 94:1–25.

Burkert, W. 1983. Itinerant Diviners and Magicians: A Neglected Element in Cultural Contacts. In *The Greek Renaissance of the Eighth Century B.C.,* ed. R. Hägg, 115–19. Stockholm: Svenska Institutet i Athen.

Burkert, W. 1985. *Greek Religion.* Trans. John Raffan. Cambridge, Mass.: Harvard University Press.

Burkert, W. 1992. *The Orientalizing Revolution: Near Eastern Influence on Greek Culture in the Early Archaic Age.* Trans. M. E. Pinder and W. Burkert. Cambridge, Mass.: Harvard University Press.

Calame, C. 1977. *Les choeurs de jeunes filles en Grèce archaïque.* Vol. 1, *Morphologie, fonction religieuse et sociale.* Rome: Ateneo & Bizzarri.

Cameron, A., and A. Kuhrt. 1983. *Images of Women in Antiquity.* Detroit: Wayne State University Press.

Campbell, J. K. 1963. The Kindred in a Greek Mountain Community. In *Mediterranean Countrymen: Essays in the Social Anthropology of the Mediterranean,* ed. J. Pitt-Rivers, 73–96. Paris: Mouton.

Campbell, J. K. 1964. *Honour, Family and Patronage: A Study of Institutions and Moral Values in a Greek Mountain Community.* Oxford: Clarendon Press.

Caraveli, Anna. 1986. The Bitter Wounding: The Lament as Social Protest in Rural Greece. In *Gender and Power in Rural Greece,* ed. Jill Dubisch, 169–94. Princeton: Princeton University Press.

Carson, Anne. 1990. Putting Her in Her Place. Woman, Dirt, and Desire. In *Before Sexuality: The Construction of Erotic Experience in the Ancient Greek World,* ed. D. M. Halperin, J. J. Winkler, and F. I. Zeitlin, 135–69. Princeton: Princeton University Press.

Chase, G. H. 1924. *Greek and Roman Sculpture in American Collections.* Cambridge, Mass.: Harvard University Press.

Chirassi, Ileana. 1964. *Miti e culti arcaici di Artemis nel Peloponneso e Grecia centrale.* Trieste Universita, Facolta di lettere e filosofia, Instituto di storia antica, no. 3. Trieste: Trieste Universita.

Chirassi, Ileana. 1979. Paides e gynaikes. Note per una tassonomia del comportamento rituale nella cultura attica. *QUCC,* n.s. 1, 30.25–58.

Clairmont, Christoph W. 1970. *Gravestone and Epigram. Greek Memorials from the Archaic and Classical Period.* Mainz: Philipp von Zabern.

Clairmont, Christoph W. 1972. Gravestone with Warriors in Boston. *GRBS* 13:49–58.

Cochrane, C. 1929. *Thucydides and the Science of History*. Oxford: Oxford University Press.

Cohen, David. 1989 Seclusion, Separation, and the Status of Women in Classical Athens. *Greece and Rome* 36:3–15.

Cohen, David. 1990 The Social Context of Adultery at Athens. In *Nomos: Essays in Athenian Law, Politics and Society*, ed. P. Cartledge, P. Millett, and S. Todd, 147–65. Cambridge. Cambridge University Press.

Cohen, David. 1991. *Law, Sexuality, and Society*. Cambridge: Cambridge University Press.

Cohen, Mark N. 1989. *Health and the Rise of Civilization*. New Haven: Yale University Press.

Cohn-Haft, Louis. 1956. *The Public Physicians of Ancient Greece*. Smith College Studies in History, vol 24. Northampton, Mass.

Cole, S. G. 1981. Could Greek Women Read and Write? In *Reflections of Women in Antiquity*, ed. Helene P. Foley, 219–45. New York: Gordon and Breach Science Publishers.

Cole, S. G. 1984. The Social Function of Rituals of Maturation: The Koureion and the Arkteia. *ZPE* 55:233–44.

Collinge, N. E. 1962. Medical Terms and Clinical Attitudes in the Tragedians. *BICS* 9:43–55.

Conze, A. 1893–1922. *Die attischen Grabreliefs*. 4 vols. in 6. Berlin: W. Spemann.

Cornford, F. M., ed. and trans. 1945. *The Republic of Plato*. New York: Oxford University Press.

Corvisier, Jean-Nicolas. 1985 *Santé et société en Grèce ancienne* Paris: Economica.

Coulton, J. J. 1976 "Brauron." In *Princeton Encyclopedia of Classical Sites*, ed. R. Stillwell, W. L. MacDonald, and M. H. McAllister, 163–64. Princeton: Princeton University Press.

Crahay, R. 1941. Les moralistes anciens et l'avortement. *AC* 10:9–23.

Culham, Phyllis. 1987. Ten Years after Pomeroy: Studies in the Image and Reality of Women in Antiquity. In *Rescuing Creusa: New Methodological Approaches to Women in Antiquity*, ed. Marilyn Skinner, 9–30 Lubbock: Texas Technical University Press

Curtius, E. 1845. Attisches Familienbild Relief im Thesion zu Athen. *Archäologische Zeitung* 34 (October):146–50

Danforth, Loring M. 1982. *The Death Rituals of Rural Greece*. Princeton: Princeton University Press.

Danforth, Loring M. 1984 The Ideological Context of the Search for Continuities in Greek Culture. *Journal of Modern Greek Studies* 2:53–85

Daux, G. 1958. Chronique des fouilles et découvertes archéologiques en 1957. *BCH* 82:808–14.

Daux, G. 1972. Stèles funéraires et épigrammes (à propos d'un livre récent). *BCH* 96.503–66.

Daux, G. 1973a. Anth. Pol. IV 280 (poupées et chevelure, Artemis Limnatis). *ZPE* 12:225–34.

Daux, G. 1973b. Les ambiguïtés de grec koph. *CRAI* 382–93.

Davies, J. K. 1971. *Athenian Propertied Families 600–300 B.C.* Oxford: Clarendon Press.

Davies, J. K. 1977–78. Athenian Citizenship: The Descent Group and the Alternatives. *CJ* 73:105–21.

Dean-Jones, L. A. 1991. The Cultural Construct of the Female Body in Classical Greek Science. In *Women's History and Ancient History*, ed. S. B. Pomeroy, 111–37. Chapel Hill: University of North Carolina Press.

Deichgräber, Karl. 1971. *Die Epidemien und das Corpus hippocraticum.* Berlin: Walter de Gruyter.

Deichgräber, Karl. 1982. *Die Patienten des Hippokrates. Historisch-prosopographische Beiträge zu den Epidemien des Corpus Hippocraticum.* Akademie der Wissenschaften und der Literatur, Mainz. Abhandlungen der Geistes- und Sozial Wissenschaftlichen Klasse, no. 9. Wiesbaden: Franz Steiner Verlag.

Delaney, Carol. 1987. Seeds of Honor, Fields of Shame. In *Honor and Shame and the Unity of the Mediterranean*, ed. D. Gilmore, 35–48. American Anthropological Association Special Publication, no. 22. Washington, D.C.: American Anthropological Association.

Delmousou, D. Peppas. 1988a. Autour des inventaires de Brauron. In *Comptes et inventaires dans la cité grecque. Actes du colloque international d'épigraphie tenu à Neuchâtel du 23 au 26 septembre 1986 en l'honneur de Jacques Tréheux*, ed. D. Knoepfler, 323–46. Neuchâtel: Faculté Des Lettres.

Delmousou, D. Peppas. 1988b The Theoria of Brauron. In *Early Greek Cult Practice: Proceedings of the Fifth International Symposium at the Swedish Institute at Athens, 26–29 June, 1986*, 255–57. Stockholm: Paul Aströms Förlag.

Demand, N. H. 1982. Plato, Aristophanes, and the Speeches of Pythagoras. *GRBS* 23:179–84.

Demangel, R. 1922. Un sanctuaire d'Artémis-Eileithyia à l'est du Cynthe. *BCH* 46:58–93.

Demosthenes. 1990 [1939]. *Private Orations.* Ed. and trans. A. T. Murray 5 vols. Loeb Classical Library. Cambridge, Mass.: Harvard University Press.

Den Boer, W. 1954. *Laconian Studies.* Amsterdam: North-Holland Publishing

Denman, Thomas. 1768. *Essays on the Puerperal Fever, and on Puerperal Convulsions.* London: J. Walter.

Detienne, M. 1977. *The Gardens of Adonis: Spices in Greek Mythology.* Trans. J. Lloyd. Hassocks, U.K.: Harvester Press.

Detienne, M. 1989. The Violence of Wellborn Ladies: Women in the Thesmophoria. In *The Cuisine of Sacrifice among the Greeks,* ed. M. Detienne and J.-P. Vernant, trans. P. Wissing, 129–47. Chicago: University of Chicago Press

Deubner, L. 1932. *Attische Feste.* Berlin: Verlag Heinrich Keller.

Devambez, P. 1955. Le motif de Phedre sur une stèle thasienne. *BCH* 79:121–33.

Di Benedetto, V. 1977. Principi metodici di Ep. II.IV.VI. In *Corpus Hippocraticum. Actes du colloque hippocratique de Mons (septembre 1975),* ed. R. Joly, 246–63. Mons: Université de Mons.

Di Benedetto, V. 1980. Cos e Cnido. In *Hippocratica. Actes du Colloque hippocratique de Paris (septembre 1978),* ed. M. D Grmek, 97–111. Paris: Éditions Du Centre National de la Recherche Scientifique.

Dikaios, P. 1961. *A Guide to the Cyprus Museum.* 3d ed. Nicosia: Nicosia Printing Works.

Diller, H. 1964. Ausdrucksformen des methodischen Bewusstseins in den hippokratischen Epidemien. *Archiv für Begriffsgeschichte* 9:133–50.

Diro, M. 1982. Malaria in Pregnancy. *Southern Medical Journal* 75:959–63.

Dohan, E. H. 1934. Some Unpublished Vases in the University Museum, Philadelphia. *AJA* 38:523–32.

Doumanis, Mariella. 1983. *Mothering in Greece: From Collectivism to Individualism.* London: Academic Press.

Dover, K. J. 1978. *Greek Homosexuality.* Cambridge, Mass : Harvard University Press.

Dowden, Ken. 1989 *Death and the Maiden: Girls' Initiation Rites in Greek Mythology.* London: Routledge.

Dubisch, Jill. 1986. Culture Enters through the Kitchen: Women, Food, and Social Boundaries in Rural Greece. In *Gender and Power in Rural Greece,* ed. Jill Dubisch, 195–214. Princeton: Princeton University Press.

Dubisch, Jill. 1991. Men's Time and Women's Time: History, Myth, and Ritual at a Modern Greek Shrine. *Journal of Ritual Studies* 5:1–26.

Du Bois, Page. 1988. *Sowing the Body: Psychoanalysis and Ancient Representations of Women.* Chicago: University of Chicago Press.

Du Boulay, J 1974. *Portrait of a Greek Mountain Village.* Oxford: Clarendon Press.

Du Boulay, J. 1983. The Meaning of Dowry: Changing Values in Rural Greece. *Journal of Modern Greek Studies* 1:243–70.

Du Boulay, J. 1986. Women—Images of Their Nature and Destiny in Rural Greece. In *Gender and Power in Rural Greece*, ed. Jill Dubisch, 139–68. Princeton: Princeton University Press

Ducrey, P., and O. Picard. 1969. Recherches à Latô. *BCH* 93:819–22, figs. 31–33.

Dye, N. S. 1980. History of Childbirth in America. *Signs* 6:97–108.

Edelstein, E. J., and L. Edelstein. 1945. *Asclepius. A Collection and Interpretation of the Testimonies*. 2 vols. Baltimore. Johns Hopkins Press.

Edelstein, L. 1943. *The Hippocratic Oath: Text, Translation and Interpretation*. Supplements to the Bulletin of the History of Medicine, no. 1. Baltimore.

Edelstein, L. 1945. The rôle of Eryximachus in Plato's Symposium. *TAPA*:85–103

Edelstein, L. 1967. *Ancient Medicine*. Ed. and trans. O. Temkin and C. L. Temkin. Baltimore: Johns Hopkins Press.

Edelstein, L. 1967. The Relation of Ancient Philosophy to Medicine. In *Ancient Medicine: Selected Papers of Ludwig Edelstein*, ed. O. Temkin and C. L. Temkin, trans. C. L. Tempkin Baltimore. Johns Hopkins University Press.

Edie, J. M. 1963 Expression and Metaphor. *Philosophy and Phenomenological Research* 23:538–61.

Edmonds, F. H. 1900. Malaria and Pregnancy. *Journal of Tropical Medicine*, May, 259–60.

Eisenberg, Leon. 1977. Disease and Illness: Distinctions between Professional and Popular Ideas of Sickness. *Culture, Medicine and Psychiatry* 1:9–23.

Engels, Donald. 1980. The Problem of Female Infanticide in the Greco-Roman World. *Classical Philology* 75:112–20.

Estes, J. Worth 1989. *The Medical Skills of Ancient Egypt*. Canton, Mass.: Science History Publications/U.S.A.

Euripides. 1955. *Medea*. Trans. Rex Warner In *The Complete Greek Tragedies*, 5 vols. ed. D. Grene and R. Lattimore. Chicago: University of Chicago Press.

Euripides. 1960. *Ten Plays by Euripides*. Ed. and trans. M Hadas and J. MacLean. New York: Bantam.

Euripides. 1964 [1912]. Ed. and trans Arthur S. Way. Loeb Classical Library. Cambridge, Mass.: Harvard University Press.

Fantham, Elaine. 1975. Sex, Status and Survival in Hellenistic Athens: A Study of Women in New Comedy. *Phoenix* 29:43–74.

Farnell, Lewis Richard 1977 [1896–1909] *The Cults of the Greek States*. 5 vols. New Rochelle, N.Y : Caratzas Brothers.

Fasbender, H. 1897. *Entwickelungslehre, Geburtshülfe und Gynäkologie in den hippokratischen Schriften.* Stuttgart: Verlag von Ferdinand Enke.

Finley, M. I. 1981. The Elderly in Classical Antiquity. *Greece and Rome* 28:156–71.

Firatli, N., and L. Robert. 1964. *Les stèles funéraires de Byzance gréco-romaine.* Paris: Librairie Adrien Maisonneuve.

Foley, Helene P. 1982. Marriage and Sacrifice in Euripides' Iphigeneia in Aulis. *Arethusa* 15:159–80.

Fontanille, M.-T. 1977. *Avortement et contraception dans la médicine gréco-romaine.* Paris: Laboratoires SEARLE.

Fontenrose, Joseph. 1978. *The Delphic Oracle: Its Responses and Operations with a Catalogue of Responses.* Berkeley: University of California Press.

Foster, George M., and Barbara G. Anderson. 1978. *Medical Anthropology* New York: John Wiley & Sons.

Foucault, Michel. 1972 [1969]. *The Archaeology of Knowledge.* Trans. A. M. Sheridan Smith. New York: Random House.

Foucault, Michel. 1979 [1975]. *Discipline and Punish: The Birth of the Prison.* Trans. Alan Sheridan. New York: Vintage Books.

Fougères, G. 1888. Stèle de Mantinée. *BCH* 12:376–80.

Fougères, G. 1898. *Mantinée et l'Arcadie orientale.* Paris: Fontemoing.

Foulkes, E. F. 1972. *The Arctic Hysterias of the North Alaskan Eskimo.* Anthropological Studies, no. 10. Washington, D.C.: American Anthropological Association.

Foxhall, Lin. 1989. Household, Gender and Property in Classical Athens. *CQ* 39:22–44.

Foy, H., and A. Kondi. 1935. Researches on Blackwater Fever in Greece: Introduction and History. *Annals of Tropical Medicine and Parasitology* 29:383–93.

Freeman, Kathleen. 1946. *The Murder of Herodes.* London: MacDonald.

Freidson, Eliot. 1975. *Profession of Medicine. A Study of the Sociology of Applied Knowledge.* New York: Dodd, Mead.

French, Valerie. 1987. Midwives and Maternity Care in the Roman World. In *Rescuing Creusa: New Methodological Approaches to Women in Antiquity,* ed. Marilyn Skinner, 69–84. *Helios* special issue 13.2, Lubbock: Texas Technical University Press.

Frenkian, Aram M. 1941. *La méthode hippocratique dans le Phèdre de Platon.* Bucharest: Imprimerie Nationale.

Friedl, Ernestine. 1958. Hospital Care in Provincial Greece. *Human Organization* 16:24–27.

Friedl, Ernestine. 1962. *Vasilika: A Village in Modern Greece.* New York: Holt, Rinehart and Winston.

Friedl, Ernestine. 1963. Some Aspects of Dowry and Inheritance in Boeotia. In *Mediterranean Countrymen: Essays in the Social Anthropology of the*

Mediterranean, ed. J. Pitt-Rivers, 113–35. Paris: Mouton.

Friedl, Ernestine. 1967. The Position of Women: Appearance and Reality. *Anthropological Quarterly* 40:97–108.

Frier, Bruce. 1982. Roman Life Expectancy: Ulpian's Evidence. *HSCP* 86:213–51.

Frier, Bruce. 1983. Roman Life Expectancy: The Pannonian Evidence. *Phoenix* 37:328–44.

Gallant, Thomas W. 1991. *Risk and Survival in Ancient Greece: Reconstructing the Rural Domestic Economy*. Stanford: Stanford University Press.

Garland, Robert. 1985. *The Greek Way of Death*. Ithaca: Cornell University Press.

Garland, Robert. 1990. *The Greek Way of Life*. Ithaca: Cornell University Press.

Gejvall, N.-G. 1983. Wear and Tear: Chronic Traumatic Lesions. In *Disease in Ancient Man: An International Symposium*, 84–96. Toronto: Clarke Irwin.

Gélis, Jacques. 1991. *History of Childbirth: Fertility, Pregnancy and Birth in Early Modern Europe*. Trans. R. Morris. Boston: Northeastern University Press.

Germain, L. R. F. 1969. Aspects du droit d'exposition in Grèce. *Revue historique de droit français étranger* 47:177–97.

Gernet, L., and M. Bizos. 1967. *Lysias. Discours*. Paris: Les Belles Lettres.

Gilmore, David D., ed. 1987. *Honor and Shame and the Unity of the Mediterranean*. American Anthropological Association Special Publication, no. 22. Washington, D.C.: American Anthropological Association.

Godelier, Maurice. 1986. *The Making of Great Men: Male Domination and Power among the New Guinea Baruya*. Trans. R. Swyer. Cambridge: Cambridge University Press.

Godwin, William. 1990 [1798]. *Memoirs of the Author of "A Vindication of the Rights of Woman."* Oxford: Woodstock Books.

Golden, Mark. 1981. Demography and the Exposure of Girls at Athens. *Phoenix* 35:316–31.

Golden, Mark. 1985a. "Donatus" and Athenian Phratries. *CQ* 35:9–13.

Golden, Mark. 1985b. Pais, "child" and "slave." *AC* 54:91–104.

Golden, Mark. 1986. Names and Naming at Athens: Three Studies. *EMC* 30:245–69.

Golden, Mark. 1990. *Children and Childhood in Classical Athens*. Baltimore: Johns Hopkins University Press.

Goldstein, Jan. 1984. Foucault among the Sociologists: The "Disciplines" and the History of the Professions. *History and Theory* 23:170–92.

Gombrich, E. H. 1977. *Art and Illusion: A Study in the Psychology of Pictorial Representation*. 5th ed. London: Phaidon Press.

Gomme, A. W. 1925. The Position of Women in Athens in the Fifth and Fourth Centuries B.C. *CP* 20:1–25.

Good, Byron. 1977. The Heart of What's the Matter: The Semantics of Illness in Iran. *Culture, Medicine and Psychiatry* 1.25–58.

Goody, Jack. 1977. *The Domestication of the Savage Mind.* Cambridge: Cambridge University Press.

Goody, Jack. 1986. *The Logic of Writing and the Organization of Society.* Cambridge: Cambridge University Press.

Goody, Jack. 1990. *The Oriental, the Ancient and the Primitive.* Cambridge: Cambridge University Press.

Gould, J. P. 1980. Law, Custom and Myth: Aspects of the Social Position of Women in Classical Athens. *JHS* 100:38–59

Gourevitch, Danielle. 1984. *La mal d'être femme: La femme et la médecine dans la Rome antique.* Paris: Société d'Édition "Les Belles Lettres."

Gourevitch, Danielle. 1987. La mort de la femme en couches et dans les suites de couches. In *La mort, les morts et l'au-delà dans le monde romain,* ed. F. Hinard, 187–93. Caen: Centre de Publications de l'Université de Caen.

Gourevitch, Danielle. 1988. La grossesse et l'accouchement dans l'iconographie antique. *Dossiers de l'archéologie* 123:42–48.

Gray, R. H. 1979. Biological Factors Other Than Nutrition and Lactation Which May Influence Natural Fertility: A Review. In *Natural Fertility,* ed. H. Leridon and J. Menken, 219–51 Liège: Ordina Editions.

The Greek Anthology. 1969 [1916]. Ed. and trans. W. R. Paton. Loeb Classical Library. Cambridge, Mass.: Harvard University Press.

Green, J. R. 1971. Choes of the Later Fifth Century. *ABSA* 66:189–228, pls. 30–33

Grensemann, Hermann. 1969. Die Krankheit der Tochter des Theodoros: Eine Studie zum siebten hippokratischen Epidemienbuch. *Clio Medica* 4:71–83.

Grensemann, Hermann. 1975. *Knidische Medizin.* Teil I, *Die Testimonien zur ältesten knidischen Lehre und Analysen knidischer Schriften im Corpus Hippocraticum.* Ars medica. Texte und Untersuchungen zur Quellenkunde der Alten Medizin, vol. 4, no. 1. Berlin.

Grensemann, Hermann. 1982. *Hippokratische Gynäkologie.* Wiesbaden. Franz Steiner Verlag.

Grensemann, Hermann 1987. *Knidische Medizin.* Teil II, *Versuch einer weiteren Analyse der Schicht A in den pseudohippokratischen Schriften de natura muliebri und de muliebribus I und II. Hermes* Einzelschriften. Wiesbaden: Franz Steiner Verlag.

Grensemann, Hermann. 1989. Kennzeichnet der erste Teil von De natura muliebri eine selbständige Stufe der griechischen Medizin? *Medizinhistorisches Journal* 24 3–24.

Griffith, F. L., ed. 1898. *The Petrie Papyri: Hieratic Papyri from Kahun and Gurob* London: Bernard Quaritch.

Grmek, M. D. 1975. La réalité nosologique au temps d'Hippocrate. In *La collection hippocratique et son rôle dans l'histoire de la médicine. Colloque de Strasbourg (23–27 octobre 1972)*, ed. L. Bourgey and J. Jouanna, 237–55. Leiden: E. J. Brill.

Grmek, M. D. 1980. La description hippocratique de la "toux epidemique" de Périnth. In *Hippocratica, Actes du Colloque hippocratique de Paris (4–9 septembre 1978)*, ed. M. D. Grmek, 199–221. Paris: Éditions Du Centre National de la Recherche Scientifique.

Grmek, M. D. 1989. *Diseases in the Ancient Greek World.* Trans M. Müllner and L. Müllner. Baltimore: Johns Hopkins University Press.

Guarducci, M. 1950 *Inscriptiones Creticae IV Tituli Gortynii.* Rome: La Libraria Dello Stato.

Gutierrez, H., and J. Houdaille 1983. La mortalité maternelle en France au XVIII siècle. *Population* 6:975–94

Hähnel, R. 1936. Der künstliche Abortus im Altertum. *Sudhoffs Archiv für Geschichte der Medizin und der Naturwissenschaften* 29:224–55.

Halliday, W. R. 1936. The Treatment of Disease in Antiquity. In *Greek Poetry and Life: Essays Presented to Gilbert Murray*, 277–94. Oxford: Clarendon Press.

Hallock, R. T. 1969. *Persepolis Fortification Tablets.* University of Chicago Oriental Institute Publications, vol. 92. Chicago: University of Chicago Press.

Halperin, D. M. 1990. *One Hundred Years of Homosexuality.* New York: Routledge.

Halperin, D. M., J. J. Winkler, and F. I Zeitlin, eds. 1990. *Before Sexuality: The Construction of Erotic Experience in the Ancient Greek World.* Princeton: Princeton University Press

Hamilton, E., and H. Cairns, eds. 1961. *The Collected Dialogues of Plato.* New York: Random House.

Hamilton, Richard. 1989. Alkman and the Athenian Arkteia. *Hesperia* 58:449–72.

Hamilton, Richard 1992. *Choes and Anthesteria· Athenian Iconography and Ritual.* Ann Arbor· University of Michigan Press.

Hammond, N. G. L. 1984. Alexander's Veterans after His Death. *GRBS* 25:51–61

Hanson, Ann Ellis. 1975. Hippocrates: Diseases of Women 1. Trans. with headnote. *Signs* 1:567–82.

Hanson, Ann Ellis. 1987. The Eight Months' Child and the Etiquette of Birth· Obsit Omen! *Bulletin of the History of Medicine* 61 (Winter): 589–602.

Hanson, Ann Ellis. 1989. Diseases of Women in the Epidemics In *Die Hip-*

pokratischen Epidemien: Theorie—Praxis—Tradition. Verhandlungen des V Colloque International Hippocratique, ed. G. Badder and R. Winau, 38–51. Sudhoffs Archiv. Beihefte 27. Stuttgart: Franz Steiner Verlag.

Hanson, Ann Ellis. 1990. The Medical Writers' Woman. In *Before Sexuality: The Construction of Erotic Experience in the Ancient Greek World*, ed. D. M. Halperin, J. J. Winkler, and F. I. Zeitlin, 309–38. Princeton: Princeton University Press.

Hanson, Ann Ellis. 1991. Continuity and Change: Three Case Studies in Hippocratic Gynecological Therapy and Theory. In *Women's History and Ancient History*, ed. S. B. Pomeroy, 73–110. Chapel Hill: University of North Carolina Press.

Hanson, Ann Ellis, and D. Armstrong. 1986. The Virgin's Voice and Neck: Aeschylus, *Agamemnon* 245 and Other Texts. *BICS* 33:97–100.

Harris, Marvin, and Eric B. Ross. 1987. *Death, Sex, and Fertility: Population Regulation in Preindustrial and Developing Societies*. New York: Columbia University Press.

Harris, W. V. 1982. The Theoretical Possibility of Extensive Infanticide in the Graeco-Roman World. *CQ* 32.114–16.

Harris, W. V. 1989. *Ancient Literacy*. Cambridge, Mass.: Harvard University Press.

Harris, William. 1845. *Lectures on Puerperal Fevers*. Philadelphia: T. and G. Town.

Harrison, A. R. W. 1968. *The Law of Athens*. Vol. 1, *The Family and Property*. Oxford: Clarendon Press.

Hassan, F. 1973. On Mechanisms of Population Growth during the Neolithic. *Current Anthropology* 14:535–42.

Havard, C. W. H., ed. 1990. *Black's Medical Dictionary*. 36th ed. Savage, Md.: Barnes and Noble.

Havelock, Eric A. 1963. *Preface to Plato*. New York. Grosset & Dunlap.

Havelock, Eric A. 1982. *The Literate Revolution in Greece and Its Cultural Consequences*. Princeton: Princeton University Press.

Helman, Cecil. 1984. *Culture, Health and Illness*. Bristol: John Wright & Sons.

Helman, Cecil. 1986. "Feed a Cold, Starve a Fever": Folk Models of Infection in an English Suburban Community, and Their Relation to Medical Treatment. In *Concepts of Health, Illness and Disease. A Comparative Perspective*, ed. C. Currer and M. Stacey, 211–29. Leamington Spa, U.K.: Berg.

Henderson, J. 1975. *The Maculate Muse: Obscene Language in Attic Comedy*. New Haven: Yale University Press.

Henderson, J., ed. 1987a. *Aristophanes Lysistrata*. Oxford: Clarendon Press.

Henderson, J. 1987b. Older Women in Attic Old Comedy. *TAPA* 117: 105–29.

Herdt, Gilbert H. 1981. *Guardians of the Flutes: Idioms of Masculity.* New York: McGraw-Hill.

Herdt, Gilbert H., ed. 1984. *Ritualized Homosexuality in Melanesia.* Berkeley: University of California Press.

Herfst, Pieter. 1979 [1922]. *Le travail de la femme dans la Grèce ancienne.* New York: Arno Press.

Herrmann, B., and T. Bergfelder. 1978. Ueber den diagnostischen Wert des sogenannten Geburtstrauma am Schambein bei der Identifikation. *Zeitschrift für Rechtsmedizin* 81:73–78.

Herzfeld, M 1980. Honor and Shame: Problems in the Comparative Analysis of Moral Systems. *Man* 15:339–51.

Herzfeld, M. 1987. *Anthropology through the Looking-glass: Critical Ethnography in the Margins of Europe.* Cambridge: Cambridge University Press.

Herzog, R. 1928. *Heilige Gesetze von Kos.* Berlin: Walter de Gruyter.

Herzog, R. 1931. *Die Wunderheilungen von Epidauros. Philologus* Suppl , vol. 22. Leipzig: Dieterich

Heuzey, L. 1882. *Catalogue des figurines antiques de terre cuite du Musée du Louvre.* 2 vols. Paris: Musées Nationaux.

Higgins, V. 1985. A Preliminary Analysis of Some of the Early Medieval Human Skeletons from San Vincenzo al Volturno. In *San Vincenzo al Volturno: The Archaeology, Art and Territory of an Early Medieval Monastery,* 111–24. BAR International Series, vol. 252. Oxford: British Archaeological Reports.

Hilts, Philip J 1990. N.I.H. Starts Women's Health Office. *New York Times* September 11, p. C9.

Hippocrates. 1923–. Ed. and trans. W. H. S. Jones and Paul Potter. 6 vols. Loeb Classical Library Cambridge, Mass.: Harvard University Press.

Hippocrates. 1961 [1839]. Ed. and trans. É. Littré. 10 vols. Amsterdam: Adolf M. Hakkert.

Hirschon, R. 1983. Women, the Aged and Religious Activity: Oppositions and Complementarity in an Urban Locality. *Journal of Modern Greek Studies* 1:113–29.

Hirschon, R. 1989. *Heirs of the Greek Catastrophe· The Social Life of Asia Minor Refugees in Piraeus.* Oxford: Clarendon Press.

Hodkinson, Stephen. 1988. Inheritance, Marriage and Demography: Perspectives upon the Success and Decline of Classical Sparta. In *Athens and Sparta: Constructing Greek Political and Social History from 478 B.C.,* ed. Anton Powell, 79–121. London· Routledge.

Holt, C. A. 1978. A Re-examination of Parturition Scars on the Human Female Pelvis. *American Journal of Physical Anthropology* 49:91–94.

Hopkins, Keith. 1966. The Probable Age Structure of the Roman Population. *Population Studies* 20:245–64.

Hopkins, Keith. 1987. Graveyards for Historians. In *La mort, les morts et l'au-delà dans le monde romain*, ed. F. Hinard, 113–26. Caen: Centre de Publications de l'Université de Caen.

Hornblower, Simon. 1987. *Thucydides*. London: Gerald Duckworth.

Humphreys, S. C. 1978. *Anthropology and the Greeks* London: Routledge & Kegan Paul.

Humphreys, Sally. 1980. Family Tombs and Tomb Cult in Ancient Athens. Tradition or Traditionalism? *JHS* 100:96–125.

Humphreys, Sally. 1981 Death and Time. In *Mortality and Immortality: The Anthropology and Archaeology of Death*, ed S. C. Humphreys and H. King, 261–83. London· Academic Press.

Hunter, Virginia. 1989a. The Athenian Widow and Her Kin. *Journal of Family History* 14·291–311.

Hunter, Virginia. 1989b. Women's Authority in Classical Athens. *EMC* 8:39–48

Isager, Signe. 1981–82. The Marriage Pattern in Classical Athens. Men and Women in Isaios *C&M* 33:81–96.

Jacobsen, Grethe. 1984. Pregnancy and Childbirth in the Medieval North: A Topology of Sources and a Preliminary Study. *Scandinavian Journal of History* 9:91–111.

Jeanmaire, Henri. 1939. *Couroi et courètes; essai sur l'education spartiate et sur les rites d'adolescence dan l'antiquité hellénique*. Travaux et mémoires de l'Université de Lille, no. 21. Lille: Bibiothèque Universitaire.

Jenkins, I. 1983. Is There Life after Marriage? A Study of the Abduction Motif in Vase Paintings of the Athenian Wedding Ceremony. *BICS* 30:137–45.

Johansen, K. F. 1951. *The Attic Grave-reliefs of the Classical Period: An Essay in Interpretation*. Copenhagen: E Munksgaard.

Jones, W. G. S. 1946. *Philosophy and Medicine in Ancient Greece Bulletin of the History of Medicine*, supplement no. 8. Baltimore.

Jones, W. G. S. 1947. *The Medical Writings of Anonymus Londinensis*. Cambridge: Cambridge University Press.

Jones, W H. S. 1907. *Malaria, a Neglected Factor in the History of Greece and Rome*. Cambridge: Cambridge University Press

Jones, W H. S. 1909. *Malaria and Greek History*. Victoria University of Manchester Historical Series, no. 8. Manchester: Sherratt & Hughes.

Jouanna, J. 1974. *Hippocrate. Pour une archéologie de l'école de Cnide* Paris· Belles Lettres

Jouanna, J 1988. Ippocrate e il sacro. *Koinonia* 12.91–113.

Jucker, I. 1963. Frauenfest in Korinth. *AK* 6:47–61

Kaempf-Dimitriadon, S 1986. Ein attisches Staatsgrabmal des 4. Jahrhunderts v. Chr. *AK* 29:23–36.

Kahil, L. 1963. Quelques vases du sanctuaire d'Artémis à Brauron. *AK* Beiheft 1:5–29.

Kahil, L. 1965. Autour de l'Artémis attique. *AK* 8.20–33.

Kahil, L. 1976. Artémis attique. *CRAI*:126–30

Kahil, L. 1977. L'Artémis de Brauron. Rites et mystère. *AK* 20:86–98.

Kahil, L. 1981. Le "cratérisque" d'Artémis et le Brauronion de l'Acropole. *Hesperia* 50:253–63.

Kahil, L. 1983. Mythological Repertoire of Brauron. In *Ancient Greek Art and Iconography*, ed. W. G. Moon, 231–44. Madison: University of Wisconsin Press.

Kallipolites, V. 1968. Une nouvelle stèle du Musée National d'Athènes. *AAA* 1:85–89.

Kein, J. H. C. 1957. An Attic "Feeding-bottle" of the 4th Century B C. in Leyden. *Mnemosyne* 10:16–21.

Keller, E. F. 1985. Baconian Science: The Arts of Mastery and Obedience. In *Reflections on Gender and Science*, ed. E. F. Keller, 33–42. New Haven: Yale University Press.

Kerényi, C. 1975. *Zeus and Hera: Archetypal Image of Father, Husband, and Wife*. Trans. C. Holme. Bollingen Series 65.5. Princeton: Princeton University Press.

Kertzer, D. J. 1987. Review of *Honor and Shame and the Unity of the Mediterranean* by D. D. Gilmore. *American Anthropologist* 89:991.

Keuls, E. C. 1985. *The Reign of the Phallus*. New York· Harper & Row.

Keuls, E. C. 1990. Review of *Studies in Girls' Transitions* by C. Sourvinou-Inwood. *AJA* 94·694–95.

King, Helen. 1983. Bound to Bleed: Artemis and Greek Women. In *Images of Women in Antiquity*, ed. A. Cameron and A. Kuhrt, 109–27. Detroit: Wayne State University Press.

King, Helen. 1985. "From Parthenos to Gyne: The Dynamics of Category." Ph.D. diss., University College London.

King, Helen. 1986. Agnodike and the Profession of Medicine. *Proceedings of the Cambridge Philological Society* 212:53–77.

King, Helen. 1987. Sacrificial Blood. The Role of the Amnion in Ancient Gynecology In *Rescuing Creusa: New Methodological Approaches to Women in Antiquity*, ed Marilyn Skinner, 117–26. *Helios* special issue 13.2. Lubbock: Texas Technical University Press.

King, Helen. 1988. The Early Anodynes. Pain in the Ancient World In *The History of the Management of Pain: From Early Principles to Present Practices*, ed. R. D Mann, 51–62. Park Ridge, N.J.: Parthenon Publishing Group.

King, Helen. 1989. The Daughter of Leonides: Reading the Hippocratic Corpus. In *History as Text*, ed. Averil Cameron, 13–32. London: Duckworth.

King, Helen. 1991. Using the Past: Nursing and the Medical Profession in Ancient Greece. In *Anthropology and Nursing*, ed. P. Holden and J. Littlewood, 7–24. London: Routledge.

Kirk, G. S., J. E. Raven, and M. Schofield. 1983. *The Presocratic Philosophers*. 2d ed. Cambridge: Cambridge University Press

Kleinman, Arthur M. 1973a. Medicine's Symbolic Reality: On a Central Problem in the Philosophy of Medicine. *Inquiry* 16:206–13.

Kleinman, Arthur M 1973b. Toward a Comparative Study of Medical Systems: An Integrated Approach to the Study of the Relations between Medicine and Culture. *Science, Medicine and Man* 1:55–65.

Kleinman, Arthur M. 1974. Cognitive structures of Traditional Medical Systems: Ordering, Explaining, and Interpreting the Human Experience of Illness. *Ethnomedizin* 1:35–49.

Kleinman, Arthur M. 1978. Concepts and a Model for the Comparison of Medical Systems as Cultural Systems. *Social Science and Medicine* 12: 85–93.

Kleinman, Arthur M. 1980. *Patients and Healers in the Context of Culture: An Exploration of the Borderland between Anthropology, Medicine, and Psychiatry.* Comparative Studies of Health Systems and Medical Care, no. 3. Berkeley: University of California Press.

Kondis, J. D. 1967. Artemis Brauronia. *AD* 22, pt. 1:156–206.

Kraemer, R S. 1979. Ecstasy and Possession. The Attraction of Women to the Cult of Dionysus *Harvard Theological Review* 72:55–80.

Krug, A. 1985. *Heilkunst und Heilkult. Medizin in der Antike.* Munich: C. H. Beck.

Kudlien, F. 1967. *Der Beginn des medizinischen Denkens bei den Griechen von Homer bis Hippokrates.* Zurich: Artemis Verlag.

Kudlien, F. 1968. *Die Sklaven in der griechischen Medizin der klassischen und hellenistischen Zeit.* Wiesbaden: Franz Steiner Verlag.

Kudlien, F. 1970. Medical Ethics and Popular Ethics in Greece and Rome. *Clio Medica* 5.91–121.

Kudlien, F. 1977. Bermerkungen zu W. D. Smith's These über die knidische Ärzteschule. In *Corpus Hippocraticum. Colloque de Mons septembre 1975*, ed. R. Joly, 95–105 Mons: Université de Mons.

Kudlien, F 1979. *Der griechische Arzt im Zeitalter des Hellenismus: Seine Stellung in Staat und Gesellschaft.* Akademie der Wissenschaften und Literatur, Mainz. Abhandlungen der Geistes- und Sozialwissenschaftlichen Klasse, no 6 Mainz: Franz Steiner Verlag.

Kuhn, Thomas S. 1970. *The Structure of Scientific Revolutions.* 2d ed Chicago. University of Chicago Press.

Kurtz, D. C., and J. Boardman. 1971 *Greek Burial Customs.* London: Thames and Hudson.

Laín Entralgo, Pedro. 1970. *The Therapy of the Word in Classical Antiquity.*

Ed. and trans. L. J. Rather and J. M. Sharp. New Haven: Yale University Press.

Lamphere, L. 1975. Women and Domestic Power: Political and Economic Strategies in Domestic Groups. In *Being Female: Reproduction, Power, and Change*, ed. D. Raphaels, 117–30. Paris: Mouton.

Lanata, Giuliana. 1967. *Medicina magica e religione popolare in Grecia fino all'età di Ippocrate*. Rome: Edizioni Dell'Ateneo.

Lancaster, H. O. 1990. *Expectations of Life: A Study of the Demography, Statistics, and History of World Mortality*. New York: Springer-Verlag.

Landy, David, ed. 1977. *Culture, Disease, and Healing: Studies in Medical Anthropology*. New York: Macmillan.

Lang, M. 1977. *Cure and Cult in Ancient Corinth: A Guide to the Asklepieion*. Princeton: American School of Classical Studies.

Lang, M. 1984. *Herodotean Narrative and Discourse*. Cambridge, Mass.: Harvard University Press.

Langholf, V. 1977. Die parallelen Texte in Epidemien V und VII. In *Corpus Hippocraticum. Actes du Colloque Hippocratique de Mons (22–26 septembre 1975)*, ed. R. Joly, 264–74. Mons: Université de Mons.

Langholf, V. 1990. *Medical Theories in Hippocrates: Early Texts and the "Epidemics."* Berlin: Walter de Gruyter.

Lefkowitz, M. R. 1981. *Heroines and Hysterics*. New York: St. Martin's Press.

Lerner, Gerda. 1986. *The Creation of Patriarchy*. Oxford: Oxford University Press.

Levy, H. L. 1963. Inheritance and Dowry in Classical Athens. In *Mediterranean Countrymen: Essays in the Social Anthropology of the Mediterranean*, ed. J. Pitt-Rivers, 137–44. Paris: Mouton.

Lewis, Gilbert. 1980. *Day of Shining Red*. Cambridge: Cambridge University Press.

Lincoln, B. 1979. The Rape of Persephone: A Greek Scenario of Women's Initiation. *Harvard Theological Review* 72:223–35.

Linders, Tullia. 1972. *Studies in the Treasure Records of Artemis Brauronia Found in Athens*. Lund: P. Åström.

Lloyd, G. E. R. 1966. *Polarity and Analogy*. Cambridge: Cambridge University Press.

Lloyd, G. E. R. 1975. The Hippocratic Question. *CQ* 25:171–92.

Lloyd, G. E. R., ed. 1978. *Hippocratic Writings*. Harmondsworth: Penguin Books.

Lloyd, G. E. R. 1979. *Magic, Reason and Experience: Studies in the Origin and Development of Greek Science*. Cambridge: Cambridge University Press.

Lloyd, G. E. R. 1983. *Science, Folklore and Ideology. Studies in the Life Sciences in Ancient Greece*. Cambridge: Cambridge University Press.

Lloyd, G. E. R. 1987. *The Revolutions of Wisdom. Studies in the Claims and Practice of Ancient Greek Science*. Berkeley: University of California Press.

Lloyd-Jones, Hugh. 1983. Artemis and Iphigeneia. *JHS* 103:87–102.

Loizos, P., and E. Papataxiarchis. 1991. Gender and Kinship in Marriage and Alternative Contexts. In *Contested Identities: Gender and Kinship in Modern Greece*, ed. P. Loizos and E. Papataxiarchis, 3–25. Princeton: Princeton University Press.

Longrigg, J. 1963. Philosophy and Medicine, Some Early Interactions. *HSCP* 67:147–75.

Lonie, Iain M. 1978. Cos Versus Cnidus and the Historians. *History of Science* 15:42–75, 77–92.

Lonie, Iain M. 1981. *The Hippocratic Treatises "On Generation," "On the Nature of the Child," "Diseases IV."* Ars Medica, vol. 7. Berlin: Walter de Gruyter.

Lonie, Iain M. 1983. Literacy and the Development of Hippocratic Medicine. In *Formes de pensée dans la collection hippocratique. Actes du IV Colloque international hippocratique (Lausanne, 21–26 septembre 1981*, ed. F. Lasserre and Philippe Mudry, 145–61. Université de Lausanne publications de la faculté des lettres. Geneva: Librairie Droz S.A.

Loraux, Nicole. 1981. Le lit, la guerre. *L'Homme* 21:37–57.

Loraux, Nicole. 1986. *The Invention of Athens: The Funeral Oration in the Classical City*. Trans. A. Sheridan. Cambridge, Mass.: Harvard University Press

Loraux, Nicole. 1987. *Tragic Ways of Killing a Woman*. Trans. A. Forster. Cambridge, Mass.: Harvard University Press.

Loudon, I. 1991. On Maternal and Infant Mortality 1900–1960. *Social History of Medicine* 4:29–73.

Luce, Judith de. 1991. Why Do We Ignore Our Elders? *Women's Classical Caucus Newsletter* 16:18–19.

MacDowell, D. M. 1978. *The Law in Classical Athens*. London: Thames and Hudson.

MacDowell, D. M. 1986. *Spartan Law*. Edinburgh: Scottish Academic Press.

Majno, G. 1975. *The Healing Hand: Man and Wound in the Ancient World* Cambridge, Mass.: Harvard University Press.

Makler, P. T. 1980. New Information on Nutrition in Ancient Greece *Klio* 62:317–19.

Malinas, Y., and D. Gourevitch. 1982. Chronique anachronique, I: Suffocation subite chez la femme enceinte *Revue Française de Gynécologie et d'Obstétrique* 77:753–55.

Manchester, K. 1984 Tuberculosis and Leprosy in Antiquity: An Interpretation. *Medical History* 28:162–73.

Manson-Bahr, F. E. C., and F. I. C. Apted. 1982. *Manson's Tropical Diseases*. 18th ed. London: Baillière Tindall.

Manuli, Paola. 1980. Fisiologia e patologia del femminile negli scritti ippocratici dell'antica ginecologia greca. In *Hippocratica. Actes du Colloque hippocratique de Paris (4–9 septembre 1978)*, ed. M D. Grmek, 393–408. Paris: Centre National de la Recherche Scientifique.

Manuli, Paola. 1983. Gli ippocratici e la malattia femminile. In *Madre Materia. Sociologia biologia della donna greca*, ed. S. Campese, P. Manuli, and G. Sissa, 154–62 Turin: Boringhieri.

Martin, Emily. 1987. *The Woman in the Body: A Cultural Analysis of Reproduction*. Boston: Beacon Press.

Mason, Peter. 1984. *The City of Men: Ideology, Sexual Politics and the Social Formation*. Göttingen. Edition Herodot.

Mason, Peter. 1987. Third Person/Second Sex: Patterns of Sexual Asymmetry in the *Theogony* of Hesiodos. In *Sexual Assymmetry: Studies in Ancient Society*, ed. J. Blok and P. Mason, 147–89 Amsterdam: J. C. Gieben.

McKee, Lauris. 1984. Sex Differentials in Survivorship and the Customary Treatment of Infants and Children. *Medical Anthropology* 8:91–108.

Megas, George A. 1958. *Greek Calendar Customs*. Athens: Press and Information Department, Prime Minister's Office.

Meinecke, Bruno. 1927. Consumption (Tuberculosis) in Classical Antiquity. *Annals of Medical History* 9:379–402.

Merck Manual. 1992. 16th ed. Ed. R. Berkow et al. Rahway, N.J.: Merck Sharp and Dohme Research Laboratories.

Merriam, A. C. 1887. Painted Sepulchral Stelai from Alexandria. *AJA* 3:259–68.

Merskey, H , and P. Potter. 1989 The Womb Lay Still in Ancient Egypt. *British Journal of Psychiatry* 154:751–53.

Meyers, Carol. 1989. Recovering Eve: Biblical Woman without Postbiblical Dogma. In *Women and a New Academy: Gender and Cultural Contexts*, ed. J. F. O'Barr, 62–80. Madison: University of Wisconsin Press.

Micale, M. S. 1989. Hysteria and Its Historiography: A Review of Past and Present Writings. *History of Science* 27:223–61, 319–51.

Micale, M. S. 1990. Hysteria and Its Historiography: The Future Perspective. *History of Psychiatry* 1:33–124.

Michon, E 1905. Lécythe funéraire en marbre de style attique Musée du Louvre. *Monuments et Mémoires (Fondation Piot)* 12 177–99.

Mihailov, G 1970. *Inscriptiones Graecae in Bulgaria repertae*. 2d ed. Academia Litterarum Bulgarica Institutum Archaeologicum. Series epigraphica, no. 10. Serdicae: In Aedibus Typographicus Academiae Litterarium Bulgaricae.

Miller, H. W. 1944. Medical Terminology in Tragedy. *TAPA* 75:156–67.

Mitropoulou, E. 1977. *Corpus I: Attic Votive Reliefs of the 6th and 5th Centuries B.C* Athens: Pyli Editions

Möbius, H 1934. Diotima. *JDAI* 49:45–60.

Möbius, H 1966. Eigenartige attische Grabreliefs. *MDAI(A)* 81.136–60.

Mommsen, August. 1898. *Feste der Stadt Athen im Altertum: geordnet nach attischem Kalender*. Leipzig: B. G. Teubner.

Mommsen, August. 1899. 'Ράκος auf attischen Inschriften. *Philologus* 58: 343–47.

Montepaone, C. 1979. L'ἀρκτεία a Brauron. *Studi Storico Religiosi* 3:342–364.

Morrison, J. S. 1964. Four Notes on Plato's *Symposium*. *CQ* 14:42–55.

Morsy, S. 1978. Sex Roles, Power, and Illness in an Egyptian Village. *American Ethnologist* 5:137–49.

Morton, N. E. 1961 Morbidity of Children from Consanguineous Marriages. *Progress in Medical Genetics* 1:261–91.

Murnaghan, Sheila. 1988. How a Woman Can Be More Like a Man· The Dialogue between Ischomachus and His wife in Xenophon's *Oeconomicus*. *Helios* 15:9–22

Myres, J. L. 1914. *Handbook of the Cesnola Collection of Antiquities from Cyprus* New York: Metropolitan Museum of Art.

Nardı, Enzo. 1971. *Procurato aborto nel mondo greco romano*. Milan: Dott A. Giuffrè Editore.

Nelson, C. 1975. Public and Private Politics: Women in the Middle Eastern World. *American Ethnologist* 1.551–64.

Newton, Judith. 1988. History as Usual?: Feminism and the "New Historicism." *Cultural Critique* 9:87–121.

Nickel, D. 1972. Ärztliche Ethik und Schwangerschaftsunterbrechung bei den Hippokratikern. *Schriftenreihe für Geschichte der Naturwissenschaften, Technik und Medizin, Leipzig* 9, no. 1:73–80.

Nickel, D. 1979. Berufsvorstellungen über weibliche Medizinalpersonen in der Antike. *Klio* 61:515–18.

Nielsen, T. H., L. Bjertrup, M. H. Hansen, L. Rubinstein, and T. Verstergaard. 1989. Athenian Grave Monuments and Social Class. *GRBS* 30. 411–20.

Nikitas, Anastasios A 1968. "Untersuchungen zu den Epidemienbüchern II IV VI des Corpus Hippocraticum." Ph.D. diss., Hamburg

Nilsson, M. P. 1957 [1906]. *Griechische Feste von religiöser Bedeutung*. Stuttgart. B. G. Teubner.

Noshy, I. 1937. *The Arts in Ptolemaic Egypt: A Study of Greek and Egyptian Influences in Ptolemaic Architecture and Sculpture*. London: Oxford University Press.

Osborne, Robin. 1985. *Demos· The Discovery of Classical Attika*. Cambridge: Cambridge University Press

Owsley, D. W , and B. Bradtmiller. 1983. Mortality of Pregnant Females in Arıkara Villages: Osteological Evidence. *American Journal of Physical Anthropology* 61:331–36.

Padel, Ruth. 1983. Women: Model for Possession by Greek Daemons. In

Images of Women in Antiquity, ed. A. Cameron and A. Kuhrt, 3–19. Detroit: Wayne State University Press.

Papademetriou, J. 1963. The Sanctuary of Artemis at Brauron. *Scientific American* 208, no. 6:111–20.

Papanikolaou, A. 1965. *Glossikai ereunai epi tou Corpus Hippocraticum.* Athens [not seen].

Parke, H. W. 1977. *Festivals of the Athenians.* Ithaca: Cornell University Press.

Parker, Robert. 1983. *Miasma: Pollution and Purification in Early Greek Religion.* Oxford: Clarendon Press.

Parry, Adam. 1969. The Language of Thucydides' Description of the Plague. *BICS* 16:106–18.

Patterson, C. 1981. *Pericles' Citizenship Law of 451–50 B.C..* New York: Arno Press.

Patterson, C. 1985. Not Worth the Rearing. *TAPA* 115:103–23.

Patterson, C. 1991. Marriage and the Married Woman in Athenian Law. In *Women's History and Ancient History*, ed. S. B. Pomeroy, 48–72. Chapel Hill: University of North Carolina Press.

Pavlides, E., and J. Hesser. 1986. Women's Roles and House Form and Decoration in Eressos, Greece. In *Gender and Power in Rural Greece*, ed. Jill Dubisch, 68–96. Princeton: Princeton University Press.

Payne, H. 1931. *Necrocorinthia: A Study of Corinthian Art of the Archaic Period.* Oxford: Clarendon Press.

Peckham, C. H. 1935. A Brief History of Puerperal Infection. *Bulletin of the History of Medicine* 3:187–212.

Peek, W. 1955. *Griechische Vers-Inschriften.* Berlin: Akademie-Verlag.

Penniston, Sarah C. 1986. "Childbed Fever in the Boston Lying-In Hospital, 1873–1889." Senior Honors Thesis, Harvard University.

Peristiany, J. G., ed. 1966. *Honour and Shame: The Values of Mediterranean Society.* Chicago: University of Chicago Press

Perlman, P. 1983. Plato's "Laws" 833C–834D and the Bears of Brauron. *GRBS* 24:115–30.

Perlman, P. 1989. Acting the She-bear for Artemis. *Arethusa* 22:111–30.

Petersen, William. 1961. *Population.* New York: Macmillan

Pfuhl, E. 1901. Alexandrinische Grabreliefs. *MDAI(A)* 26.268–70.

Pfuhl, E., and H. Möbius 1977. *Die ostgriechischen Grabreliefs.* Mainz: Von Zaubern.

Philadelpheus, A. 1927. Le sanctuaire d'Artémis Kallistè et l'ancienne rue de l'Académie. *BCH* 51:155–63.

Phillips, E. D. 1973. *Greek Medicine.* London: Thames and Hudson.

Pingiatoglou, S. 1981. *Eileithyia.* Würzburg: Königshausen & Neumann

Plato. 1953. *Dialogues.* Trans. B. Jowett. Oxford: Clarendon Press.

Ploss, H. H. 1891. *Das Weib in der Natur- und Völkerkunde, anthropologische Studien.* 3d ed. Leipzig: T Brieben.

Polgar, S. 1972. Population History and Population Policies from an Anthropological Perspective *Current Anthropology* 13:203–11.

Pomeroy, Sarah. 1975 *Goddesses, Whores, Wives, and Slaves: Women in Classical Antiquity.* New York: Schocken.

Pomeroy, Sarah. 1978. Plato and the Female Physician (*Republic* 454d2). *AJP* 99.496–500.

Pomeroy, Sarah. 1983. Infanticide in Hellenistic Greece. In *Images of Women in Antiquity,* eds A Cameron and A. Kuhrt, 207–22. Detroit: Wayne State University Press.

Pomeroy, Sarah. 1991. *Women's History and Ancient History* Chapel Hill: University of North Carolina Press.

Potter, P. 1980. *Hippokrates, Ueber die Krankheiten III.* Berlin: Akademie Verlag.

Potter, P., G. Maloney, and J. Desautels, eds. 1990. *La maladie et les maladies dans la collection hippocratique.* Actes du VI Colloque international hippocratique. Sillery, Quebec: Editions Du Sphinx.

Pouilloux, J. 1954. *Recherches sur l'histoire et les cultes de Thasos I. De la fondation de la cité à 196 avant J.-C.* Études Thasiennes. Paris. De Boccard.

Powell, Anton. 1988. *Athens and Sparta: Constructing Greek Political and Social History from 478 B.C.* London: Routledge.

Preus, Anthony. 1975. Biomedical Techniques for Influencing Human Reproduction in the Fourth Century B.C. *Arethusa* 8·237–63.

Price, T. Hadzisteliou. 1978. *Kourotrophos: Cults and Representations of the Greek Nursing Deities.* Leiden: E. J. Brill.

Prukakis-Christodulopulos, A. 1970. Einige Marmorlekythen. *MDAI(A)* 85:54–99.

Randall, R. H., Jr. 1953. The Erechtheum Workers. *AJA* 57:199–210.

Redfield, James. 1982. Notes on the Greek Wedding. *Arethusa* 15:181–201.

Reynolds, E., and F. S. Newell. 1902. *Practical Obstetrics: A Text-book for Practitioners and Students.* Philadelphia: Lea Brothers.

Richardson, Nicholas James, ed. 1974. *The Homeric Hymn to Demeter.* Oxford: Clarendon Press

Richlin, Amy. 1991. Zeus and Metis: Foucault, Feminism, Classics. *Helios* 18·160–80.

Richter, G. M. A. 1954. *Catalogue of Greek Sculptures in the Metropolitan Museum of Art* Cambridge, Mass.· Harvard University Press.

Riddle, John. 1992. *Contraception and Abortion from the Ancient World to the Renaissance.* Cambridge, Mass.: Harvard University Press.

Riemann, H. 1940. *Kerameikos: Ergebnisse der Ausgrabungen.* Vol. 2, *Die*

Skulpturen vom 5. Jahrhundert bis in Römische Zeit. Berlin: Walter de Gruyter.

Robert, F. 1973. La bataille de Délos. *BCH* Suppl. 1:427–33.

Robert, F. 1975. Les adresses de malades dans les Épidémies II, IV, et VI. In *La collection hippocratique et son rôle dans l'histoire de la médecine. Colloque de Strasbourg (23–27 octobre 1972),* ed. L. Bourgey and J. Jouanna, 173–94. Leiden: E. J. Brill.

Robert, F. 1989. Médecine d'équipe dans les Épidémies V. In *Die hippokratischen Epidemien. Theorie—Praxis—Tradition. Verhandlungen des V Colloque international Hippocratique,* ed. G. Badder and R. Winau, 20–27. Stuttgart: Franz Steiner Verlag.

Robinson, David M. 1942. *Necrolynthia: A study in Greek Burial Customs and Anthropology.* Excavations at Olynthus, vol. 11. Baltimore. Johns Hopkins Press.

Roebuck, C. 1951. *The Asklepieion and Lerna.* Excavations at Corinth, vol. XIV. Princeton: American School of Classical Studies.

Rogers, Spencer L. 1942. The Methods, Results, and Values in Shamanistic Therapy. *Ciba Symposia* 4 (April):1215–24.

Rouse, William H. D. 1902. *Greek Votive Offerings.* Cambridge: Cambridge University Press.

Rousselle, Aline. 1980. Observation féminine et idéologie masculine: le corps de la femme d'après les médecins grecs. *Annales (ESC)* 35, no. 6:1089–115.

Rousselle, Aline. 1988. *Porneia: On Desire and the Body in Antiquity.* Trans. F. Pheasant. Oxford: Basil Blackwell.

Rubel, A. J. 1964. The Epidemiology of a Folk Illness: Susto in Hispanic America. *Ethnology* 3·268–83.

Rubel, A. J., Carl W. O'Nell, and Rolando Collado-Ardón. 1984. *Susto, a Folk Illness.* Comparative Studies of Health Systems and Medical Care. Berkeley: University of California Press.

Rumpf, A. 1961. Attische Feste—Attische Vasen. *Bonner Jahrbücher* 161: 208–14.

Russell, W. M. S. 1983. The Palaeodemographic View. In *Disease in Ancient Man,* ed. G. D. Hart, 217–53. Toronto: Clarke Irwin.

Rutman, Darrett B., and Anita H. Rutman. 1976. Of Agues and Fevers: Malaria in the Early Chesapeake *William and Mary Quarterly* 3:31–60.

Sale, W. 1975. The Temple Legends of the Arkteia. *RhM* 118:265–84.

Sallares, Robert. 1991. *The Ecology of the Ancient Greek World.* Ithaca: Cornell University Press.

Salviat, F. 1959. Décrets pour Épié fille de Dionysios: Déesses et sanctuaires Thasien. *BCH* 83:362–97.

Sanders, I. T. 1962. *Rainbow in the Rock: The People of Rural Greece.* Cambridge, Mass.: Harvard University Press.

Sawicki, Jana. 1991. *Disciplining Foucault: Feminism, Power, and the Body.* New York: Routledge.

Schaps, D. M. 1977. The Woman Least Mentioned. *CQ* 27:323–30.

Schaps, D. M. 1979. *Economic Rights of Women in Ancient Greece.* Edinburgh: University of Edinburgh Press.

Schmaltz, B. 1970. *Untersuchungen zu den attischen Marmorlekythen.* Berlin: Mann.

Schmaltz, B. 1983. *Griechische Grabreliefs.* Darmstadt: Wissenschaftliche Buchgesellschaft.

Schofield, R. 1986. Did the Mothers Really Die? Three Centuries of Maternal Mortality in "The World We Have Lost." In *The World We Have Gained: Histories of Population and Social Structure: Essays Presented to Peter Laslett on His Seventieth Birthday,* ed. L. Bonfield, R. M. Smith, and K. Wrightson, 231–60. Oxford: Basil Blackwell.

Schweitzer, B. 1941. Krieger in der Grabkunst des Fünften Jahrhunderts. *Die Antike* 17:35–48.

Scarborough, J. 1979. Nicander's *Toxicology* II: Spiders, Scorpions, Insects and Myriapods *Pharmacy in History* 21:73–92.

Scurlock, J. A. 1991. Baby-snatching Demons, Restless Souls and the Dangers of Childbirth: Medico-magical Means of Dealing with Some of the Perils of Motherhood in Ancient Mesopotamia. *Incognita* 2:137–85.

Seligman, S. A. 1991 The Lesser Pestilence: Non-epidemic Puerperal Fever. *Medical History* 35:89–102.

Semmelweis, Ignaz. 1983 [1860]. *The Etiology, Concept, and Prophylaxis of Childbed Fever.* Ed. and trans. K. Codell Carter. Madison: University of Wisconsin Press.

Sergent, B. 1987. *Homosexuality in Greek Myth* Trans. A. Goldhammer. London: Athlone Press.

Shapiro, H. A. 1991. The Iconography of Mourning in Athenian Art. *AJA* 95:629–56.

Shaw, M.. 1975. The Female Intruder: Women in Fifth-century Drama. *CP* 70:255–66.

Sherwin-White, S. M. 1978. *Ancient Cos: An Historical Study from the Dorian Settlement to the Imperial Period. Hypomnemata.* Untersuchungen zur Antike und zu ihrem Nachleben, vol. 51. Göttingen: Vandenhoeck & Ruprecht.

Shorter, Edward. 1986. Paralysis: The Rise and Fall of a "Hysterical" Symptom. *Journal of Social History* 19:549–82.

Sillen, A. and P. Smith. 1984 Weaning Patterns Are Reflected in Strontium-calcium Ratios of Juvenile Skeletons. *Journal of Archaeological Science* 11:237–45.

Simon, B. 1978. *Mind and Madness in Ancient Greece: The Classical Roots of Modern Psychiatry* Ithaca. Cornell University Press.

Simon, Erika. 1983. *Festivals of Attica: An Archaeological Commentary* Madison: University of Wisconsin Press.

Sissa, Giulia. 1990. *Greek Virginity*. Trans. A. Goldhammer. Cambridge, Mass.: Harvard University Press.

Slater, P. E. 1968. *The Glory of Hera: Greek Mythology and the Greek Family*. Boston: Beacon Press.

Smith, Wesley D. 1973. Galen on Coans and Cnidians. *Bulletin of the History of Medicine* 47:569–85.

Smith, Wesley D. 1979. *The Hippocratic Tradition*. Cornell Publications in the History of Science. Ithaca: Cornell University Press.

Smith, Wesley D. 1989. Generic Form in Epidemics I to VII. In *Die Hippokratischen Epidemien: Theorie—Praxis—Tradition. Verhandlungen des V Colloque International Hippocratique*, ed. G. Badder and R. Winau, 144–58. *Sudhoffs Archiv*, Beihefte 27. Stuttgart: Franz Steiner Verlag.

Sokolowski, F. 1962. *Lois sacrées des cités grecques. Supplément*. Paris: De Boccard.

Sourvinou, C. 1971. Aristophanes, *Lysistrata*, 641–647. *CQ* 21·339–42.

Sourvinou-Inwood, C. 1987a. Erotic Pursuit: Images and Meanings. *JHS* 107:131–53.

Sourvinou-Inwood, C. 1987b. Menace and Pursuit: Differentiation and the Creation of Meaning. In *Images et société en Grèce ancienne. L'iconographie comme méthod d'analyse*, ed. C. Bérard, C. Bron, and A. Pomari, 41–58. Lausanne: Institut d'Archéologie et d'Histoire Ancienne, University de Lausanne.

Sourvinou-Inwood, C. 1988. *Studies in Girls' Transitions: Aspects of the Arkteia and Age Representation in Attic Iconography*. Athens: Kardamitsa.

Sourvinou-Inwood, C. 1990. Myths in Images: Theseus and Medea as a Case Study. In *Approaches to Greek Myth*, ed. Lowell Edmunds, 395–445. Baltimore: Johns Hopkins University Press.

Speier, H. 1932. Zweifiguren-Gruppen im fünften und vierten Jahrhundert vor Christus. *MDAI(R)* 47:1–94.

Stanworth, M., ed. 1987. *Reproductive Technologies: Gender, Motherhood, and Medicine*. Minneapolis: University of Minnesota Press.

Starr, C. G. 1978. An Evening with the Flute-girls. *PP* 183:401–10.

Stinton, T. C. W. 1976. Iphigeneia and the Bears of Brauron. *CQ*, n.s , 26:11–13.

Stoddart, Simon, and James Whitley. 1988. The Social Context of Literacy in Archaic Greece and Etruria. *Antiquity* 62:761–72.

Stoop, M. W. 1960. *Floral Figurines from South Italy*. Assen: Royal Van-Gorcum.

Strauss, Barry S. 1985. Ritual, Social Drama and Politics. *AJAH* 67–83.

Stupperich. 1977. "Staatsbegrabnis und Privatgrabmal im klassischen Athen." Dissertation, Westälischer Wilhelms Universität.

Suchey, J M., D. V. Wiseley, R. F. Gree, and T. T. Noguchi 1979. Analysis of Dorsal Pitting in the *Os Pubis* in an Extensive Sample of Modern American Females. *American Journal of Physical Anthropology* 51: 517–23.

Sybel, Ludwig von. 1881. *Katalog der Sculpturen zu Athen*. Marburg: N. G. Elwert'sche.

Tarrant, H. 1988. Midwifery and *Clouds*. *CQ* 38:116–22.

Themelis, Petros G. 1971. *Brauron: Guide to the Site and Museum*. Athens· E. Tzaferis.

Thomas, Rosalind. 1989. *Oral Tradition and Written Record in Classical Athens* Cambridge: Cambridge University Press.

Thompson, Homer. 1936. Pynx and Thesmophorion. *Hesperia* 5:151–200

Thompson, W. E. 1967. The Marriage of First Cousins in Athenian Society. *Phoenix* 21:273–82.

Thompson, W. E. 1972. Athenian Marriage Patterns: Remarriage *CSCA* 5:211–25.

Timken-Zinkann, R F 1968. Black Bile: A Review of Recent Attempts to Trace the Origin of the Teaching on Melancholia to Medical Observations. *Medical History* 12:288–92.

Tomin, Julius. 1987. Socratic Midwifery. *CQ* 37:97–102

Trillat, E. 1986. *Histoire de l'hysterie*. Paris: Seghers.

Turner, J. A. 1983. "Hiereiai: Acquisition of Feminine Priesthoods in Ancient Greece." Ph.D. diss., University of California, Santa Barbara

United Nations. 1954. Foetal, Infant and Early Childhood Mortality Vol. 2, Biological, social and economic factors. *United Nations Population Studies* 13. New York: United Nations.

United Nations. 1955. Age and Sex Patterns of Mortality: Model Life-tables for Underdeveloped Countries. *United Nations Population Studies* 22. New York· United Nations.

Ussher, R. G., ed and comm. 1973. *Aristophanes Ecclesiazusae*. Oxford. Clarendon Press.

Van Straten, R. T. 1981. Gifts for the Gods. In *Faith, Hope and Worship*, ed. H. S. Versnel, 65–151. Leiden: E. J. Brill

Vedder, U. 1988. Frauentod-Kriegertod im Spiegel der attischen Grabkunst den 4. Jhr.v.Chr. *MDAI(A)* 103:161–91, pls. 21–25.

Vedder, U. 1989. "Szenenwechsel"—Beobachtungen an zwei Grabstelen in Cambridge (Mass.) und Athen. In *Festschrift für Nikolaus Himmelmann*, ed H.-U. Cain, H. Gabelmann, and D. Salzmann, 169–77. Mainz: Philipp von Zabern.

Veith, Ilza 1965. *Hysteria: The History of a Disease*. Chicago: University of Chicago Press.

Vernant, J -P. 1980–81. Étude comparée des religious antiques. *ACF* 81:391–405.

Versnel, H. S. 1987. Wife and Helpmate: Women of Ancient Athens in Anthropological Perspective. In *Sexual Asymmetry: Studies in Ancient Society*, ed. J. Blok and P. Mason, 59–86. Amsterdam: J. C. Gieben.

Veyne, Paul. 1987. The Roman Empire. In *A History of Private Life*. Vol. 1, *From Pagan Rome to Byzantium*, ed. Paul Veyne, trans. A. Goldhammer, 5–312. Cambridge, Mass.: Harvard University Press.

Von Staden, Heinrich. 1989. *Herophilus: The Art of Medicine in Early Alexandria*. Cambridge: Cambridge University Press.

Von Staden, Heinrich. 1990. Incurability and Hopelessness: The Hippocratic Corpus. In *La maladie et les maladies dans la collection hippocratique*, ed. P. Potter, G. Maloney, and J. Desautels, 75–112. Actes du VI Colloque international hippocratique. Sillery, Quebec: Editions Du Sphinx.

Von Sybel, Ludwig. 1881. *Katalog der Sculpturen zu Athen*. Marburg. N. G. Elwert'sche Verlags.

Vitrac, Bernard. 1989. *Médicine et philosophie au temps d'Hippocrate* Paris. Presses Universitaires de Vincennes.

Walbank, M. B. 1981. Artemis Bear-Leader *CQ*, n s., 31:276–81.

Walcot, P. 1970 *Greek Peasants, Ancient and Modern: A Comparison of Social and Moral Values*. Manchester: Manchester University Press

Waldstein, Charles 1892. *Excavations of the American School at the Heraion of Argos*. New York: Ginn.

Walker, James, Ian MacGillivray, and Malcolm C. Macnaughton. 1976 *Combined Textbook of Obstetrics and Gynaecology*. 9th ed. Edinburgh: Churchill Livingston.

Wallace, M. B. 1970. Notes on Early Greek Grave Epigrams. *Phoenix* 24:95–105.

Walton, J., P B. Beeson, and R Scott. 1986. *The Oxford Companion to Medicine*. Oxford: Oxford University Press.

Watkinson, M., and D. Rushton 1983. Plasmodial Pigmentation of Placenta and Outcome of Pregnancy in West African Mothers. *British Medical Journal* 287:251–54.

Weidauer, K. 1953. *Thukydides und die hippokratische Schriften*. Heidelberg: C. Winter

Weill, Nicole. 1985. *La plastique archaïque de Thasos*. Ecole française d'Athènes. Paris Boccard.

Weinberg, Eugene D. 1984. Pregnancy-associated Depression of Cell-mediated Immunity. *Reviews of infectious diseases* 6 (November–December):814–31

Weinberg, Eugene D. 1987. Pregnancy-associated Immune Suppression: Risks and Mechanisms. *Microbial Pathogenesis* 3.393–97

Wells, C. 1964. *Bones, Bodies and Disease*. London: Thames and Hudson.

Wells, C. 1975. Ancient Obstetric Hazards and Female Mortality. *Bulletin of the New York Academy of Medicine* 51:1235–41.

Wernicke, K. 1895a. Arkteia. *RE* 3:1970–72.

Wernicke, K. 1895b. Artemis. *RE* 3:1335–1440.

Willetts, R F. 1967. *The Law Code of Gortyn*. Berlin: Walter de Gruyter.

Winkler, John J 1990. *The Constraints of Desire*. New York: Routledge.

Wolters, Paul. 1892. Boiotikaí archaiotêtes. *AE*:214–40.

Wolters, Paul, and C. Friederichs. 1885 *Die Gipsabgüsse antiker Bildwerke in historischen Folge erklärt* Berlin: W Spemann.

Yap, Pow Meng. 1977. The Culture-bound Reactive Syndrome. In *Culture, Disease, and Healing: Studies in Medical Anthropology*, ed. David Landy, 340–49. New York: Macmillan.

Youmans, G P. 1979. *Tuberculosis*. Philadelphia W. B. Saunders.

Young, Allan. 1976. Internalizing and Externalizing Medical Belief Systems: An Ethiopian Example. *Social Science and Medicine* 10, nos. 3–4:147–56.

Zeitlin, Froma I. 1981. Travesties of Gender and Genre in Aristophanes' "Thesmophoriazousae." In *Reflections of Women in Antiquity*, ed. Helene Foley, 119–67. New York: Gordon and Breach Science Publishers.

Zeitlin, Froma I. 1982. Cultic Models of the Female: Rites of Dionysus and Demeter. *Arethusa* 15.129–57.

Zulueta, Julian de. 1973 Malaria and Mediterranean History. *Parassitologia* 15·1–15.

General Index

Hippocratic Index Locorum

ANCIENT SOCIETY AND HISTORY

The series Ancient Society and History offers books, relatively brief
in compass, on selected topics in the history of ancient Greece and
Rome, broadly conceived, with a special emphasis on comparative
and other nontraditional approaches and methods. The series,
which includes both works of synthesis and works of original
scholarship, is aimed at the widest possible range of specialist and
nonspecialist readers.

Published in the Series:
Eva Cantarella, *Pandora's Daughters: The Role and Status of Women
    in Greek and Roman Antiquity*
Alan Watson, *Roman Slave Law*
John E. Stambaugh, *The Ancient Roman City*
Géza Alföldy, *The Social History of Rome*
Giovanni Comotti, *Music in Greek and Roman Culture*
Christian Habicht, *Cicero the Politician*
Mark Golden, *Children and Childhood in Classical Athens*
Thomas Cole, *The Origins of Rhetoric in Ancient Greece*
Maurizio Bettini, *Anthropology and Roman Culture: Kinship, Time,
    Images of the Soul*
Suzanne Dixon, *The Roman Family*
Stephen L. Dyson, *Community and Society in Roman Italy*
Tim G. Parkin, *Demography and Roman Society*
Alison Burford, *Land and Labor in the Greek World*
Alan Watson, *International Law in Archaic Rome: War and
    Religion*
Stephen H. Lonsdale, *Dance and Ritual Play in Greek Religion*
J. Donald Hughes, *Pan's Travail: Environmental Problems of the
    Ancient Greeks and Romans*
C. R. Whittaker, *Frontiers of the Roman Empire: A Social and
    Economic Study*
Pericles Georges, *Barbarian Asia and the Greek Experience*
Nancy Demand, *Birth, Death, and Motherhood in Classical Greece*

The Library of Congress has cataloged the hardcover edition of this book as follows:

Demand, Nancy H.
    Birth, death, and motherhood in Classical Greece / Nancy Demand.
        p. cm.
    Includes bibliographical references (p.   ) and index.
    ISBN 0-8018-4762-1 (hc : acid-free paper)
        1. Women—Greece—History. 2. Women—Greece—Social conditions.
3. Pregnancy—Greece—History. 4. Childbirth—Greece—History.
5. Greece—Civilization. 6. Feminist theory. I. Title.
HQ1134.D36   1994
305.4′09495—dc20   93-39828

ISBN 0-8018-8053-X (pbk.)

DATE DUE

APR 1 7			

Printed in the United States
22085LVS00005B/1-48

9 780801 880537